Register for Free Membership to

solutions@syngress.com

Over the last few years, Syngress has published many best-selling and critically acclaimed books, including Tom Shinder's *Configuring ISA Server 2000*, Brian Caswell and Jay Beale's *Snort 2.1 Intrusion Detection*, and Angela Orebaugh and Gilbert Ramirez's *Ethereal Packet Sniffing*. One of the reasons for the success of these books has been our unique **solutions@syngress.com** program. Through this site, we've been able to provide readers a real time extension to the printed book.

As a registered owner of this book, you will qualify for free access to our members-only solutions@syngress.com program. Once you have registered, you will enjoy several benefits, including:

- Four downloadable e-booklets on topics related to the book. Each booklet is approximately 20-30 pages in Adobe PDF format. They have been selected by our editors from other best-selling Syngress books as providing topic coverage that is directly related to the coverage in this book.

- A comprehensive FAQ page that consolidates all of the key points of this book into an easy to search web page, providing you with the concise, easy to access data you need to perform your job.

- A "From the Author" Forum that allows the authors of this book to post timely updates links to related sites, or additional topic coverage that may have been requested by readers.

Just visit us at **www.syngress.com/solutions** and follow the simple registration process. You will need to have this book with you when you register.

Thank you for giving us the opportunity to serve your needs. And be sure to let us know if there is anything else we can do to make your job easier.

SYNGRESS®

APPLE I
REPLICA CREATION

Back to the Garage

Tom Owad

with Foreword by
Steve Wozniak, Co-Founder of Apple Computer

KEY	SERIAL NUMBER
001	HJIRTCV764
002	PO9873D5FG
003	829KM8NJH2
004	BNB3288BN6
005	CVPLQ6WQ23
006	VBP965T5T5
007	HJJJ863WD3E
008	2987GVTWMK
009	629MP5SDJT
010	IMWQ295T6T

PUBLISHED BY
Syngress Publishing, Inc.
800 Hingham Street
Rockland, MA 02370

Apple I Replica Creation: Back to the Garage

Printed in the United States of America
1 2 3 4 5 6 7 8 9 0
ISBN: 1-931836-40-X

Publisher: Andrew Williams
Acquisitions Editor: Gary Byrne
Technical Editor: John Greco
Cover Designer: Michael Kavish

Page Layout and Art: Patricia Lupien
Copy Editor: Darlene Bordwell
Indexer: J. Edmund Rush

Acknowledgments

Syngress would like to acknowledge the following people for their kindness and support in making this book possible.

Thank you to Steve Wozniak for contributing his insights.

Thank you to John Soluk of VAMP Inc., for contributing both his software and expertise to this project.

Syngress books are now distributed in the United States and Canada by O'Reilly Media, Inc. The enthusiasm and work ethic at O'Reilly is incredible and we would like to thank everyone there for their time and efforts to bring Syngress books to market: Tim O'Reilly, Laura Baldwin, Mark Brokering, Mike Leonard, Donna Selenko, Bonnie Sheehan, Cindy Davis, Grant Kikkert, Opol Matsutaro, Steve Hazelwood, Mark Wilson, Rick Brown, Leslie Becker, Jill Lothrop, Tim Hinton, Kyle Hart, Sara Winge, C. J. Rayhill, Peter Pardo, Leslie Crandell, Valerie Dow, Regina Aggio, Pascal Honscher, Preston Paull, Susan Thompson, Bruce Stewart, Laura Schmier, Sue Willing, Mark Jacobsen, Betsy Waliszewski, Dawn Mann, Kathryn Barrett, John Chodacki, and Rob Bullington. And a hearty welcome to Aileen Berg—glad to be working with you.

The incredibly hard working team at Elsevier Science, including Jonathan Bunkell, Ian Seager, Duncan Enright, David Burton, Rosanna Ramacciotti, Robert Fairbrother, Miguel Sanchez, Klaus Beran, Emma Wyatt, Rosie Moss, Chris Hossack, Mark Hunt, and Krista Leppiko, for making certain that our vision remains worldwide in scope.

David Buckland, Marie Chieng, Lucy Chong, Leslie Lim, Audrey Gan, Pang Ai Hua, and Joseph Chan of STP Distributors for the enthusiasm with which they receive our books.

Kwon Sung June at Acorn Publishing for his support.

David Scott, Tricia Wilden, Marilla Burgess, Annette Scott, Andrew Swaffer, Stephen O'Donoghue, Bec Lowe, and Mark Langley of Woodslane for distributing our books throughout Australia, New Zealand, Papua New Guinea, Fiji Tonga, Solomon Islands, and the Cook Islands.

Winston Lim of Global Publishing for his help and support with distribution of Syngress books in the Philippines.

Author

Tom Owad is a Macintosh consultant in southern Pennsylvania and the D.C., area and vice president of Keystone MacCentral. He serves on the board of directors of the Apple I Owners Club, where he is also Webmaster and archivist. Tom is the owner and Webmaster of Applefritter, a Macintosh community of artists and engineers. Applefritter provides its members with discussion boards for the exchange of ideas and hosts countless member-contributed hardware hacks and other projects. Tom holds a BA in computer science and international affairs from Lafayette College, PA.

Technical Editor

John Greco is a professor of electrical and computer engineering at Lafayette College, where he has taught digital circuit and system design for 28 years. He holds a Ph.D. in electrical engineering from the City University of New York. In addition, John has taught at the University of Petroleum and Minerals in Saudi Arabia. He has worked for GTE-Sylvania and has performed consulting work for (the former) Bell Laboratories and Moore Products.

Foreword Contributor

Steve Wozniak, a Silicon Valley icon and philanthropist for the past three decades, Founder, Chairman and CEO of Wheels of Zeus (wOz), helped shape the computing industry with his design of Apple's first line of products (the Apple I and II) and influenced the popular design of Macintosh. For his achievements at Apple Computer, Steve was awarded the National Medal of Technology by the President of the United States in 1985; the highest honor bestowed upon America's leading innovators.

In 2000 Steve was inducted into the Inventors Hall of Fame and was awarded the prestigious Heinz Award for Technology, The Economy and Employment for "single-handedly designing the first personal computer, and for then redirecting his lifelong passion for mathematics and electronics toward lighting the fires of excitement for education in grade school students and their teachers."

Making significant investments of both his time and resources in education, Wozniak "adopted" the Los Gatos School District, providing students and teachers with hands-on teaching and donations of state-of-the-art technology equipment. Wozniak founded the Electronic Frontier Foundation, and was the founding sponsor of the Tech Museum, Silicon Valley Ballet, and Children's Discovery Museum of San Jose.

Steve is currently a member of the board of directors for Jacent, a developer of cost-effective telephony solutions, and Danger, Inc., developer of an end-to-end wireless Internet platform.

Author Acknowledgments

Much thanks goes to my parents, John and Cindy Owad, who always supported my interests but nevertheless are happy that my racks of PDP-11 equipment no longer fill their living room. Were it not for their munificent toleration of my hobby, this book would not exist.

Dr. John Greco, my technical editor, has offered great guidance and been of immeasurable help in structuring and error-checking this book. Sandra Veresink deserves thanks for her editing and stylistic help. Should any part of this book resemble 19th century Irish prose, I owe it to her influence.

Vince Briel designed the Replica I circuit described in this book and has generously shared his design with us. Sarah McMenomy wrote the plot for the BASIC game in chapter five.

John and George Soluk at VAMP Inc. provided valuable assistance in moving our designs to McCAD EDS and have generously allowed us to include their software with this book.

Thanks also to Achim Breidenbach, who provided the image for Figure 1.1 in Chapter 1.

Joe Torzewski founded the Apple I Owners Club back in 1977 and kept it alive all these years. And thanks to Steve Wozniak, who started it all.

Contents

Foreword

I was in the sixth grade when I got my first transistor radio. That might have been the most important gift of my life. I found out about music, and I knew that it was a big thing in my life, all from this small, handheld, 10-transistor radio. I could sleep with music all night long, and did so that entire year. My father was working on missile guidance technology for military projects around this time and showed me how tightly transistors could be packed. He also told me how chips were coming with more than one transistor on them, for even more space and weight savings. I commented that they were designing these things to make better and smaller radios, and he told me, "no," that they were being designed for military and commercial uses and that only after a long time they'd filter down to consumer products that we used in our lives and homes. That thought bummed me out—that normal people in their homes wanting good products were not driving technology.

My introduction to electronics was accidental. I lived in a new community surrounded by orchards. It was Santa Clara Valley, California, but it is now called Silicon Valley. I had lots of local childhood friends who were interested in electronics, and we'd do gardening to be paid in parts, like resistors. I read a book about a ham radio operator solving a kidnapping and found that anyone of any age could be a ham. You didn't have to be older as with car licenses. So by sixth grade I had my ham license and was learning electronics back in the days of tubes.

One day I stumbled across a journal in a hall closet of my home. It had articles about early computing projects. This was around 1960, when computers were unknown to mortals and filled entire rooms. I read articles on strange storage devices, Boolean algebra, and logic gates, and how they could be combined. What amazed me most was that none of this stuff was too hard for a fifth grader to follow. You didn't need advanced math to understand binary arithmetic or logic gates. I became fascinated by what I'd stumbled onto. Based on what I'd read and what my father could teach me, I worked on a couple of large science fair projects in sixth and eighth grade demonstrating hundreds of transistors and diodes, all doing logic. One played tic-tac-toe, which I thought was a game of logic (I now know that it's more a game of psychology). The other project added and subtracted 10-bit numbers. I had no idea that I was on the right path to learning how to design computers or that there were jobs in this field. In fact, I was on a search to find out what a computer was. I myself was too shy to ask or read to get such answers.

At another science fair I stumbled onto a project with a stepping motor advancing a pointer to switches where you could set up operations to be done. This motor could loop or back up, depending on results. This was the first time in my life that I learned that computers had instructions to do things like my adder/subtractor did, and that it could repeat those instructions.

We had no computer at our high school, but because I was so advanced by then in electronics, my teacher, John C. McCullum, a great teacher, arranged for me to learn more by programming a computer at a company in Sunnyvale. In those days just the word "computer" brought looks of awe. I came to love all that I could do in FORTRAN that year. I also stumbled upon a manual at Sylvania titled *The Small Computer Handbook*. It described a real minicomputer, the PDP-8. The engineers let me have that manual, and it changed my life forever.

Now I had a manual that described a real computer and its architecture and included instructions. I also had some chip catalogs, back when you could get only one gate on a chip. And I had my knowledge of how to combine gates into things like adders. So for the rest of high school, my favorite pastime became designing minicomputers on paper. When a single chip cost $50 (maybe that's $500 today), you don't have the parts to build your own computer. I found how to get manuals describing various minicomputers from Digital, HP, Varian, DEC, and so on. I designed my own versions of these machines over and over. As chips got better, my designs took fewer and fewer parts. My goal became to beat my prior design whenever I redesigned the same computer again. I got very skilled at digital design this way. I had no endpoint; you can always think of one more way to save another chip in a design.

I had no friends, parents, or teachers doing this with me, nor was anyone even aware that I was doing it. My computer designs were weekend projects in my room with my door shut. I sometimes would go late into the night, and it helped to drink cokes. The Data General Nova was introduced. When I finally got around to designing this computer, I found that it took half as many chips as my other designs, due to a unique architecture. That changed my life a lot, too. If you design a computer architecture based on what chips are available, it can save a lot of parts.

All these minicomputers had front rectangular plates full of switches and lights. They were intimidating and commercial looking and belonged in racks on factory floors. But if they could run FORTRAN, that could even enable a mere mortal to use them to play games and solve problems. I knew what I needed and told my father that someday I'd have a 4K NOVA computer. When he pointed out that it cost as much as a house, I said I'd live in an apartment, but I'd have my own computer someday.

I could design computers but couldn't afford the parts to build them.

After some college, I wound up designing chips for HP's early scientific calculators. I worked on a lot of interesting side projects, but lost track of minicomputers and overlooked the introduction and advancement of microprocessors. In 1974 I saw my first Pong game in a bowling alley. As I stared, mesmerized, at the screen, it occurred to me that I could build a Pong. I could never afford an output device, but like everyone else, I had a color TV at home. There was no video-in jack, but in those open days, you got schematics with your TV. I knew TV signals and how they worked from high school electronics, and I knew digital design, so it wasn't long before I built my own Pong, using very few chips.

Later in 1974 I visited an old friend, famous phone phreak John Draper, aka Captain Crunch. He was typing on a teletype, an input/output device that I myself could never afford. He was playing chess with a computer in Boston. Then he showed me how he could have the teletype type out a list of computers, and he could switch to one at Berkeley. It was the early Arpanet, and you dialed into a number at Stanford using a modem to get onto it.

I absolutely had to do this thing that made you like a king, doing what nobody else could do. I had just built my Pong and knew how to get signals onto a TV screen. So I designed and built a terminal that could put letters and numbers on my home TV. I had to buy a keyboard for $60 and that was very expensive for me, but was barely affordable. I did indeed access the Arpanet a few times, but wasn't so much interested in using those computers as just in knowing that I could reach out to such distant places. It was like ham radio, and also like phone phreaking, in that sense.

So a $60 uppercase-only keyboard and my Sears color TV gave me the input/output I needed at an affordable cost. Steve Jobs said "let's sell it," and we did sell a number to a local timeshare outfit called Call Computer.

Next, in 1975, the Homebrew Computer club started. I got tricked into going. I never would have gone to something based on microprocessors because I didn't know what a microprocessor was. I didn't know that you could buy an enhanced microprocessor, a CPU, in a case called the Altair. I didn't know that you could add enough to this processor to make it a computer. I was told that a new club was being formed for people with terminals and the like. I figured it would be a great chance for a shy guy to show off with his own video terminal based on very cheap chips.

I got scared the first night at the Homebrew Computer Club. Everyone knew what was going on with these new affordable "computers." I took home a micro-processor data sheet, and to my surprise, this chip was the CPU that I'd grown up designing in high school. I was back in business. I saw that night that soon I'd design or buy a 4KB computer and run FORTRAN for myself finally.

Rather than design a computer from scratch, I saw a shortcut. I could take my terminal with human input and output, and combine it with a microprocessor and some RAM. I'd actually built a computer of my own design five years earlier, one equivalent to the Altair with 256 bytes of RAM and switches and lights on a front panel. I didn't want to do that again. I didn't need to wire dozens of switches and have the chips to get them to the memory of a computer. That took too many parts and chips and money. Our calculators at HP had ROMs, and they ran a program when you turned them on that waited for a user to press human buttons and then the program did the right things. I saw that I could write a short program that monitored the keyboard for input to do what the old front panels had done. I called this program a monitor. It took 256 bytes, which was two PROM chips in 1975.

I first got working on what was to be the Apple I, using static 1K RAM chips. But it took 32 of these chips to have 4KB of RAM, enough for a computer language. The 4K dynamic RAMs were just being introduced, the first RAMs to be cheaper than magnetic core memories. I bought some from a fellow at our club and got them working on my computer. I had to design some refresh circuitry, but overall, I saved so many chips and dollars that it was the right way to go. If you look back, you'll find that every single other hobby computer back then used static RAMs because they involved less design work.

I passed out schematics and code listings freely at our club, hoping that others would now be able to build their own computers. It took another four months for me to write a BASIC program for this computer. I'd never studied computer language writing, but figured out good approaches for that. Steve Jobs said that there was a lot of interest in having computers but not in wiring them up, so why don't we start a company to make PC boards for $20 and sell them for $40. We'd have our own company and all. Steve came up with the name Apple Computer. I sold my most valuable possession, my HP-65 calculator. We came up with a few hundred dollars and started this company.

After the PC board was done, Steve struck up a partnership with Paul Terrell at the Byte Shop, the only computer store in our region, to sell it fully built and assembled computer boards for $500 each. I was into repeating digits, so we priced it at $666.66 retail.

We did not make or sell a lot of Apple I computers over the next year, but we had other jobs. We did get our name and computer characteristics in many articles over that year, and it was easy to see that Apple Computer was getting very well known in some circles.

I look back on my Apple I design and actually have trouble figuring out some of it. My designs back then were sometimes too clever to figure out. They were designed to save parts and cost.

The Apple][was really the computer designed from the ground up that would kick off personal computing on a large scale. But the Apple I took the biggest step of all. Some very simple concepts are very hard to do the first time. This computer told the world that small computers should never again come with geeky front panels, but rather with human keyboards, ready to type on. After the Apple I, Processor Technology introduced the SOL computer, and it also came with a keyboard and monitor and became the hottest selling Intel-based hobby computer, selling thousands a month. Contrast that with the Apple I, of which we sold maybe only 150. The Apple][was to be the third low-cost computer to come with a human keyboard.

—Steve Wozniak
January, 2005

About the CD Contents

Simply copy the entire contents of the CD to your computer's hard disk. You will need about 70 megabytes of hard disk space. At the root level of the CD, there are two folders.

McCAD_EDS_SE_for_MacOS Folder

This folder contains the development tools for those who wish to create or modify designs of their own making. All the documents necessary to create the Apple I replica circuit board can be found in their respective subfolders contained therein. The software tools provided within this folder will work only on Macintosh operating systems. Those wishing to have tools that run under other operating systems can visit **www.McCAD.com** to view the other products and versions offered by VAMP Inc., the publisher of McCAD electronic design tools.

Once copied to your hard disk, the McCAD tools will run in their initial mode. However, it is very important that you fill out the enclosed registration card and send it to VAMP Inc. Once VAMP receives it, the company will send you your authorization code, which will allow you to enable the expanded capabilities of the SE400 series. See the registration card for more details.

XA-2.1.4h Folder

In this folder you will find XA 2.1.4. It is a 6502 Cross-Assembler that you can use to write Apple I assembly programs on your Mac or PC. Sample assembly programs from the book are included on the disk. An introduction to XA can be found in Chapter 6.

## Chapter 1

The History of the Apple I

Topics in this Chapter:

- The Apple I
- The Apple I Owners Club
- Apple I Pioneer Interviews
- Summary

Introduction

Steve Wozniak's microcomputer, the Apple I, launched the Apple Computer Co. and generated an outburst of innovation that revolutionized the way people use computers. This book won't tell you who provided the venture capital or what date Apple was incorporated. Instead, this book is about *computers*, how to build them, and how to program them. In this first chapter, we examine the history of the Apple I but not the history of the company. We'll be looking at the computer itself—the peripherals, the modifications, and the community of users who were the first in the world to own a *personal* computer.

The Apple I

Merely finding an Apple I to buy was a daunting task in 1976. Two hundred were made. The Byte Shop purchased 100 of these. Most of the remaining computers were sold at other stores and through an ad in *Interface Age*. The computer's retail price, $666.66, wasn't much, but all that bought you was the circuit board (see Figure 1.1). It was up to the user to find a keyboard, power supply, and video monitor.

Figure 1.1 The Apple I Circuit Board

With a user base of fewer than 200, nobody was making peripherals specifically for the Apple I. The power supply could be built with standard parts. For an ASCII keyboard, a Datanetics Corp. keyboard was the most common choice (see Figure 1.2). The user had to make the cable on his own. A video monitor could be used for the display, but the cheapest option was to buy an RF modulator and connect the computer to a television. The Apple I was the first computer of its kind to use a keyboard and monitor as standard in/out (I/O) devices. Most competing systems, such as the Altair, used rows of lights and switches to communicate with the user or provided a serial port for use with an expensive teletype unit.

Programs were loaded onto the Apple I either by typing the machine code in by hand or by transferring the program from an audio cassette. Apple BASIC was only available on cassette, and most users were not keen on loading their programs by hand; therefore, the Apple I's cassette interface (see Figure 1.3) was a ubiquitous option. Apple sold a handful of games on cassette, but in 1976 nobody bought a microcomputer to run commercial software.

Figure 1.2 The Apple I with Datanetics Keyboard

Figure 1.3 The Apple I Cassette Interface

The concept of commercial software barely existed in 1976. Companies like Apple made their money from hardware sales. Nine programs were available on cassette: BASIC, Mastermind, Lunar Lander, Blackjack, Hamurabi, Mini-Startrek, 16K-Startrek, Dis-Assembler, and Extended Monitor. Apple sold these programs for just $5 apiece to encourage interest in the Apple I. Hobbyists wrote their own software and shared it freely with one another, eager for the opportunity to show off their innovations and share what they learned. Equal liberty was taken with other manufacturers' software. Microsoft, which wrote BASIC for the Altair, was the first company to have a financial interest in software sales. "I would appreciate letters from anyone who wants to pay up," Bill Gates wrote in his poorly received *Open Letter to Hobbyists*.

With the exception of those nine programs that Apple sold on cassette, any software programs that the Apple I user wanted to buy or copy from a book had to be laboriously translated by hand from their original format into Apple I BASIC or Assembly language. A similar situation existed for the hardware. There were few microcomputer peripherals that the competent engineer couldn't interface to his or her computer, but none of these were actually intended for the Apple I.

One popular device was the Southwest Technical Products Corporation (SWTPC) PR-40 alphanumeric printer (see Figure 1.4). This printer cost $250 and, like the Apple I, did not support lowercase characters. It used standard adding machine paper and could print 40 characters per line. The Apple I had no parallel port, but users could build a small circuit that would redirect video output to the printer.

Another peripheral, called the KIMSI (see Figure 1.5), was an interface that allowed popular S-100 peripherals to be used with the MOS KIM-1 computer. With only minor adaptations, the KIMSI could be attached to the Apple I's 44-pin expansion bus. Any S-100 card could be used with this interface, but writing programs that used the cards was up to the Apple I user.

Figure 1.4 The SWTPC PR-40 Printer

Figure 1.5 An Ad for the KIMSI Interface

The most ambitious upgrade to the Apple I was the addition of an SWTPC GT-6144 Graphics Board (see Figure 1.6). The graphics board allowed the system to display a 64 × 96 *array*, or rectangles (pixels) in black and white. It was available only as a kit and, like the PR-40 printer, it interfaced to the computer via a parallel port. After building a simple custom interface to attach the graphics board, the user could write programs that drew graphics to the screen or even performed simple animations.

Figure 1.6 The GT-6144 Terminal System

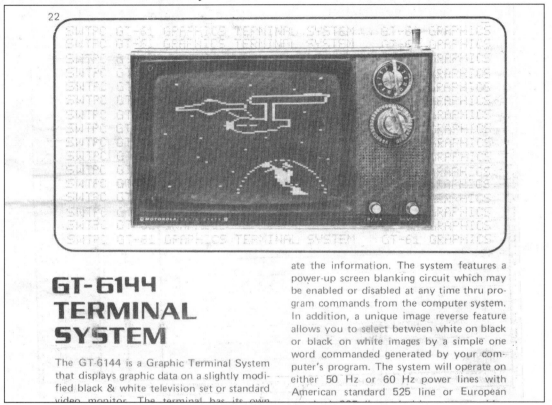

GT-6144 TERMINAL SYSTEM

The GT-6144 is a Graphic Terminal System that displays graphic data on a slightly modified black & white television set or standard video monitor. The terminal has its own ate the information. The system features a power-up screen blanking circuit which may be enabled or disabled at any time thru program commands from the computer system. In addition, a unique image reverse feature allows you to select between white on black or black on white images by a simple one word commanded generated by your computer's program. The system will operate on either 50 Hz or 60 Hz power lines with American standard 525 line or European

The Apple I Owners Club

In the earliest days of the Apple I, Steve Wozniak would visit the Homebrew Computer Club, sharing schematics and giving away code. Fellow hobbyists could even expect hands-on support from "Woz" as they experimented with their early Apple I computers. As Apple grew as a company, the new Apple II quickly became the center of attention, and interest in the Apple I fell to the wayside.

In 1977, Joe Torzewski decided to found the Apple I Owners Club to support users of the Apple I. Joe sent announcements to *Interface Age* and *Byte*. Apple happily sent out letters to Apple I customers, instructing them to direct further inquiries to Joe. The club was expected not only to provide peer support but also to take over distribution of Apple I software.

Five people—Joe Torzewski, Larry Nelson, Richard Drennan, Fred Hatfield, and Dr. Arthur Schawlow of Stanford University—made up the core of the group, which had roughly 30 members altogether. Members exchanged programs that they'd written and compiled a software library. They ported the Focal programming language to the Apple I and developed methods for memory expansion. As interesting new hardware and peripherals were released, Owners Club members shared their strategies and schematics for getting the equipment working with the Apple I.

The Apple I Owners Club continues today, with founder Joe Torzewski, original member Larry Nelson, and many new members who have never used a real Apple I. With message boards, file libraries, and member Web pages, the Owners Club continues to serve hobbyists and offer a community to people who are eager to learn about computers.

The Apple I Owners Club welcomes new members who are interested in building replicas of the Apple I, as well as those simply interested in learning more about how computers work. With the help of new members, the Owners Club hopes to provide many fascinating new articles on hardware expansion, programming, and other projects. If interested, you can join them at www.applefritter.com/apple1.

THE APPLE I OWNERS CLUB PREMIER NEWSLETTER

APPLE 1 POWER

Well, this is our start, and I hope it's just one of many. So far, there are about 30 of us. First of all, I would like to put out a list of names of persons who want to get in touch with other Apple 1 owners and are working on projects, also a list of persons who would be willing to help others with their hardware or software projects.

We need hardware articles on anything that you have hooked up to your Apple. Memory expansion is high on the list.

Where is our Apple 1 hardware expert? I need someone who can devote his time on a project for us. Needs access to a slide projector or should have one. I have 35mm slides and some notes on how Apple put the 16K chips on the Apple 1 board. Someone has to figure out from this (mainly the slides) and try to write it up so we can pass it along to everyone. So, don't be bashful; we need you.

Would like to hear from you guys with the new monitor and what you have done with it and the commands and such. Trying to get all the details from everyone and trying to piece it together.

Software programs in basic and machine language are needed. Maybe, we should work on certain types of programs together as a group for a month or two and then go to another area. Take one type of program and try to modify it and see what we can come up with. Open for ideas on this, so input now. How about sending a list of your program so we can see what is out there?

Here is a basic (Apple-Basic) challenge from Larry Nelson. What is the best Apple-Basic solution to the problem with the following program?

Continued

```
75 DATA 13, 14, 15, 22, 23, 24, 29, 30, 31
77 For W-1 to 9
79 HEAD K
81 B(N)—7
32 NEXT W
```

There is a program, 4 pages, a primitive, line-oriented text editor that you can use to draw pictures or text and store them, from Professor Schawlow. Well that's about it for now, remember to send in your inputs and program and a stamp or so if you can. Till next time …

Apple I Pioneer Interviews

The most fascinating stories of the Apple I come from those who were there at the beginning. These interviews with original Apple I owners attempt to capture the experience of using an Apple I when it was new in 1976. Joe Torzewski, Larry Nelson, Ray Borril, Liza Loop, Steve Fish, and Allen Baum discuss their first experiences with the Apple I, their programs, and their hardware projects.

Joe Torzewski

Joe Torzewski is the founder of the Apple I Owners Club. Now retired from industry, he remains an active hobbyist with the Apple I. Pictures of Joe's Apple system are shown in Figures 1.7–1.9.

Figure 1.7 Assembling the System

Figure 1.8 Joe Torzewski's Apple I

Figure 1.9 Inside Joe Torzewski's Apple I

TO: When did you first learn about the Apple I?

JT: I believe I first learned of the Apple I through an ad in one of the older computer magazines, *Interface Age*. When I saw their ad, I thought having video, memory, and processor on the same board was a great idea. The S-100 bus depended on a separate card for everything.

TO: How did your background as an engineer affect your interest in the Apple I?

JT: I liked the idea that everything was there on the board. At that time, they were having problems with the S-100 bus, and the Apple I's 44-pin bus looked good for expansion. The 6502 CPU was also easier to program.

TO: Why did you start the Apple I Owners Club?

JT: I was having problems with Apple Co. over support. The Apple II was all that interested them, and the Apple I was something they did not want to support anymore. So, Apple started giving my name and address to any Apple I computer owners who contacted them for help. One of the first persons that I met was Larry Nelson, who was an outstanding programmer for the 6502 chip and the Apple I.

TO: How did you learn to program for the Apple I?

JT: Everything was self-taught; that's how it was back then. One of the main references to use for machine language programming at the time was from MOS Technology, the maker of the 6502 chip. It explained how to use each command. Larry Nelson and Richard Drennan did a lot of programming and hardware mods.

TO: What programs did you write?

JT: I did write a few games in BASIC and modified a few for the Apple I computer. I also did some machine language mods to add more commands to programs.

I adapted the game Gomoko in BASIC to run on the Apple I. When you played the game, you had to enter your row and column that you wanted and then the computer would draw the boxes, using dashes going across and exclamation points going down. Then it put your *X* or *O* into the box, depending if you moved first or second. You had 100 squares and had to get five in a row, diagonal, vertical, or horizontal, in order to win.

TO: What hardware modifications did you perform?

JT: I added the extra 16KB of memory to the board. This involved adding two more chips in the work area on the board and wiring and cutting tracks on the motherboard to make it work. I got that info from Professor Arthur L. Schawlow. I put in the expansion board with three extra slots and then built an EPROM board (see Figure 1.10) and burned in a better monitor ROM for the Apple I.

Others in the club added the GT-6144 graphics card and even the Kim-1 memory board.

Figure 1.10 Joe's Homebrew EPROM Card

Larry Nelson

Larry Nelson has been an active participant in the Apple I Owners Club since 1977. The owner of an Apple I for many years, he has been an enthusiastic user, programmer, and hardware hacker. He is currently retired and living in southern Indiana and continues to use a replica of the Apple I computer for hobby purposes.

TO: When did you first learn about the Apple I? Why did you want a computer, and why the Apple I?

LN: I took courses in electronics in the early '60s and, although I didn't go to work in the industry, I did have an interest in the field. In 1977 I began to see articles in electronic magazines about the new computers for individual use. When I discovered that the Byte Shop had a store there, I drove 60 miles to Fort Wayne, Indiana. They had displays of several personal computers, and I looked at several. The Apple computer was the one that interested me the most, as it came with a great cassette interface, BASIC, and lots of memory. Soon after I discovered it, I returned to buy one for myself. This would have been in the summer of 1977. The purchase included the computer circuit board with 8 kilobytes of dynamic RAM, a cassette interface, an ASCII keyboard, an RF modulator to adapt the video output to the input of a television, and a book, *101 BASIC Computer Games,* by David Ahl. Back home, I still had to acquire two power supply transformers, build the RF converter (it was in kit form, [see Figure 1.11]), and wire switches and power cords to the unit. I built a case for the Apple from sheet metal, since I was operating an HVAC business at the time.

Figure 1.11 VD-1 Building the Video Modulator

TO: Could you describe the process of writing a program for the Apple I?

LN: I had no programs (other than a tape of BASIC), so the book by David Ahl was my only source of input material. My son, a junior in high school, was interested in computer programming and went to a "computer camp" at nearby Anderson College for a couple of weeks while I assembled the Apple. The emphasis at the computer camp was on BASIC programming. The Apple was completed when he came home, and he helped me learn to program in BASIC. Most of the listings I had were for "standard" BASIC, which, of course, Apple BASIC was not. The limitations of Apple BASIC included integer-only math, single-dimension arrays, and a nonstandard method of string manipulation.

But with careful editing, many corrections of "syntax error" messages, and a lot of guesswork, I got a couple of games up and running, the first being "HELLO." Most games in the David Ahl book were too large for my Apple's memory.

I subscribed to *Byte* magazine and *Interface Age* magazine to gain more knowledge. I finally tried a little programming in Assembly language, although it required assembling a program manually, then converting the listing to machine code and typing the resulting hexadecimal into the Apple. Many hours were spent hunched over the keyboard just to see the results of a simple game. Several times, I copied hexadecimal listings from magazines into the computer, one byte at a time.

A fellow named Peter Jennings wrote a chess-playing program for the KIM-1 computer, another 6502-based microcomputer. I sent off for a listing of his program and successfully adapted it to the Apple-1.

TO: What hardware modifications did you perform?

LN: I added a printer (the PR-40) that had 40 columns of width on a 4-inch paper roll. Then I replaced 4K of RAM with a 16K set of chips. Now I had an amazing 20K of memory, more that I would ever need! However, at a swap meet in Fort Wayne, I got another 4K of static RAM on a separate board, which I wired to a connector to plug into the Apple I's expansion connector. I don't think I ever had another "MEM FULL ERROR" message after that.

TO: *Tell us about the Apple I community.*

LN: In response to an inquiry to the Apple Computing Co. in late 1977, I found Joe Torzewski. Joe now had the Apple I Computer library (about a half-dozen games, routines, and programs), and he began sending me lots of material from other Apple I owners.

Other than Joe Torzewski, I have never met another Apple I owner in person. I did happen upon a local fellow with a KIM-1 and we spent some time discussing the various things we could do with our micros. I was pleased to learn that the Apple I was far more flexible in its abilities to be programmed, and the monitor output was superior to the LED display of the KIM-1.

Ray Borril

Ray Borril began his career in electronics after leaving the U.S. Army in 1956. Employed as a technician at Brookhaven National Labs, he constructed digital systems for nuclear research. Ray enlisted in the U.S. Air Force in 1958 and attended courses on the computers used in the SAGE system. Honorably discharged from the Air Force in July 1959, Ray soon founded Applied Digital Data Systems (ADDS), which became one of the leading suppliers of IBM- and teletype-compatible CRT terminals. He moved to Indiana in 1973 to work as a systems engineer, designing and developing computer-based systems for psychological research. In February 1976, Ray opened The Data Domain, one of the pioneering retail computer stores. He retired in 1984.

TO: *What is your background in computers?*

RB: If I have any talent at all, it is the task of telling or writing "war stories" of the computer industry, which I have been directly involved with since the fall of 1958. I got into the personal computer business sort of passively in 1975, when in November I attended the famous Kansas City meeting sponsored by *Byte* magazine. The purpose was to develop a specification describing the operating parameters of an interface between a serial data port on a personal computer and an audiocassette player so that data could be compatible between systems. It was a lofty but naive objective because virtually every manufacturer in the industry already had a product on the market or at least on the drawing boards.

There were more than 25 people there, but I was the only one who did not represent anyone but myself. I met and became somewhat acquainted with Don Tarbell, Don Lancaster, Harry Garland of Cromemco, Hal Chamberlain of The Computer Hobbyist, Lee Felsenstein, the people from Processor Technology and IMSAI, and more. I decided there and then to open a computer store as soon as possible. It took me almost three months, but The Data Domain started in about 750 square feet just off Court House Square in Bloomington, Indiana, on February 12, 1976. At that time we were authorized dealers for IMSAI, Processor Technology, Cromemco, and several makers of after-market add-ons, as well as TV monitors, keyboards, every computer book we could find, every computer magazine on the market, and even computer-generated works of art!

www.syngress.com

At the World Altair Convention in March, I met and became friends with Ted Nelson, author of *Compute Lib/Dream Machine*. Ted was the keynote speaker and kept the large audience in hysterics for an hour, giving his somewhat risqué predictions of the future digital world. Ted was there with his friend Jim Banish, and they told me that they were opening a store in Evanston, Illinois, and thought we should establish some sort of relationship. They were interested in my experience and talent for selling computers, and I could take advantage of their great financial management group. The result was that I became the vice president of the "itty bitty machine company" as well as the sole proprietor of The Data Domain.

I have a picture (Figure 1.12) of The Data Domain that I took in April or May of 1976. It is my firm belief that we were the first to use the term Personal Computer commercially. DEC used it internally in 1972 or 73. amd Apple used it in a Wall Street Journal ad in 1978 and got the credit for making it catch on, but I used it first!

Figure 1.12. The Data Domain

TO: How did you become involved with the Apple I?

RB: By June the store was going great guns and I was always on the lookout for new products to sell. One day, I got a call from a young man named Steve Jobs. He had just spoken with Jim Banish of the itty bitty machine company, who told Steve that I was the guy he would have to convince, since I made all the purchasing decisions. He went into his spiel about what a great computer he had, since there was no assembly required (a slight exaggeration since one had to wire a power supply, keyboard cable, display monitor, and some other ancillary stuff, then find a way to package it all up nicely). But Steve is a good talker and we needed some more product to sell. So, as was routine in those early days, I ordered 15 Apple I computers with the optional cassette interface card, sight unseen, on the word of a guy I had never met or heard of, and which would be delivered C.O.D. "soon." And thus,

The Data Domain and the itty bitty machine company became two of the first four dealers for Apple Computer Co. The first dealer was The Byte Shop and the second was Stan Viet's store in New York.

The Apple I was hard to sell because of the packaging problem, and for some reason we were never supplied with the cassette version of Apple BASIC, which made some buyers very unhappy. But, eventually, all 15 were sold, except for two. One of these was a machine we gave away to the U.S. Olympic tennis team. Only a few weeks later, it went down with a plane that killed several members and destroyed the Apple I. The other one stayed in my display case for a couple of years. When it began to gain fame for its design, I decided to take it home and keep it. There it stayed for 25 years until I decided to auction it off in 2001.

TO: What was your impression of the Apple I? Did you do any programming for it?

RB: Of course, in my case, there was no real personal decision in choosing and purchasing the Apple I over some competitor. I listened to Steve's sales pitch, and it seemed like a good idea to be able to offer a computer that did not require any soldering skill. It was inexpensive enough to sell, and we had the opportunity to increase the value of the total sale (and increase the profit margins) by selling the things needed to make a complete system, such as a cassette recorder, power supply components, keyboard, monitor, and a case—or a further option: we offered to assemble the whole thing. While my techs wrote some programs for the Apple I, I did not and only learned to run some demos that we wrote and things like that. I spent more of my time teaching people how to make interfaces, etc., for all our computers. I didn't get closely involved with the Apple I like I did with the Apple II and S-100 bus computers.

TO: What were some common peripherals and modifications for the Apple I?

RB: Printers were popular, but in those days about the only printers available to the general public were teletypewriters and lots of surplus units, both serial and parallel. You wouldn't believe the confusion and frustration of hooking up a simple Model 33 ASR teletype to a serial interface when you had no idea how a teletype works and never heard of RS-232C! One of the nice things about the Apple I was that it required no modifications to make it run and was a complete, working system, once the ancillary stuff was assembled. Occasionally, someone would wish to change from the 6502 processor to the Motorola 6800, which the motherboard was designed to allow, or add a serial RS232C interface in the "kludge" area, but these were not ordinary modifications and were rarely done.

The real fact is that the Apple I's potential never was exploited by Apple. At the Atlantic City convention in August, all attending dealers were shown a demonstration of the color graphics of the future Apple II, and that was the end of orders for the Apple I.

Liza Loop

Liza Loop is a social scientist with a focus on how individuals adapt to changing social and physical technologies. She draws her data from the everyday life that surrounds her and often sets up venues, such as LO*OP Center's public access computer center, so that she can be an up-close participant observer. "Every phenomenon can be interpreted as a complex system," she explains. "By paying attention to the characteristics of the elements inside the system, the relationships, both real and possible, among those elements and the emergent properties of the system as a whole, we can learn how to shape our world in positive ways."

TO: When did you first learn about the Apple I?

LL: I went to a homebrew computer club meeting in early 1976 and announced that I had a storefront computer center and was planning to take my machines into elementary and secondary schools. I was looking for computing equipment to use to demystify computing to children and the general public. Woz heard my comments and brought the Apple I to a Sonoma County Computer Club meeting for a demonstration. At that time, he gave us the computer. Before then, I knew nothing about the Apple I.

TO: *Why did you choose the Apple I over other computers?*

LL: Because Woz gave it to us. Actually, I found it very difficult to use. Our Apple I wouldn't stay running for a 45-minute class period and caused no end of frustration. I took it back to Woz and asked him to fix it. He made it a little better, but still not very serviceable. Eventually, he provided us with an Apple II to replace it.

TO: *Did you do much programming in the classroom?*

LL: I only used the machine to demonstrate simple BASIC routines and to play a few games. It was easy to take around to different schools because it was small and light. Probably 50 to 100 students ran their first five-line BASIC programs on our Apple I. For many of them, the Apple I was the first computer they had ever seen. The workhorse of our classes, however, was a PDP-8e.

TO: *What hardware modifications did you perform?*

LL: Apple I, number one, came to LO*OP Center as a naked motherboard (Figure 1.13). One of our computer club members built it a box and a power supply. I drove from our storefront in Cotati to Palo Alto, California (two hours), to buy a Cherry Pro keyboard. We used an audiotape recorder for "mass" storage.

I believe Woz added some jumper wires when he had the machine back for repair. Today, we would probably call that an upgrade! Other than that it is still in original condition.

Figure 1.13 The LO*OP Center's Apple I

TO: Did you know any other Apple I owners or microcomputer hobbyists? Could you tell us about the community?

LL: In the fall of 1975, when I opened LO★OP Center (LO★OP stands for *Learning Options ★ Open Portal*), I knew next to nothing about computers. I began the Sonoma County Computer Club simultaneously so that I could create a nearby hobbyist community. Out of the Sonoma County woodwork came about 30 folks, mostly men; however, I was not the only woman who knew a lot about programming and electronics. Everyone was very excited when the MITS Altair arrived, and the participants taught each other about the machines they knew. Those club members fanned out across the microcomputer industry as it grew. One worked on the original WordStar. Another developed the first TRS-80 disk drive. Someone else wrote a stock market analysis program and retired on the bundle he made. The guy who built the Altair is still crafting acoustic guitars in the Sonoma County hills. I see some of them occasionally when I go to the Vintage Computer Festival. We're grayer, but there's a glint in our eyes that says we were involved in something really revolutionary.

For me, computers were a means to an end and not an independent interest. I needed the hobbyists to teach me and to provide hardware support. They did it happily and were very tolerant when I tuned out on the endless discussions of which capacitor applied where would increase throughput how much.

For most of 1976, LO★OP's Apple I was the only Apple in the North Bay, although there were several in Berkeley and on the Peninsula. By the time the Apple II came out, there were several single-board computers on the market that kept the hardware enthusiasts engaged. The Apple II was not a kit, so it didn't appeal as much to the Club's group of tinkerers. There was also a growing demand for a plug 'n play computer among science-minded high schoolers, a few teachers, and many forward-looking business types. The Apple II filled that niche in a way the Apple I never could have.

TO: What motivated you to become so involved with computers?

LL: Because I grew up among linguists and electronics pioneers, I always believed that computers would become pervasive within our society. My concern was that we would follow a path leading to all the machine-control and information-handling power of computers in the hands of a tiny scientific elite. When, in 1972, I discovered a Montessori primary school that was using a terminal attached to Lawrence Hall of Science as an educational "toy," I was delighted. Making sure that youngsters knew exactly how programs got into computers was the best possible vaccination against public intimidation by that elite (Figure 1.14). From then on, I put all of my available energy into finding ways to get ordinary people to take control of those mysterious machines, computers.

Figure 1.14 Learning at the LO*OP Center

Steve Wozniak was on a similar track. He also wanted to provide broad public access to and understanding of computers. Luckily our paths crossed at Homebrew. I'd like to think that by keeping in touch with him and sharing my woes trying to use the Apple I in educational settings, I contributed, in a small way, to the birth of the Apple II and its success in making the computer an everyday tool.

The task of harnessing the power of computing to the needs of sustainable human society is not complete. Humanity is still in danger of computing its way to extinction. Perhaps, by following the life history of those 200 Apple Is that existed for a short time, we can learn a lesson in the appropriate use of technology.

Steve Fish

Steve Fish was introduced to computers in the U.S. Navy in 1972. He worked for Burroughs Corp. as a computer systems technician in the mid '70s in its Santa Barbara, California-based minicomputer assembly plant. He attended Brooks Institute in Santa Barbara and graduated with a degree in professional photography. He became immediately involved in the microcomputer revolution and founded Peripheral Visions Inc., which specialized in photographic and audio/visual software and hardware until the early 1990s. Steve now works as a freelance underwater photographer, filmmaker, and Web designer.

TO: Did you have any background in computers previous to the Apple I?

SF: In the mid-1970s, I spent a lot of time prowling the few computer stores that existed in those days, looking for a way to get back into computers. In the Navy, I had worked a little bit with Super Nova Micro computers around 1972–73. After the Navy, I used that experience and worked for a few months as a computer systems technician for Burroughs before returning to college to get a degree in professional photography. Though I had repaired quite a lot of computer processors and peripherals, I hadn't ever really done any programming. Running maintenance routines wasn't all that much fun. I took a "programming" class, but it consisted mostly of punching cards and sorting them into stacks. Not very satisfying.

TO: When did you first learn of the Apple I?

SF: In 1976, when the Apple I was first introduced, a small computer store called Computer Playground had just opened in Orange County, California, near where I was working. In addition to selling the Apple I and the limited other hardware items that were available at that time, they had a number of Apple I systems installed as "workstations" that you could rent time on by the hour to play games or write your own programs. I started frequenting the establishment to play games (much more fun than sorting a stack of punch cards) and took a BASIC programming course taught by Dr. Will Otaguro, one of the owners. While I don't remember the first program I wrote, I definitely remember the feeling of instant gratification when I ran it without having to run a stack of cards through a teletype and wait for a line printer to churn out a ream of paper. These computers were cool! They were self-contained, and when you hit the Return key, execution was immediate.

The Apple I workstations [at Computer Playground] were built into a false wall with a keyboard shelf and a monitor behind a window. Everything else was in the back; you never actually saw the hardware. You could play Star Trek, Life, Lunar Lander, or several other games. When you wanted to play a different game or tinker in BASIC, a staff member (usually Will) would go into the back room where the motherboards and monitors were and load the program for you. The Apple I systems that they had for sale were a bit fancier. They had custom-made walnut cases with built-in keyboards. They looked a little like wooden versions of the (future) Apple II.

The store gained quite a following. Any evening you would find several users sitting at their keyboards either banging away at a program or playing one of the games. Not many were programming anything in machine language at that point—pretty much all BASIC because there wasn't an assembler for the Apple I in the early days. Heck, even the Woz was handcoding his machine language at that point; BASIC was written on paper!

TO: When did you decide to buy an Apple I?

SF: I didn't buy an Apple I immediately. I rented a lot of time on them, though. When the Apple II came out, I decided to take the plunge and bought a 4K Apple II motherboard. Yes, initially, you could just buy an Apple II board and add your own keyboard and power supplies, just like the Apple I. That stopped after the Apple II was on the market a few months, but I got one out of the first production run (SN 468), and I still have it. When the Apple II was introduced, the Apple I market dried up pretty fast. Everyone (me included) was hot for the II. Computer Playground merged with another LA-area computer store called Computer Components Inc. and moved into much larger quarters. In the move, the idea of workstations that you could rent time on sort of died off (until the revival of the cybercafé 20 years later). All of the workstation Apple Is and a couple of the nice walnut-cased units were sold off at clearance prices. I bought one of the nice Apple Is in the walnut case in late

1977, mostly out of nostalgia (see Figures 1.15 and 1.16). It was the machine that I learned to program on, and they were dirt cheap by that time. I believe that the bare board systems were donated to an Explorer Post in the area for geek scouts to play with.

Figure 1.15 Steve Fish's Apple I

Figure 1.16 Inside Steve Fish's Apple I

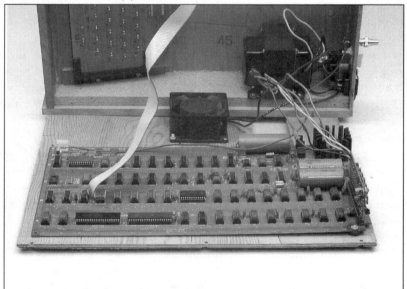

TO: How did you use your Apple I?

SF: I'm not sure if I ever even powered up my Apple I after I bought it. I think I probably just put it in the closet, figuring I'd get it out and play with it someday. That day didn't happen until about 28 years later, when I found the Apple I Owners Club on Applefritter by chance and was inspired to get [the computer] out and dust it off. I had a few minor problems getting it running, but mostly it was just a couple wires broken from being moved around and a minor keyboard problem. At any rate, it's now alive and well and in pretty much the same condition it was when it was brand new. No hacks or mods [modifications] on the motherboard. It's as close to being mint as a 28-year-old computer can be. It was never owned by anyone else, or even used until 2005. I have the original Sanyo 9-inch BW monitor that was originally used on my Apple II, but it is of the same vintage as the Apple I. Also, the Panasonic cassette was originally used with my Apple II, but is the same model that was being used with the Apple I at that time for loading programs. The cassette interface on the Apple I was always a little bit on the fussy side, but once you get the input and output levels set correctly, it hums along quite nicely. It's only about 1500 baud, but in those days that was quite fast. Mine still has the original 8K RAM configuration. In 1977, 16K RAM chips cost about $500 for a set of eight. Though I have a box full of 16K chips now, I'm choosing to leave the Apple I in its original 8K configuration.

I've been an Apple user continuously since 1976. I suspect that there aren't a lot of us left who have never, ever gone over to "the dark side." Heck, even Steve Jobs was a NeXT user for a few years. When I compare the capabilities of my Apple I of 1977 with my current Mac PowerBook, it's almost like a science fiction story come true. I feel very privileged to have been involved with personal computing literally from the very start. I wonder what the next 30 years will bring; I bet it will be wickedly cool.

Allen Baum

Allen J. Baum is a principal engineer at Intel working on enterprise processor architectures. Previously, he worked at Digital Equipment Corp. and Compaq Computer on the StrongArm (SA1500) and Alpha EV7 and EV8 processor designs. Prior to his position at DEC he worked on the Newton, Apple II, and proprietary processors at Apple and was a designer of the PA-RISC architecture and HP45 calculator at HP. He received his BSEE and MSEE from MIT in 1974. He is named on over 17 patents in the area of processor architectures and is chair of the IEEE Technical Committee on Microprocessors and Microcomputers, which oversees the Hot Chips conference.

TO: Could you tell us about the Homebrew Computer Club and your involvement with it?

AB: My involvement was as a "charter" (I guess) member. I saw a flyer for the first meeting (probably at the People's Computer Center) and thought that Steve would be interested and dragged him along.

The Homebrew Computer Club was arguably the earliest meeting place for hobbyists who had, or dreamed of having, their own personal computer. It started in Gordon French's garage, where he demonstrated his Altair to us. Most of the early personal computer companies got their start there.

The club was later "conducted" by ringmaster Lee Felsenstein (himself greatly responsible for many early personal computer successes) and grew to fill the auditorium of Stanford's Linear Accelerator Center. It served as a forum for product (and project) introductions and demos, software and information exchanges (back when that was still legal …), asking and getting advice on problems (both in design and use of products), and just being able to mingle with other like-minded people.

TO: What did you use your Apple I for? What programs did you write?

AB: I was mostly writing development utilities for it. Steve was hand-assembling his code and typing it in hex. He could do that in his head, and he was an extremely fast and accurate typist. I wasn't; so, even after hand-assembling, trying to figure out whether what I typed in was what I had intended was tough. So, the first thing I wrote was the disassembler, which would allow me to see whether I typed the right thing in.

The next thing was a mini-assembler, which used the disassembler as a subroutine (basically, the assembler guessed all possible values, ran it through the disassembler, and stopped when it matched). Steve and I worked over those and got the sizes down to under 256 bytes each. I credit Steve for saving most of the bytes.

After that, I started working on a debugger and a Fortran compiler, but got bogged down with engineer's disease (kept designing it trying to get it perfect, but never actually finishing) so never finished.

TO: Any stories to share?

AB: I remember Steve sitting in the lobby of Homebrew with his hand-wired Apple I (in addition to being an incredibly fast, accurate typist, he's the best technician I know—his wiring and soldering were unbelievably neat and careful), typing in his BASIC interpreter in hex—all 4K, trying to get it done before the break. He'd type a bunch and then would have to check it all character by character to make sure he hadn't blown it (he didn't very often).

I think that's when I decided to write the disassembler and when he decided he'd better get a cassette interface working.

Apple contracted with one of Woz's fellow HP employees (I don't recall if this was before or after Woz left HP) to design the cassette interface. It was a board full of op amps and analog parts. I think Woz was pretty disgusted—it was way overkill, so he chucked it and redesigned it to work with a few really simple parts, cutting down to a tenth its original size and cost. Steve was always really focused on getting the absolute simplest, lowest-cost design.

Summary

The Apple I is so primitive compared with computers today that it's difficult to imagine a time when users entered programs in machine code and connecting a printer required use of a soldering iron. Nothing about the Apple I was a mystery to its users. They knew how to determine the function of every wire on the motherboard and every byte of code in their programs. As you learn to program and build your replica of the Apple I, you too will have the opportunity to learn all the secrets of its inner workings.

Chapter 2

Tools and Materials

Topics in this Chapter:

- Introduction: Tools You'll Need
- Multimeter
- Logic Probe
- Breadboard
- Wire-Wrap Tools
- Soldering Iron and Materials
- Power Supply
- TTL Chips
- Circuit Boards and Software Tools
- Chip Pullers and Straighteners
- Ambience

Introduction: Tools You'll Need

Before we get started building an Apple I replica, let's take a look at a few of the tools and materials that we'll need to complete this project. Some are more necessary than others, and several won't be needed until later in the book. If you don't have the parts you need to build an Apple I readily available or you have trouble obtaining them, you might consider skipping ahead to the programming section for the time being and simply using an emulator instead.

Multimeter

The digital multimeter is the first item on our list and a tool everyone should own. We're about to spend a few hundred pages talking about electricity, so it's important to be familiar with the tool we use to measure it. We'll use the multimeter primarily to measure DC voltage and, occasionally, resistance. If you don't have a multimeter, consider buying one at once. It doesn't need to be anything fancy; it should merely be functional for use in these projects. An inexpensive meter from Harbor Freight or eBay can be had for under $10 and will work just fine.

Figure 2.1 A Cen-Tech Multimeter

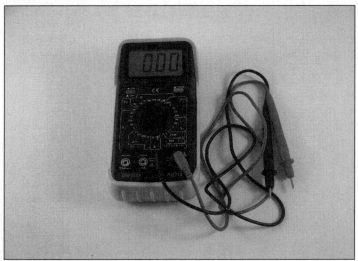

Figure 2.1 shows the meter I normally use. I almost ordered it from Jameco when I saw Harbor Freight had the same unit on sale at half the cost. Be sure to shop around to find the best price. This meter is made by Cen-Tech, which seems to dominate the cheap multimeter market.

Shown in Figure 2.2 is one of the less expensive meters you'll find on eBay or at an import store. It is also made by Cen-Tech and works moderately well, but it is of a significantly lesser quality than its pricier counterparts. I've already broken one of the cables, and when the batteries died in this unit, I lost patience and wired it up to the AC using a power adapter from an old modem. A less expensive model like this one can be good to have around as a practical backup unit.

Figure 2.2 A Cen-Tech Seven-Function Multimeter

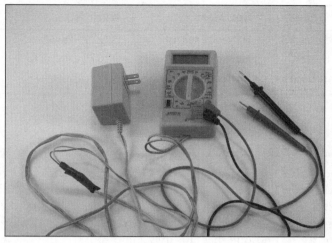

Finally, if you're feeling especially geeky, large, older meters such as the Racal-Dana (see Figure 2.3) can be fun. They're more precise and more reliable than the cheap, modern versions, and you can get them for a song from surplus sellers. Of course, they are kind of big. (This particular unit was Navy surplus and came out of a system for testing aircraft circuitry. It's about 20 years old.) Table 2.1 lists various types of multimeters and retailers you can buy them from.

Figure 2.3 A Racal-Dana Multimeter

Table 2.1 Multimeters

Product Type	Retailer	Item No.	Price
Cen-Tech Multimeter	Harbor Freight	37772-3VGA	$19.99
Cen-Tech 7-Func Multimeter	Harbor Freight	92020-0VGA	$9.99
EZ Digital Benchtop Multimeter	Jameco	132564	$219.95

Logic Probe

Digital signals are either on or off, high or low, zero or one. Touch the point of a logic probe to a wire and it will respond with either "high" or "low." This is an invaluable tool for building circuits and one you'll use frequently. Most logic probes have two light-emitting diodes (LEDs)—one that lights when the line is high and one that lights when it's low. Depending on how the pen-shaped logic probe is positioned, the LEDs can be hard to see while you're working. Look for a probe that has its LEDs close to the tip or try to find one that also uses audio tones as an indicator. In addition, try to find one that looks like it could double as a murder weapon, because if the point isn't sharp (thin) enough, it could be difficult getting it into the breadboard holes, as we'll see in the next section.

In Figure 2.4, you can see my logic probe, which is a bit awkward to work with because of the positioning of the LEDs. Figure 2.5 shows a classic Hewlett-Packard logic probe. These are no longer available new, but you can still find them on eBay, and they are often a better value than the majority of the newer probes.

A logic probe can be purchased for less than $20. If you'd rather not spend the money, it is possible to get by with just a multimeter. In this case, 2.4 to 5 volts is a digital high, and 0 to 0.4 volts is a digital low. Table 2.2 lists various types of logic probes.

Figure 2.4 The LP-900 Logic Probe

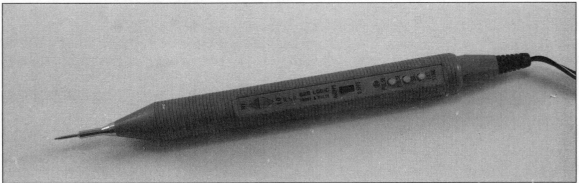

Figure 2.5 A Hewlett-Packard Logic Probe

Table 2.2 Logic Probes

Product Type	Retailer	Item No.	Price
Logic Probe Kit	Ocean State Electronics	LP-525K	$15.95
Logic Probe	Ocean State Electronics	LP-550	$18.95
Logic Probe	Ocean State Electronics	LP-900	$27.95
Logic Probe	Jameco	149930	$29.95

Breadboard

Before building the replica, let's do a few basic experiments in electronics. A breadboard is almost essential for these exercises and is also ideal for making quick prototypes. Breadboards come in a variety of sizes, as outlined in Table 2.3. In Figure 2.6, you'll see three models that Circuit Specialists sells. The medium–sized unit on the left is the one that I would recommend. It's large enough to handle all the projects in this book, and it has banana plugs for connecting the power supply. The smaller unit on the right will work fine as well; it's just not as convenient.

Table 2.3 Breadboards

Size	Retailer	Item No.	Price
Small	Circuit Specialists	WB-102+J	$6.25
Medium	Circuit Specialists	WB-104-1+J	$12.99
Large	Circuit Specialists	WB-108+J	$22.90

Figure 2.6 Breadboards

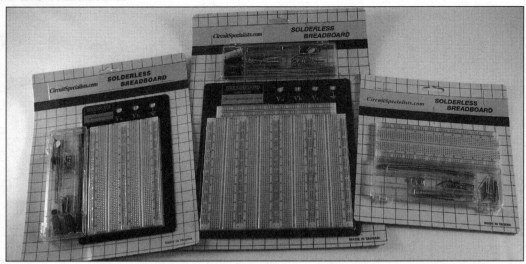

Wire-Wrap Tools

Wire wrapping is useful if you have unique designs that you want to build, play with for a few months, and then take apart. Breadboards are much more convenient for quick, temporary designs, whereas circuit boards are more reliable for long-term setups (especially if your wire-wrapping abilities are anything like mine!). If, however, you're designing your circuit as you're building it or you just don't have the patience to wait around for a printed circuit board, wire-wrap may be your best option.

The basic wrapping tool from Radio Shack (see Table 2.4) works considerably well. Be sure to get a few different colors of wire so you can tell them apart. There is nothing worse than trying to trace a tangled mess of thousands of wire-wrapped lines—this cheapskate knows!

Table 2.4 Wire-Wrap Tools

Type of Tool	Retailer	Item No.	Price
Wire-wrapping tool	Radio Shack	276-1570	$6.99
Red wire wrap	Radio Shack	278-501	$3.29
White wire wrap	Radio Shack	278-502	$3.29
Blue wire wrap	Radio Shack	278-503	$3.29
8-pin DIP socket	Radio Shack	900-7242	$0.80
14-pin DIP socket	Radio Shack	900-7243	$1.20
16-pin DIP socket	Radio Shack	900-7244	$1.35
18-pin DIP socket	Radio Shack	900-7245	$1.56
20-pin DIP socket	Radio Shack	900-7246	$1.75

Continued

Table 2.4 Wire-Wrap Tools

Type of Tool	Retailer	Item No.	Price
24-pin DIP socket	Radio Shack	900-7249	$2.00
28-pin DIP socket	Radio Shack	900-7250	$2.42
40-pin DIP socket	Jameco	41187	$3.15

If you expect to do a lot of wire wrapping, consider getting a Cooper automatic wire-wrapping tool. These sell as new for a few hundred dollars but can often be found at very affordable prices on eBay.

Finally, you're going to need sockets, which hold the chips, as well as a wire-wrap board. Sockets cost anywhere from $0.80 to a little over $3.00, which means that their cost can add up fast. For circuit boards, try the 32-DE-STD wire-wrap board from Douglas Electronics, which is available for $21.53. Douglas is a reliable company. I have a brochure of theirs from 1983 in which the same board is advertised with the same part number—and the price has only gone up $1.53 in the last 22 years.

Soldering Iron and Materials

Soldering components to a circuit board is the most reliable and permanent method for building your Apple I replica. The process requires a potentially expensive printed circuit board, discussed later in this chapter, but the soldering equipment itself can be very affordable. A good soldering job on a printed circuit board will result in a product indistinguishable from a professionally made board.

When choosing a soldering iron, make sure to get one with adequate power. The inexpensive 15W irons (Figure 2.7), which can be found for around $5, can be adequate, but they are exceedingly frustrating if you don't know what you're doing. A 40W iron can be purchased for under $10 and will save you a world of frustration. These "pencil irons" are entirely contained within the handle. In Figure 2.8 you can see the simple coil-heating mechanism of a standard pencil iron.

Figure 2.7 A 15W Soldering Iron

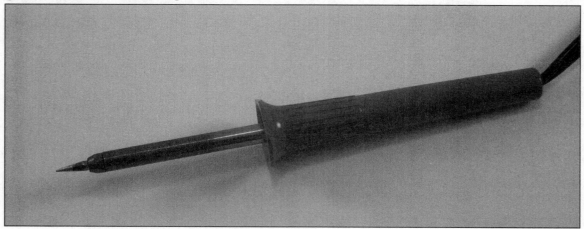

Figure 2.8 A Disassembled Soldering Iron

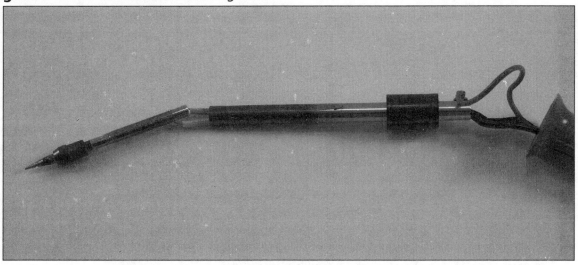

If you plan to do a lot of soldering, consider a more expensive, temperature-controlled iron. Temperature-controlled irons allow you to precisely set the temperature of your iron and ensure that the temperature stays within a narrow range. Shown in Figure 2.9 is a Hakko FP-102 soldering station. This tool, as well as similar high-end soldering irons, is very reliable and pleasant to work with.

Figure 2.9 The Hakko FP-102 Soldering Station

WARNING

Don't neglect safety. Molten solder on the eyeball is sure to ruin your day; so always wear your safety goggles. Likewise, be sure to work in a well-ventilated room and keep a fan on to blow the fumes away from you. And if the iron starts to fall—*don't* try to catch it!

Solder is inexpensive and can be found at any electronics store. However, be certain that you purchase rosin-core and not acid-core solder (see Figure 2.10). Even though it's doubtful you'd find it in an electronic store, acid core will ruin your circuits.

Figure 2.10 Rosin-Core Solder

Mistakes are made, and components die. For whatever reason, sometimes it's necessary to remove a component that has been soldered in. There are two different methods for removing components. One is to heat the solder and then suck it into a desoldering pump (see Figure 2.11). The other method is to wick the solder out with a desoldering braid (see Figure 2.12). The braid is placed against the solder and then heated. As the solder melts, it diffuses into the braid. Table 2.5 lists various types of soldering supplies.

Figure 2.11 A Desoldering Pump

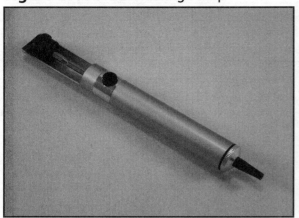

Figure 2.12 Desoldering Braid

Table 2.5 Soldering Supplies

Type of Tool	Retailer	Item No.	Price
Hakko Soldering Station	Hakko USA	FP-102-01	$249.97
40W pencil iron	Radio Shack	#64-2071	$8.39
15W with grounded tip	Radio Shack	#64-2051	$8.39
Xytronix Soldering Iron, 40W	Jameco	#224602	$9.95
Rosin Core Solder, 8.0 oz.	Radio Shack	#64-007	$7.29
Solder Roll, 1.1 lbs.	Jameco	#141786	$7.95
Desoldering tool	Radio Shack	#64-2098	$7.29
Desoldering pump	Jameco	#19166	$4.95
Desoldering braid	Radio Shack	#64-2090	$3.19
Desoldering braid	Jameco	#63695	$1.95

Power Supply

To power your Apple I replica as well as your other experiments, you'll need an AT power supply. An AT power supply is distinguished by the connectors shown in Figure 2.13.

Figure 2.13 AT Motherboard Connectors

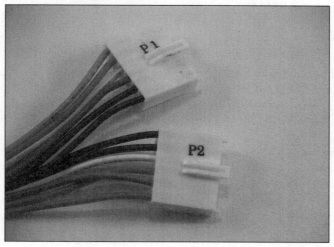

An AT power supply like the one shown in Figure 2.14 is extremely easy to find. Any pre-ATX computer will have one, and systems like these get thrown away every day. Go to a Hamfest www.arrl.org/hamfests.html, and you'll find one for no more than a couple dollars. On eBay you can purchase one for around $5. New ones can run anywhere from $35 to $50. When looking at power supplies, you'll usually see the wattage rating advertised. For our simple project, any rating will work. If you already have a spare ATX power supply, you only need to find an adapter similar to the one pictured in Figure 2.15.

Figure 2.14 An AT Power Supply	**Figure 2.15** An ATX-to-AT Adapter
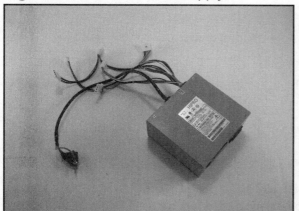	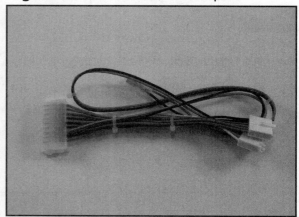

AT supplies are "switching power supplies" and should require a load to operate properly. With nothing connected to your power supply, check the output voltage on the 5 volt (red) line. It should be 5 volts. If it's not, try connecting it to something like a spare hard drive to create a load and regulate the voltage. With the AT power supplies I've tried, this hasn't been necessary, but it's a good idea to check before you connect anything important.

TTL Chips

We'll be doing many experiments in the first couple chapters, so it's good to have chips readily available. The chips you'll need to complete the introductory projects are:

Table 2.6 lists the transistor-transistor logic (TTL) chips that you'll need for the projects in this book.

Table 2.6 Needed TTL Chips

IC	Type	Jameco#	Price
74LS00	NAND	46252	$0.29
74LS02	NOR	46287	$0.29
74LS04	INV	46316	$0.29
74LS08	AND	46375	$0.36
74LS32	OR	47466	$0.29
74LS74	Flip-Flop	48004	$0.29
74LS86	XOR	48098	$0.35

TTL chips will be labeled 74xx, where 74 is the series of chips that we'll be using and xx is a number that specifies the particular chip. Often you'll see a few letters between 74 and xx, such as 74LSxx. These classifications are described as follows:

- **74Lxx, low power** Requires 1/10 the power and runs at 1/10 the speed of a standard TTL IC
- **74Hxx, high power** Requires twice the power and operates at twice the speed
- **74Sxx, Schottky** Runs at higher speed
- **74LSxx, low-power Schottky** Runs at high speed and requires 1/5 the power
- **74ALSxx** Advanced low-power Schottky
- **74HCxx** CMOS chips; equivalent to the CMOS 4xxx series

NEED TO KNOW...

Transistor-transistor logic (TTL) is a method for creating the logic gates in integrated circuits using two transistors at the output circuit. The primary alternative to TTL is complementary metal oxide semiconductor (CMOS). CMOS circuits use less power than TTL but are also more prone to static damage.

You can get most TTL chips for less than a dollar from Jameco. You can also buy bags of mixed chips very affordably from Jameco and on eBay. If you're planning to do more projects, these bags are a good deal.

Another option is to take the chips out of old computers and other electronics that are being discarded. Don't let any piece of hardware make it to the trash without being thoroughly dismantled. Circuit boards are always a great place to find chips; printers and disk drives are a great source for small motors.

Circuit Boards and Software Tools

To get the total design experience you should design a printed circuit board for your Apple I Replica. The schematic and board layout shown in this book were done using the McCAD EDS SE software tools made by VAMP Inc. For those of you wishing to expand your experience, VAMP Inc. has provided you with the McCAD EDS SE bundle on the CD that comes with this book. Also on the CD you will find the libraries and design files that were used to create the printed circuit board for the Replica I.

While wire wrap remains a cost-effective solution for those looking to make only a single board, the argument that getting prototype boards made is too expensive just isn't true any more. In single quantities the cost will range from $50 to $100, depending on what options you request at the board fabricator facility (Table 2.7). In larger quantities the cost per item will drop significantly. If you total the cost of special wire-wrap sockets and cheese board used in wire wrapping, a printed circuit board is often less money. You also might wish to consider that if you plan on making more than one Apple Replica I, wire wrapping does not save any time. In fact with wire-wrap versions you usually have two or more projects that have to be debugged.

I encourage you to use the McCAD EDS SE bundle that we have provided on the CD. You will find it extremely easy to master and use, while having a robust set of capabilities at your disposal. While there are numerous other free tools available on the Web, none offers the combination of ease of use and power that McCAD does.

HISTORY OF McCAD

The McCAD series of computer-aided design tools have being in continuous development since 1984. This division of VAMP Inc. was one of the original 39 developers for the Macintosh. Its long history with Apple's Human Interface Guidelines clearly shows in the design of the tools and enables quick mastery of the tool sets. To see a full listing of the company's products, which expand upon those included with the book, you may visit its Web site at http://www.McCAD.com.

Table 2.7 PCB Manufacturers

Manufacturer	Web Site
ExpressPCB	www.expresspcb.com
Overnite Protos	www.pcborder.com
PCB Express	www.pcbexpress.com
PCB Express	www.pcbontime.us

Chip Pullers and Straighteners

As you work, you'll frequently find yourself in a situation in which you want to remove chips from their sockets. The best way to do this is to take a small flat screwdriver, insert it under the chip, and gently pry upward. If the chip is soldered onto the board, you can use an IC extraction tool (about $2) to gently pull it up as you unsolder. However, you should not use the extraction tool to remove socketed chips because it will put pressure on solder joints.

One tool that is very helpful is a chip straightener. Invariably, the pins on the chip you're attempting to insert will all be bent out just a little bit further than what you need. Bending them back (don't go too far!) can be an onerous task without a straightener. Table 2.8 lists some chip pullers and straighteners.

Table 2.8 Chip Pullers and Straighteners

Type of Tool	Retailer	Item No.	Price
IC pin straightener	Jameco	#99362	$6.95
DIP IC extractor	Jameco	#16838	$1.49

Need to Know...

Sockets (see Figure 2.16) allow you to easily insert and remove chips without soldering them directly to the circuit board. Instead of the chip, the socket gets soldered to the board. This facilitates the replacement of chips and spares the chips the extreme heat of being directly soldered in.

Figure 2.16 DIP Socket

Keyboard and Monitor

Whether you end up building the Replica I from a kit or using your own design, you are going to want a keyboard and a monitor. The original Apple I used an ASCII keyboard, and this option remains today. Unfortunately, ASCII keyboards are all but impossible to find. Figure 2.17 shows an ASCII keyboard taken from an Apple II+, but these machines are becoming collectibles in their own right. As an alternative, Vince Briel designed an interface for a PS/2 keyboard, which is now part of the Replica I design. With this, any modern PS/2 keyboard, such as that in Figure 2.18, can be used with the Replica I.

Figure 2.17 An ASCII Keyboard

Figure 2.18 A PS/2 Keyboard

Video output is via a standard composite video signal. If you have an old composite monitor (Figure 2.19), such as from an Apple IIe or Commodore 64, it will work perfectly. If not, composite monitors can also be found on eBay for a pittance, or a television equipped with composite video will work just as well.

Figure 2.19 A Video Monitor

Ambience

What are you neighbors doing right now? Probably something ordinary. By contrast, you're designing a computer in your garage or perhaps even in your bedroom. Wherever you are, it's important that you begin referring to this location as your *laboratory*. Pronunciation is equally important. Lower your voice and deeply enunciate each syllable of the word. Practice explaining to your parents or spouse that you are "working in your laboratory." Because, let's face it, ordinary folks don't build computers—you're a scientist now.

Now that you've got a laboratory (did you pronounce that right?), a lab coat is clearly in order. There are a plethora of new lab coats on eBay, often factory seconds, that sell for less than $10. Many lab coats now come in blue, but I strongly recommend white for that quintessential mad scientist look. Order a spare—you never know when you might acquire an assistant.

Let's not forget safety glasses! Sure, we mentioned them earlier in regard to soldering, but safety glasses can be quite stylish, too. For the best reactions, be sure to get colored lenses. Mine are tinted green.

Next we need music—something ominous to set the mood. I asked my fellow mad scientists what they listen to and came up with a few suggestions. Dr. Webster recommends Orff's classical *Camina Burana*. Reverend Darkness is a fan of *Night on Bald Mountain* as well as *Tocatta and Fugue in D Minor*, played by an orchestra, not by the usual pipe organ. Deadelvis listens to *Danse Macabre* by Saint-Saens and Mozart's *Requiem Mass*. Also worthy of consideration are the soundtracks to *The Twilight Zone* and *2001: A Space Odyssey*. Stuka recommends the MIDI soundtrack to the game *Doom*, which is available for free online.

## Chapter 3

Digital Logic

Topics in this Chapter:

- Breadboarding
- Electricity
- Gates
- Circuits with Algebra
- Latches and Flip-Flops
- What Is Data?
- A Few More Chips
- Summary

Introduction

This chapter provides an introduction to digital logic, the basis of microcomputer design. Although it is *not* critical that you understand everything in this chapter, to gain a full understanding of the microcomputer a background in digital logic is imperative. Each level that we'll cover (digital logic, microcomputer, and software) contains a certain degree of abstraction from the layer following it.

Breadboarding

We'll perform all the experiments in this chapter using breadboards. To begin, perform the following steps:

1. Find a power supply and snip off one of the hard drive connectors.

2. Strip down the end of the red wire (5 volts) and the black wire (ground).

3. Turn the power supply on and check these cables with your multimeter to ensure that they really are 5 volts and ground.

4. On your breadboard, you'll see a series of red and blue lines running the length of the plastic. Connect the power supply cables to the banana plugs, and connect the banana plugs to these lines (see Figure 3.1)

Figure 3.1 Connecting Power and Ground

The holes beside these lines are for power and ground, respectively. A look inside may help us understand how these boards work (see Figure 3.2).

Figure 3.2 Inside the Breadboard

Inside each hole is a metallic socket into which you can plug a wire or component. Every socket in the ground strip is connected; therefore, if you connect one socket to your ground supply, all sockets in the strip are grounded. The same rule applies to the power strip. We have three columns of power and ground strips with nothing connecting them, so we need to use jumper wires across the bottom (see Figure 3.3).

Figure 3.3 Jumpering Power and Ground Lines

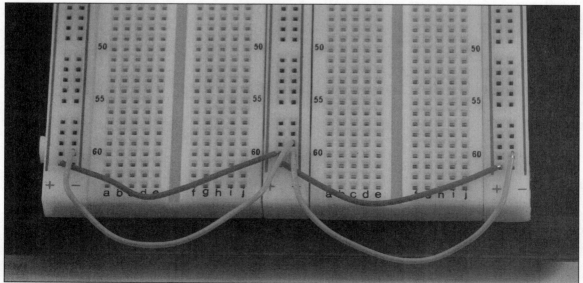

To help gain an understanding of the rest of the board, take a look at Figure 3.2 once again. Each horizontal row of five sockets is connected. Therefore, if we wanted to connect three resistors in a series (one after the other), we could configure them as shown in Figure 3.4.

Figure 3.4 Resistors in Series

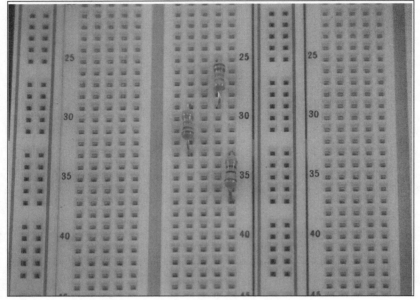

Next, let's make sure everything's configured correctly by running some tests using the logic probe:

1.   Connect your probe's alligator clips to the power and ground lines (see Figure 3.5).

Figure 3.5 Connecting the Logic Probe

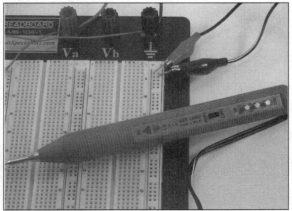

2. Touch the point of the probe to any socket on the power line. The "HI" light should come on.

3. Test a socket in each strip by repeating Step 2.

4. Repeat Step 2 yet another time for the ground sockets; for these, the "LOW" light should come on (see Figure 3.6). The sockets connected to neither power nor ground should produce no light at all.

Figure 3.6 Testing with the Logic Probe

Electricity

Here you'll find a very brief, hands-on introduction to electronics fundamentals. This chapter provides enough of the basics that you shouldn't have too much difficulty completing the Apple I. However, a more substantial understanding of electronics will serve you well in the future. If you'd like to do some further reading, *The Art of Electronics,* by Paul Horowitz and Winfield Hill (Cambridge University Press, 1989), is the most widely acclaimed book on the topic but is perhaps too difficult for the beginner. A more appropriate book for the novice is *Hands-On Electronics,* by Daniel M. Kaplan and Christopher G. White (Cambridge University Press, 2003).

Voltage and Current

Voltage (*V*) is the potential difference between two points, measured in volts. When you set your multimeter to Volts DC and touch the probes to the breadboard, negative to negative and positive to positive, you'll get a reading of 5 volts. That is related to the amount of energy it takes to move charge from the lower point (ground) to the higher.

Current (*I*) is used to measure the rate of flow of electrical charge and can be thought of in terms of a water current. Current is measured in amperes (*A*). Whereas voltage is measured *between* two points, current measures the rate of flow *at* a particular point. DC voltage is steady (hook your circuit up to a 5-volt supply, and 5 volts is what you'll get), but current only "pulls" as much as you need. If you have a power supply capable of 10 amps and your circuit only needs 5 amps, then 5 amps is all that it will pull.

Power (*P*) is voltage multiplied by current. Power is measured in watts, which you're probably familiar with seeing on light bulbs. In fact, light bulbs serve as an excellent example. Consider a 20W and a 50W halogen bulb (see Figure 3.7). Both require 12 volts. The difference is in the current, which we can calculate using $P = V \cdot I$.

$I = P/V$ 20 watts / 12 volts = 1.6 amps   50 watts / 12 volts = 4.16 amps

Appropriately, we see that the brighter light bulb draws significantly more current than the dimmer one. Here's an exercise: Replace all the 40W lights in your house with 200W bulbs and see what happens to your electricity bill.

Figure 3.7 A Light Bulb Circuit

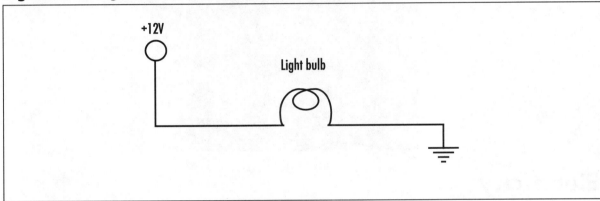

NEED TO KNOW...

If you have two wires you want to connect in a schematic, place a large dot at the point of connection. If there is no dot, readers (and the schematic software) will assume there is no physical connection between the two lines. See Figure 3.8.

Figure 3.8 Intersections

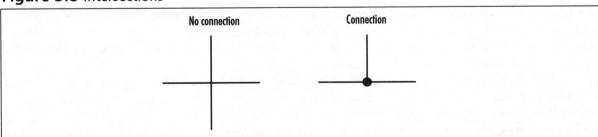

Resistors and Diodes

Now that we've explained the basics of current and voltage, we can take a more hands-on approach to resistance. Let's wire up a light-emitting diode (LED). A *diode* is a device that allows current to flow in only one direction. For this experiment, let's use a standard red LED, such as Model #276-041 from Radio Shack. These LEDs have a recommended voltage of about 2.25 volts, with a maximum voltage of 2.6 volts (you'll find all this information on the packaging). The maximum current is 28 mA. Our power supply provides 5 volts; therefore, if we hook the LED up directly to the power supply, it will probably burn out. (If you have a spare, try this!)

To reduce the voltage, use a resistor. A *resistor* is a partial conductor, usually made of carbon. We can calculate resistance using the equation:

R = V/I

where R (resistance) is calculated in ohms, V (voltage) in volts, and I (current) in amps.

Our circuit is shown in Figure 3.9. In moving from our 5-volt supply to ground, we have 5 volts we need to dispose of. The LED uses 2.25 volts, which leaves 2.75 volts for the resistor. This is the value we want to use for V in this equation. Now we can calculate:

R = (5v − 2.25v) / .028 A = 98 ohms

If you calculated decimal places, you're taking these numbers too seriously. Next, we need to find a 98-ohm resistor. A resistor with a smaller value will provide less resistance and potentially damage your LED. One with greater resistance merely means that your LED won't be quite as bright. We're just experimenting, so brightness level isn't a major concern. I used the nearest resistor I had available, which happened to be 300 ohm.

Now it's time to wire it up:

1. Snip off the ends of the resistor, making it fit conveniently into your breadboard.

2. Hook up the resistor and the LED in series. It doesn't matter which one you connect first; however, be aware that the orientation of the LED does matter (see the "LED Polarity" sidebar). The finished circuit is displayed in Figure 3.10.

Try swapping your current resistor with some resistors of varying sizes to see what happens. Also try putting the LED in backward.

Figure 3.9 LED Circuit

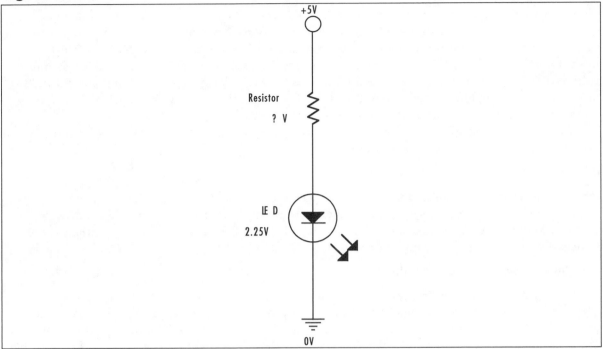

Figure 3.10 Wired LED

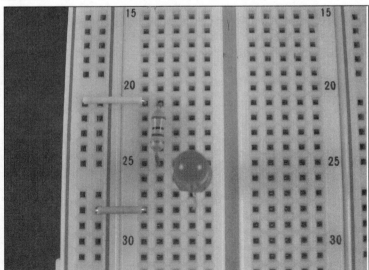

NEED TO KNOW...

An LED typically has two leads projecting from its base (see Figure 3.11). The longer lead is the positive lead (also known as the *anode*), and the shorter lead is the negative lead (also known as the *cathode*). The cathode is also denoted by a flat edge on the plastic LED housing. The anode will connect to a positive voltage (5V in this case), and the cathode will connect to ground.

Figure 3.11 LED Diagram

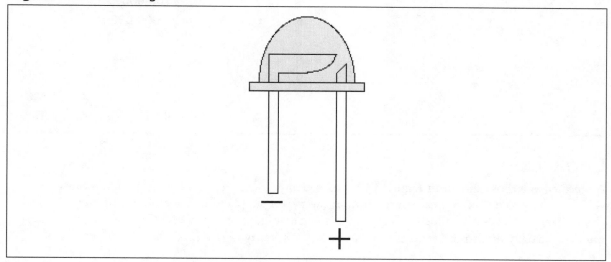

NEED TO KNOW...

Most resistors have four colored bars that will give you the value in ohms, as shown in Table 3.1. A resistor of Yellow, Red, Red, Gold would be 4,200 ohms, with an accuracy of 5%. If we needed a 30-ohm resistor, we would search for the colors Orange, Black, Black, Gold.

Memorizing Table 3.1 will save you time if you're going to do a lot of work with resistors. At the very least, knowing the values in column three will help prevent you from using an exponentially incorrect resistor. If you don't have the time to memorize the table or have no desire to haul the chart around with you, there are a multitude of Java applets on the Web that will do the conversions for you. There are also many applications for graphing calculators that allow you to complete the conversion without the work, including the RCOL for the HP 48, which is available at hpcalc.org. You can also simply use your multimeter to measure the ohms.

Table 3.1 Resistor Codes

Color	Bar 1	Bar 2	Bar 3	Bar 4
Black	0	0	x1	
Brown	1	1	x10	
Red	2	2	x100	
Orange	3	3	x1,000	
Yellow	4	4	x10,000	
Green	5	5	x100,000	
Blue	6	6	x1,000,000	
Magenta	7	7		
Gray	8	8		
White	9	9		
Gold			x0.1	5%
Silver			x0.01	10%

Capacitors

A *capacitor*, like those shown in Figure 3.12, stores energy in an electric field. In building our circuits, we'll use these as de-spiking capacitors to filter the power supply. When the output of one of our chips changes, it causes a sudden voltage drop (a negative-going spike). When this occurs, the capacitor will partially discharge its energy to eliminate the severity of this spike.

Figure 3.12 Capacitors

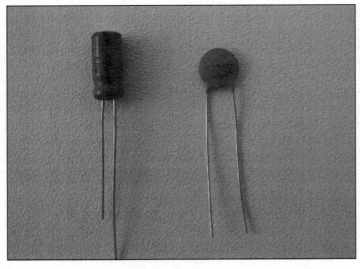

Gates

Those little black chips that cover circuit boards look extremely complex. Today, most of these *integrated circuits*, or ICs, are quite intricate, but there are still many chips available of the simpler variety. If you examine the chips in a modern computer, you will notice that many of them have hundreds of pins placed so closely that they appear almost impossible to work with. Open an older computer, and you'll discover chips that look much more accessible, with few pins and great spacing. We'll be working with these older, more "classic" chips throughout this book.

The 7400 series of ICs serves as the basis for digital logic and is very easy to understand. Throughout the rest of this chapter we'll concentrate on building a few very basic digital circuits using 7400 series ICs, resistors, and LEDs.

AND

IF it is dark *AND IF* there is a car in the driveway *THEN* turn on the porch light.

Under what circumstances is the porch light turned on? Only if both statements are true—it must be dark, and there must be a car in the driveway. One of the two is not enough. In a schematic, we'd express this idea as shown in Figure 3.13. The *D* symbol is a logical *AND*. We can also use a truth table. Follow along with the truth tables in Table 3.2 and see if they match the aforementioned assertions. You'll note that all three tables contain the same data. True is a logical 1, which is implemented with a 5-volt signal. False is a logical 0 and is implemented by a 0-volt signal.

Figure 3.13 An *AND* Gate

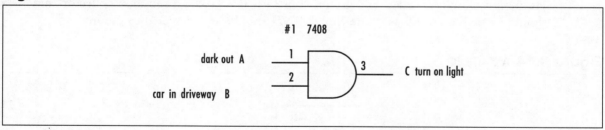

Table 3.2 *AND* Truth Tables

Input A	Input B	Output C
False	False	False
False	True	False
True	False	False
True	True	True

Continued

Table 3.2 *AND* Truth Tables

Input A	Input B	Output C
0	0	0
0	1	0
1	0	0
1	1	1

Input A	Input B	Output C
0v	0v	0v
0v	5v	0v
5v	0v	0v
5v	5v	5v

With all this in mind, perform the following steps:

1. Take a 7408 IC and insert it into your breadboard. This chip has four *AND* gates, arranged as you see in Figure 3.14. Note the location of the notch in the diagram.

2. Orient all chips so that the notch is at the top, and pin 1 will always be in the upper-left corner.

3. Hook up the supply voltage and ground. Pin 14 is Vcc (Voltage common collector) and should be tied to your 5-volt line. Pin 7, *GND*, should be connected to ground.

Figure 3.14 A 7408 IC

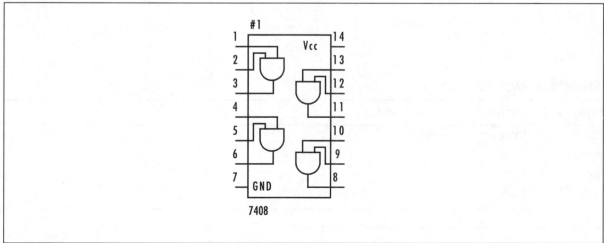

NEED TO KNOW...

Pin numbering always starts in the upper-left corner, goes down the left side, and follows up the right side. Pin 1 is marked either by a circle in the upper-left corner or by a notch in the top center (at which point it's up to you to know left from right). See Figure 3.15.

Figure 3.15 Pin Arrangement

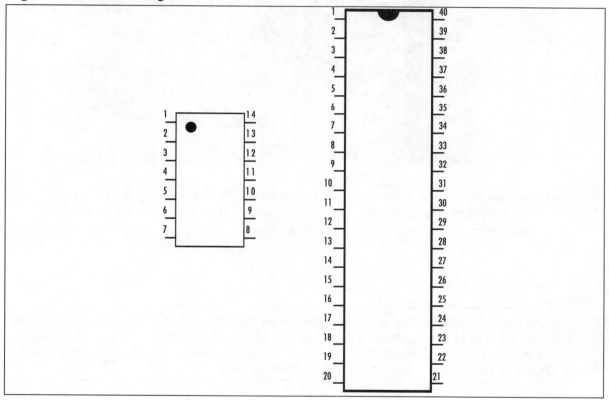

Now let's wire the first *AND* gate on the chip:

1. Connect pins 1 and 2 (inputs to the *AND* gate) to the supply voltage line.

2. Then, connect pin 3 to the input of the LED that was wired up earlier.

3. Turn on the power, wait a few nanoseconds for the signal to propagate, and the LED should light up (see Figure 3.16). Since both Input A and Input B are high, the output will also be high and the LED will be powered on.

Figure 3.16 The Lit LED

4. Next, take the wire from pin 2 (or pin 1) and move it from supply voltage to ground. To grasp the importance of this step, imagine that instead of moving the cable by hand, it's hooked up to a light sensor that outputs 0 volts when it's light out and 5 volts when it's dark.

NOTE

When a chip's inputs are changed, the output does not change instantaneously. The new signals take time to propagate throughout the chip. This propagation varies depending on the speed and complexity of the design, but TTL gates tend to take about 10 nanoseconds (ns) to complete propagation. There are 1 billion nanoseconds in a second.

If you like a challenge, try playing around with the chip a bit more by wiring the inputs of some gates to the outputs of others. Create the equivalent of a four-input *AND* gate. You can also examine the logic table in Table 3.3 to find patterns.

Table 3.3 A 4-Input *AND* Gate

Input A	Input B	Input C	Input D	Output E
0	0	0	0	0
0	0	0	1	0
0	0	1	0	0
0	0	1	1	0
0	1	0	0	0
0	1	0	1	0
0	1	1	0	0
0	1	1	1	0
1	0	0	0	0
1	0	0	1	0
1	0	1	0	0
1	0	1	1	0
1	1	0	0	0
1	1	0	1	0
1	1	1	0	0
1	1	1	1	1

Inverter, *NAND*

IF it is dark *AND IF* there is a car in the driveway, *THEN* turn *OFF* the porch light.

This statement is almost identical to the one in previous section, even though our goal has changed to produce the opposite effect. The only change that needs to be made is the addition of an inverter (see Table 3.4). The inverter takes whatever signal it is given and outputs the opposite; therefore, if you put 0 volts in, you'll get 5 volts out, and vice versa. In Figure 3.17, you'll see the symbol for an inverter along with an *AND* gate. The triangle means "buffer" (replicate the signal), and the small circle means "invert it." Find a 7404 (shown in Figure 3.18) and connect the voltage to supply and ground. Now connect the output of your *AND* gate (pin 3) to the input of the 7404's inverter (pin 1). The output of the inverter (pin 2) goes to the LED to complete our circuit, shown in Figure 3.19.

Table 3.4 Inverter Truth Table

Input A	Output B
0	1
1	0

Figure 3.17 An Inverter and an *AND* Gate

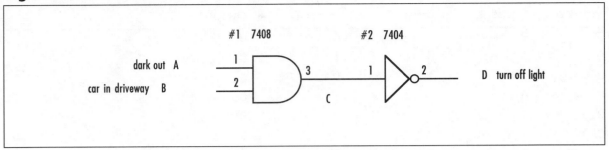

Figure 3.18 A 7404 IC

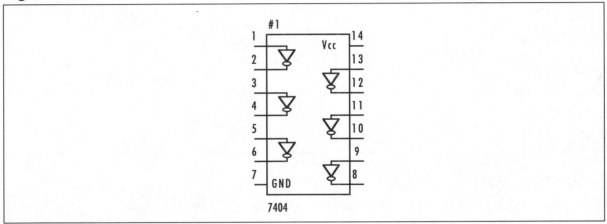

Figure 3.19 *AND* and *NAND* Gates, Wired to LED

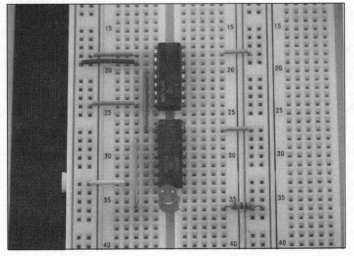

The inverted *AND* is so common that it has its own gate, the *NAND* (*not AND*) gate. This gate is functionally equivalent to an *AND* followed by an inverter. The *NAND* is pictured in Figure 3.20, with its layout in Figure 3.21. Table 3.5 displays its operation, which, hopefully, you were able to surmise.

Figure 3.20 The *NAND* Gate

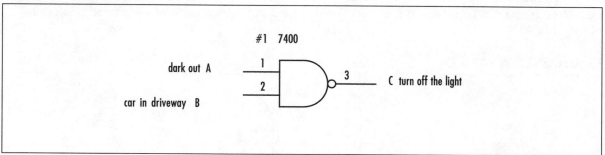

Figure 3.21 A 7400 IC

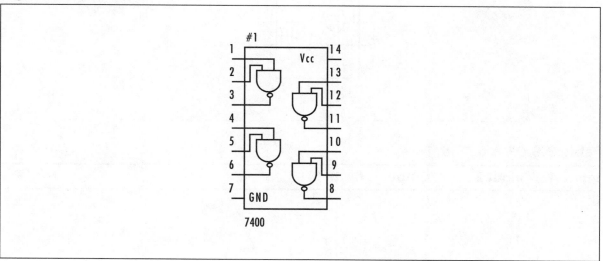

Table 3.5 *NAND* Truth Table

Input A	Input B	Output C
0	0	1
0	1	1
1	0	1
1	1	0

OR, NOR

IF it is dark *AND IF* there is a car in the driveway *OR* if the light switch is on, *THEN* turn on the porch light.

Here we take our output from the *AND* gate already wired up and *OR* it with "the light switch is on." The *OR* gate in TTL logic is the 7432 (see Figure 3.22), which exhibits the characteristics provided in Table 3.6.

Figure 3.22 A 7432 IC

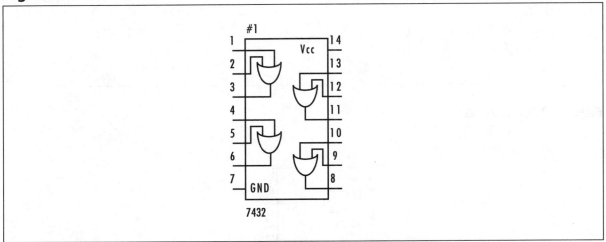

7432

Table 3.6 *OR* Gate Truth Table

Input A	Input B	Output C (A OR B)
0	0	0
0	1	1
1	0	1
1	1	1

Perform the following steps:

1. Take your 7432 and connect power and ground.

2. Using the *AND* circuit that you already wired, hook the output of the *AND* gate to an input of the *OR* (pin 1). The other *OR* input (pin 2) should be connected directly to power or ground to simulate the light switch being on or off.

3. Next, wire the *OR's* output (pin 3) to the LED (see Figure 3.23). Table 3.7 describes the behavior of this entire circuit. Note that the light comes on for five out of eight possible combinations.

Figure 3.23 *AND* and *OR*, Wired

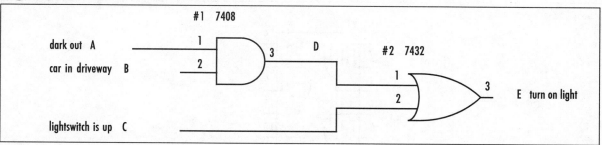

Table 3.7 Truth Table for Figure 3.23

Input A	Input B	A AND B	Input C	Output E ((A AND B) OR C)
0	0	0	0	0
0	1	0	0	0
1	0	0	0	0
1	1	1	0	1
0	0	0	1	1
0	1	0	1	1
1	0	0	1	1
1	1	1	1	1

As with *NAND*, there is also a *NOR* gate (see Figure 3.24), which is *OR* followed by an inverter. You can find *NOR* gates on the 7402 (see Figure 3.25). Table 3.8 shows a *NOR* gate truth table.

Figure 3.24 A *NOR* Gate

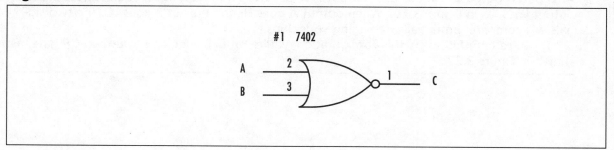

Figure 3.25 A 7402 IC

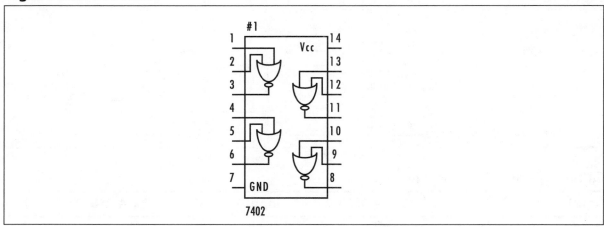

7402

Table 3.8 *NOR* Gate Truth Table

Input A	Input B	Output C (A NOR B)
0	0	1
0	1	0
1	0	0
1	1	0

Need to Know...

Let's say you have two *AND* gates and you want to combine their outputs so that if either *AND* gate's output is HI, our final output is HI as well. What happens if you connect the two output lines, as in Figure 3.26? When output A goes HI and output B goes LO, the two signals will compete, potentially damaging your chips.

If you're tempted to try this configuration, you're probably looking to use an *OR* gate, as shown in Figure 3.27.

Figure 3.26 A Bad Circuit

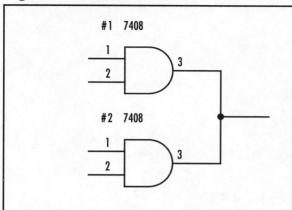

Figure 3.27 A Good Circuit

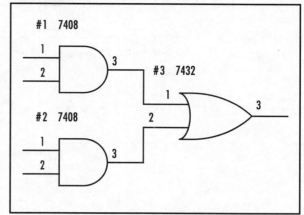

XOR

IF it is dark *OR IF* there is a car in the driveway—but *NOT* if both—*THEN* turn on the porch light.

Perhaps this behavior would be desirable if you wanted to discourage visitors after dusk? *XOR* is short for *exclusive OR* and means "if one or the other is true, but not if both are true." You can find *XOR* gates on the 7486 (see Figure 3.28). In Figure 3.29 you see the schematic for this circuit, along with an equivalent circuit that does not use the *XOR* gate but achieves the same effect. Table 3.9 shows an *XOR* truth table.

Figure 3.28 A 7486 IC

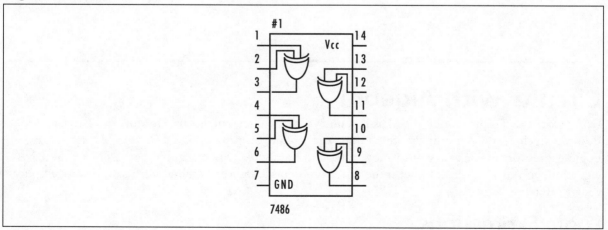

Figure 3.29 Schematic of Circuits with and without *XOR* Gates

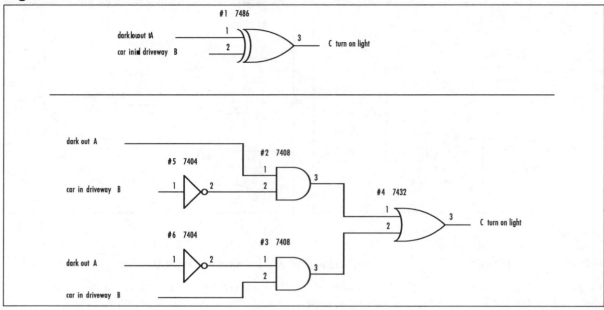

Table 3.9 *XOR* Truth Table

Input A	Input B	Output C (A XOR B)
0	0	0
0	1	1
1	0	1
1	1	0

Circuits with Algebra

Don't worry, this topics is not as bad as it sounds. Using logic expressions, DeMorgan's Laws, and Boolean algebra, you can quickly sketch out basic circuits on paper or even in a simple text editor. Logic expressions will allow you to show gates and lines with symbols and letters. DeMorgan's Laws will allow you to swap gates to get more efficient circuits. Boolean algebra will allow you to simplify your circuits.

Logic Expressions

Ambiguities in the English language can make it very difficult to precisely express digital logic; therefore, an algebra has been developed for this purpose. Understanding this algebra is merely a matter of getting accustomed to the symbols. Table 3.10 displays these symbols, listed in order of precedence.

Table 3.10 Algebraic Symbols for Expressing Digital Logic

Symbol	Meaning
'	NOT
•	AND
+	OR
⊕	XOR

Figure 3.30 shows a few logic expressions and their equivalent circuits. Take a good look at these and make sure you understand them. Try writing a few of your own.

Figure 3.30 Logic Expressions

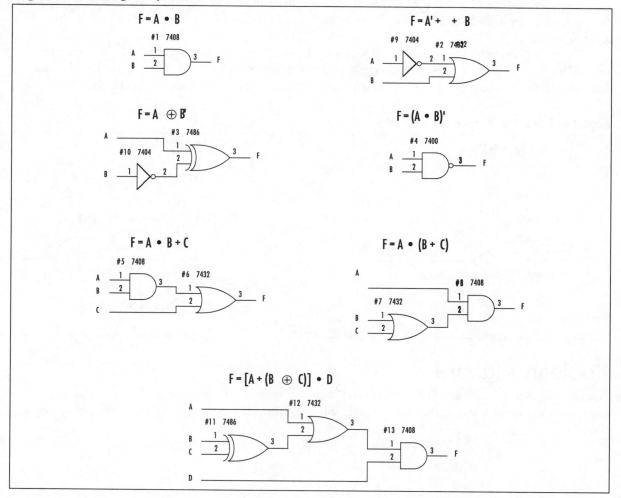

DeMorgan's Laws

The term *DeMorgan's Laws* sounds dull and tedious, but these laws are a real boon for the improvising hacker. DeMorgan's laws explain how we can substitute different combinations of gates to best use our available resources. They can be expressed as:

(A + B) ' = A' • B'

(A • B) ' = A' + B'

Let's take (A • B) ' (a *NAND* gate), for example. This statement means that A and B are not both true; therefore, at least one of them is false. Consequently, it follows that A is not true or B is not true, which we can write as A' + B'. This looks like a slight change from the first equation, but it can make a huge difference. Consider, for example, that the signals you are receiving may already be inverted or that you may not even have any *NAND* gates. Also note that each of the chips we've been using contains multiple gates. DeMorgan's Laws allow us to more fully utilize the chips with which we're already working.

There's an easy way to remember DeMorgan's Laws in practice (see Figure 3.31). To find the equivalent for any gate, first swap the symbol (*OR* to *AND*, *AND* to *OR*). Then look at each input and output. Everywhere there's an inverter, remove it, and everywhere there isn't, add one.

Figure 3.31 DeMorgan's Laws

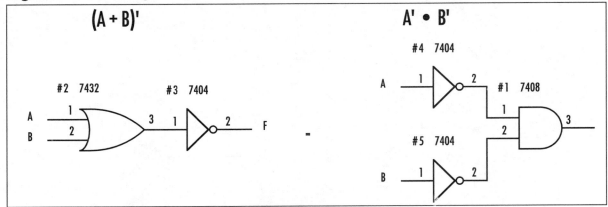

Boolean Algebra

Boolean algebra is a method for manipulating logic expressions. It allows us to reduce complex expressions to simpler statements that are logically equivalent. Some useful equivalences are shown in Table 3.11.

Table 3.11 Equivalences

Equivalence	Equivalence
A • 1 = A	A + 0 = A
A • 0 = 0	A + 1 = 1
A • A = A	A + A = A
A • A' = 0	A + A' = 1
(A') ' = A	((A') ') ' = A'
A • B + A • C = A • (B + C)	(A + B) • (A + C) = A + (B • C)
A • (A + B) = A	A + (A • B) = A
A • (A' + B) = A • B	A + (A' • B) = A + B
(A • B) ' = A' + B'	(A + B) ' = A' • B'

Make sure you understand why all these equivalences are true. Let's take

A + 1 = 1

as an example. The statement reads "if A is 1 or if 1 is 1." Given that 1 is always 1, this statement is always true and we can simply assert 1.

All You Need Is *NAND*

We've already shown that *XOR* can be expressed as a combination of *AND* and *OR* gates (refer back to Figure 3.29). Likewise, *NAND* and *NOR* can be expressed using an inverter along with *AND* and *OR*, respectively. Thanks to DeMorgan's Laws, we can use a combination of inverters and *OR* gates to produce an *AND* gate or a combination of inverters and *AND* gates to produce an *OR* gate. At this point, we have a means of re-expressing every gate except the inverter. We can do that with a *NAND* gate. Connect both inputs of your *NAND* gate to the same line (we'll call it *P*). A *NAND* gate is expressed:

(A • B) ' = C

Since in our case, *A* and *B* are the same line, we can write:

(P • P) ' = C

Using the equivalence

A • A = A

given in the previous section, we can reduce this to

(P) ' = C

which means that our *NAND* gate now functions as an inverter.

A *complete set* is a collection of chips that can be used to produce any logical statement. One example of a complete set is the 7408 (*AND*), the 7432 (*OR*), and the 7404 (*NOT*). Another example is the 7400 (*NAND*). Any circuit can be built using nothing but *NAND*. This means that any computer of any complexity could be built using only 7400 ICs. This is not practical when you consider the colossal size such a computer would have to be, but it is interesting to consider the magnitude of the concepts you can express using nothing but *NAND*.

A second *NAND* gate is used to negate the negation, and we're back to an ordinary *AND* (Figure 3.32).

Figure 3.32 *AND* with *NANDs*

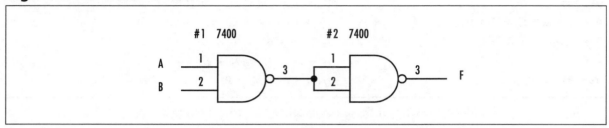

Thanks to DeMorgan's Laws, we know that an *AND* gate surrounded by inverters is equivalent to an *OR* (see Figure 3.33).

Figure 3.33 *OR* with *NANDs*

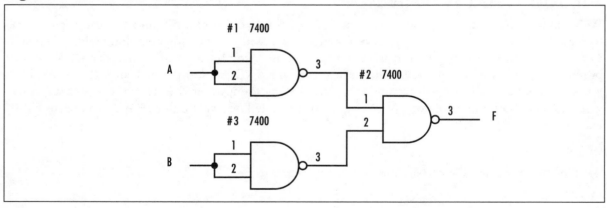

An *XOR* gate can be expressed as (*A* • *B'*) + (*A'* • *B*). Using that equivalency and the previous examples as parts, we can express an *XOR* using nine *NAND* gates (see Figure 3.34). This circuit, by the way, can be reduced to five *NAND* gates pretty easily, and there's also a way to do it with just four.

Figure 3.34 *XOR* with *NANDs*

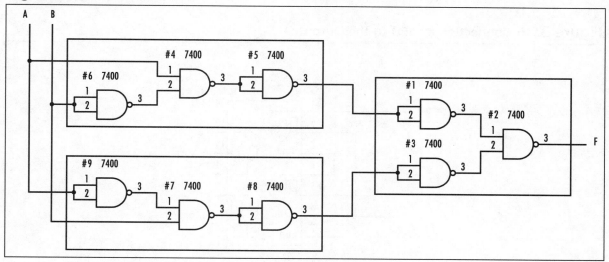

Latches and Flip-Flops

You might have noticed a shortcoming in the circuits we've described thus far. What if we want the porch light to *stay on* after it detects a car in the driveway? The circuits we've covered have no memory. In this section we discuss ways to add memory to our circuits, using only the gates we've covered in previous sections.

SR Latch

A *set-reset (SR) latch* allows us to set a bit to 1 or reset it to 0 (see Figure 3.35). We can do this using ordinary logic gates. The trick is to loop the output back into the input:

Figure 3.35 An SR Latch

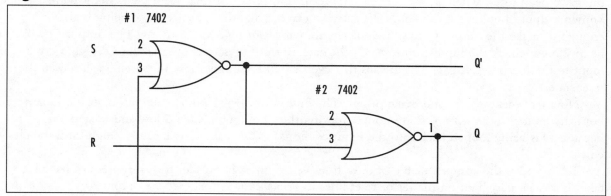

Grab a 7402 and wire up this circuit. Connect an LED to the output Q (see Figure 3.36).

Figure 3.36 Connecting an LED to the Output Q

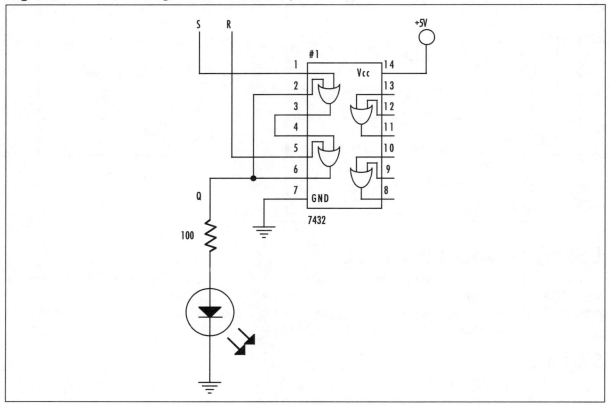

This circuit is confusing because our outputs are determining our inputs. Consequently, the first thing we need to do when we power this circuit on is to reset it so that we have a circuit with known outputs. Looking at the #2 *NOR* gate, we can see that the input *R* alone being high is enough to make the output Q low. In your circuit, wire *R* to high and *S* to low. The output Q will be low. Now check the inputs to the #1 *NOR* gate. Both of these are low, making Q' high. Q' is an input to the lower *NOR* gate. This means that even when Reset goes low, the circuit will stay in the reset state.

Now, let's make *R* low and make *S* high. The output of the #1 *NOR* becomes 0, which means both the inputs to the #2 *NOR* are now 0, making the Q output 1. Take *S* low and Q stays high, because Q is being looped back into the input of the #1 *NOR* gate. Q will remain high until the circuit is reset.

Table 3.12 is the complete table of operation. What's most important to realize here is that all it takes is a *momentary* high on the set or reset lines to *permanently* set or reset the output Q.

Table 3.12 Latch Operation

S	R	Q
0	0	Previous value of Q
0	1	0
1	0	1
1	1	Not used

Flip-Flop

Imagine we have a situation where we want to grab a value at a certain instant and then hold onto it. For example, every hour, we want check to see if the water level in a container is above a certain indicator. If it is, sound the alarm for a full hour, then check again. We can accomplish this using a *D flip-flop*.

Figure 3.37 shows the circuit to help you build it on your breadboard. We're not going to examine its operation, but if you want to figure it out, follow the levels in your mind or with a logic probe. Normally, when you see a flip-flop in a schematic, it'll look like Figure 3.38.

If you don't want to wire up all those *NAND* gates, use a 7474 TTL flip-flop, which is shown in Figure 3.39. Notice the inverters at the inputs to the Preset and Clear lines. Due to their presence, we use a high signal instead of a low to deactivate these lines.

Figure 3.37 A Flip-Flop in Logic Gates

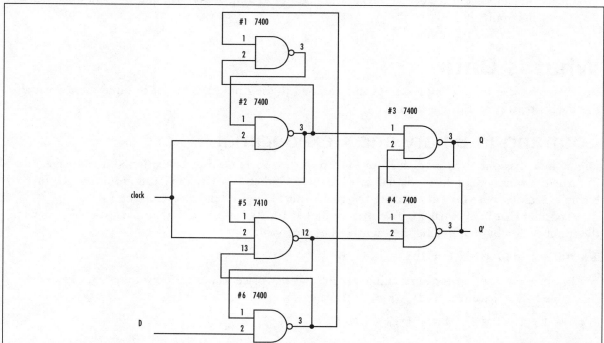

Figure 3.38 A D Flip-Flop

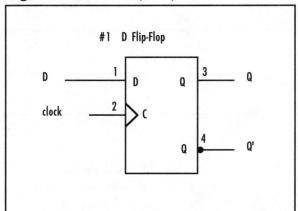

Figure 3.39 A 74LS74 IC

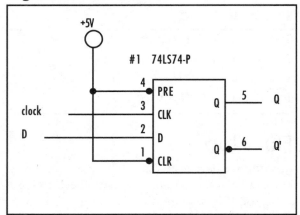

To use the circuit, perform the following steps:

1. Connect the clock input to low and the D input to whatever value you want (let's say 1, in this case).

2. Now we want to pulse the clock. Disconnect the clock from low, touch it to high, then move it back to low. That's a pulse. In a D flip-flop, a pulse is detected at the moment of the change from low to high.

3. You can leave the clock connected to high for as long as you like and it is still only seen as a single pulse.

What Is Data?

Before we look at more complex chips that are used in the Apple I, we need to understand what all this data is that we're passing around.

Counting in Binary and Hexadecimal

Digital logic has only two states, high or low; so our numbers need to be expressed in a binary (base 2) format. A binary digit, like a digital signal, is always either 1 or 0. Converting from decimal to binary is tedious, but you can calculate the values quickly by adding up each place value.

Consider that in decimal we have place values 1, 10, 100, and so on, such that we could calculate the number 203 by multiplying the digit by the place value:

2 x 100 + 0 x 10 + 3 x 1 = 203

In binary, we can do the same thing, except that our place values are now 1, 2, 4, 8, and so on (see Table 3.13). If we take 1101, we can calculate:

1 x 8 + 1 x 4 + 0 x 2 + 1 x 1 = 13

Table 3.13 Values Expressed as Decimals, Binary Numbers, and Hexadecimals

Decimal	Binary	Hexadecimal
1,000,000	64	16,777,216
100,000	32	1,048,576
10,000	16	65,536
1,000	8	4,096
100	4	256
10	2	16
1	1	1

NOTE

If we write 10, is it a decimal 10 or a binary 2? To distinguish binary numbers from decimal numbers, append a *b* to the end so that it reads *10b*. Hexadecimal numbers are prefixed with a dollar sign ($) or sometimes with *0x*; hence, a hexadecimal 10 would look like this: $10 or 0x10.

Each digit in binary is called a *bit*. With 10 bits, we can express 0 through 1023 in binary. Note that you also have 10 fingers. Counting on your fingers, with each finger corresponding to a bit, is a good way to get used to the binary system (see Figure 3.40). As you count, you'll also notice some patterns, which are also apparent in Table 3.14. The ones column alternates 0 and 1 with each row; the twos column alternates every two rows, and so on.

Figure 3.40 Counting Binary Numbers with Your Fingers

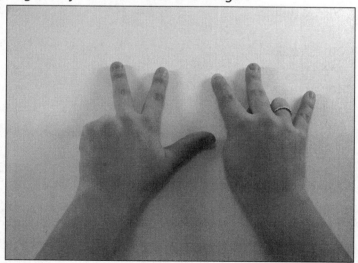

Table 3.14 Patterns in Values Expressed as Decimals, Binary Numbers, Exponents, and Hexadecimals

Decimal	Binary	Exponential	Hexadecimal
0	0000 0000b	0	$00
1	0000 0001b	2^0	$01
2	0000 0010b	2^1	$02
3	0000 0011b	$2^1 + 2^0$	$03
4	0000 0100b	2^2	$04
5	0000 0101b	$2^2 + 2^0$	$05
6	0000 0110b	$2^2 + 2^1$	$06
7	0000 0111b	$2^2 + 2^1 + 2^0$	$07
8	0000 1000b	2^3	$08
9	0000 1001b	$2^3 + 2^0$	$09
10	0000 1010b	$2^3 + 2^1$	$0A
11	0000 1011b	$2^3 + 2^1 + 2^0$	$0B
12	0000 1100b	$2^3 + 2^2$	$0C
13	0000 1101b	$2^3 + 2^2 + 2^0$	$0D
14	0000 1110b	$2^3 + 2^2 + 2^1$	$0E
15	0000 1111b	$2^3 + 2^2 + 2^1 + 2^0$	$0F
16	0001 0000b	2^4	$10
17	0001 0001b	$2^4 + 2^0$	$11
18	0001 0010b	$2^4 + 2^1$	$12
19	0001 0011b	$2^4 + 2^1 + 2^0$	$13
20	0001 0100b	$2^4 + 2^2$	$14
32	0010 0000b		$20
64	0100 0000b		$40
128	1000 0000b		$80
255	1111 1111b		$FF
256	0000 0001 0000 0000b		$01 00
1000	0000 0011 1110 1000b		$03 E8
1023	0000 0011 1111 1111b		$03 FF
1024	0000 0100 0000 0000b		$04 00
14287	0011 0111 1100 1111b		$37 CF
65535	1111 1111 1111 1111b		$FF FF

Binary numbers are difficult to read and write, not to mention pronounce. Fortunately, they are very easy to translate into the more convenient hexadecimal (base 16). Note that each binary number in the table is divided into groups of four bits. With 4 bits, we can count up to 15, which correlates perfectly to hexadecimal. Since we only have 10 symbols (0–9) in decimal, we need to create six more for hexadecimal. For these last six symbols, the letters *A* through *F* are used. For example, *B* is 11, *C* is 12, and *F* is 15. Let's take a look at a couple of hexadecimal examples using place-value calculations:

$CF = 12 \times 16 + 15 \times 1 = 207$

$10 = 1 \times 16 + 0 \times 1 = 16$

$FFFF = 15 \times 4,096 + 15 \times 256 + 15 \times 16 + 15 \times 1 = 65,535$

Bytes

There's not much that can be expressed with a single bit; so, computers examine a collection of bits at one time. This collection of bits is called a *word*. Modern computers have 32- or 64-bit words. Traditionally, personal computers such as the Apple I have used an 8-bit word, which is why you'll often hear computers from the 1970s and early '80s referred to as "8-bit microcomputers." This 8-bit word is known as a *byte*.

Eight bits can be used to represent any letter in the alphabet, a computer instruction, a number, the color of a pixel, or data in countless other formats. A byte is not significantly harder to work with than a single bit. An 8-bit flip-flop (called a *register*), for example, is just eight flip-flops connected to the same clock (see Figure 3.41).

Figure 3.41 An 8-Bit Flip-Flop (Register)

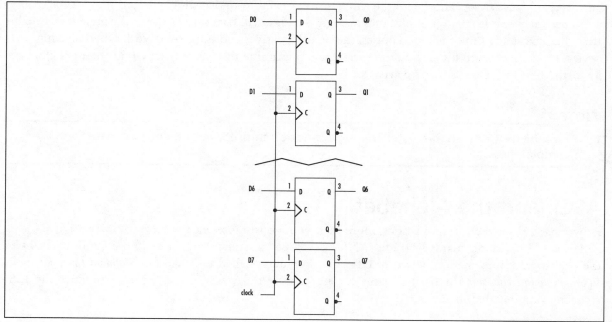

When we work with eight bits, it can become very repetitive drawing identical objects one after the other, eight times. A shortcut is therefore adopted whereby we use a single (usually thicker) line to represent multiple lines. The circuit in Figure 3.42 is equivalent to that in Figure 3.41, but it takes less space and is quicker to read. If you're using schematic software such as McCAD, it may forgo the slash and merely use a thicker line.

Figure 3.42 A Compact 8-Bit Flip-Flop

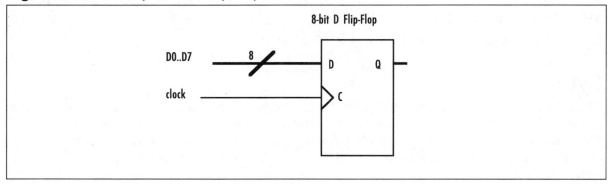

A selection of lines (such as D0 through D7) treated as a group is called a *bus*. Since our Apple I circuit is based on the byte, we will be using the 8-bit bus quite extensively. A bus can be either parallel or serial. If you're familiar with the parallel and serial ports used on the PC and the Apple II, you probably already have an idea of the difference between the two. In a parallel bus, which you've see in Figures 3.41 and 3.42, every bit is on its own line and arrives at the same time. At each clock pulse, a new byte of data arrives. This bus is the simplest to use and to understand.

The other option, the serial bus, uses a single data line. All data arrives over this single line, one bit after the next. Each time the clock pulses, the next bit arrives and must be saved by the receiving device. Once the eighth bit arrives, the recipient can examine the entire byte. Upon the next clock pulse, the first bit of the next byte arrives.

NOTE

A *nibble* is 4 bits—half a byte. The term is not often used, but I mention it here for completeness.

ASCII and the Alphabet

A byte has 256 possible combinations, more than enough to represent the entire alphabet. The American National Standards Institute (ANSI) developed a standardized code in the 1960s to facilitate the exchange of information between different computers. Called the *American Standard Code for Information Interchange (ASCII)*, it remains in common use today. ASCII uses 7 bits to produce the 128 characters enumerated in Table 3.15.

Table 3.15 ASCII Chart

Dec	Hex	Char	Dec	Hex	Char	Dec	Hex	Char	Dec	Hex	Char
0	0	NUL (null)	32	20	Space	64	40	@	96	60	`
1	1	SOH (start of heading)	33	21	!	65	41	A	97	61	a
2	2	STX (start of text)	34	22	"	66	42	B	98	62	b
3	3	ETX (end of text)	35	23	#	67	43	C	99	63	c
4	4	EOT (end of trans.)	36	24	$	68	44	D	100	64	d
5	5	ENQ (enquiry)	37	25	%	69	45	E	101	65	e
6	6	ACK (acknowledge)	38	26	&	70	46	F	102	66	f
7	7	BEL (bell)	39	27	'	71	47	G	103	67	g
8	8	BS (backspace)	40	28	(	72	48	H	104	68	h
9	9	TAB (horizontal tab)	41	29	)	73	49	I	105	69	i
10	A	LF (line feed)	42	2A	*	74	4A	J	106	6A	j
11	B	VT (vertical tab)	43	2B	+	75	4B	K	107	6B	k
12	C	FF (form feed)	44	2C	,	76	4C	L	108	6C	l
13	D	CR (carriage return)	45	2D	-	77	4D	M	109	6D	m
14	E	SO (shift out)	46	2E	.	78	4E	N	110	6E	n
15	F	SI (shift in)	47	2F	/	79	4F	O	111	6F	o
16	10	DLE (data link escape)	48	30	0	80	50	P	112	70	p
17	11	DC1 (device control 1)	49	31	1	81	51	Q	113	71	q
18	12	DC2 (device control 2)	50	32	2	82	52	R	114	72	r
19	13	DC3 (device control 3)	51	33	3	83	53	S	115	73	s
20	14	DC4 (device control 4)	52	34	4	84	54	T	116	74	t
21	15	NAK (neg. acknowledge)	53	35	5	85	55	U	117	75	u
22	16	SYN (synchronous idle)	54	36	6	86	56	V	118	76	v
23	17	ETB (end of trans.)	55	37	7	87	57	W	119	77	w
24	18	CAN (cancel)	56	38	8	88	58	X	120	78	x
25	19	EM (end of medium)	57	39	9	89	59	Y	121	79	y
26	1A	SUB (substitute)	58	3A	:	90	5A	Z	122	7A	z

Continued

Table 3.15 ASCII Chart

Dec	Hex	Char	Dec	Hex	Char	Dec	Hex	Char	Dec	Hex	Char
027	1B	ESC (escape)	59	3B	;	91	5B	[	123	7B	{
28	1C	FS (file separator)	60	3C	<	92	5C	\	124	7C	|
29	1D	GS (group separator)	61	3D	=	92	5D	]	125	7D	}
30	1E	RS (record separator)	62	3E	>	94	5E	^	126	7E	~
31	1F	US (unit separator)	63	3F	?	95	5F	_	127	7F	Del

A Few More Chips

We will now discuss shift registers, buffers, tri-state buffers, encoders, and decoders.

Shift Register

A *shift register* is a collection of flip-flops hooked up in a row such that the output of one is the input to the next (see Figure 3.43). This allows us to store a series of data, as it comes in—1 bit for every clock pulse. Let's assume that at every pulse of the clock, a new bit of data arrives on the input line, which is, in fact, usually the case. This data will be:

101100000...

Though most shift registers have a "clear" input, to reset all the flip-flops to 0, ours does not; therefore, we're going to assume that the content of the flip-flops before we enter our data is unknown (either 0 or 1). This will be represented in our table by an x. We also use t to represent time. For example, $t0$ is when we start, $t1$ is immediately after the first clock pulse, $t2$ after the second pulse, and so on.

Figure 3.43 Shift Register with D Flip-Flops

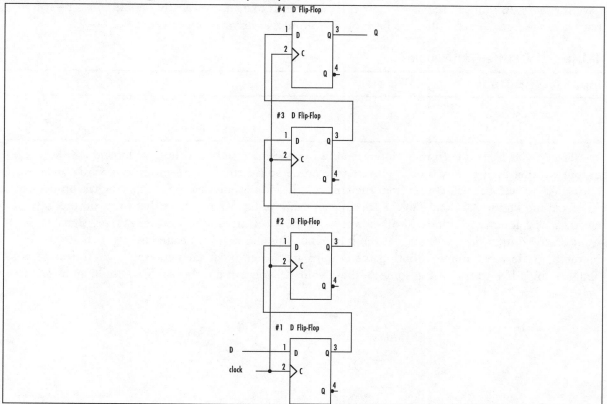

At *t0* we don't know the contents of any of the flip-flops, but some time before the first clock pulse a 1 arrives on the D input line. At *t1* the clock pulses, and this 1 is loaded into the first flop-flop. As soon as it is loaded into that flip-flop, it becomes present on the Q output. At *t2*, the clock pulses again. At this instant, 1 is loaded into flip-flop #2 and the next 0 is loaded into flip-flop #1. You can see the full continuation of this process in Table 3.16.

Table 3.16 Shift Register Output

	t0	t1	t2	t3	t4	t5	t6	t7	t8	t9
FF #1	x	1	0	1	1	0	0	0	0	0
FF #2	x	x	1	0	1	1	0	0	0	0
FF #3	x	x	x	1	0	1	1	0	0	0
FF #4	x	x	x	x	1	0	1	1	0	0

Buffer and Tri-State Buffer

On occasion, we want to use the output of one gate as the input to quite a few other gates, but we are limited by the fact that a TTL gate can drive only 10 other gates. To alleviate this problem, we have the *buffer*. As you can see from Table 3.17, a buffer is like an inverter that doesn't invert—it just replicates the signal. Each buffer we have on an output can drive 10 more gates.

Table 3.17 Buffer Truth Table

Input A	Output Y
0	0
1	1

The *tri-state buffer* is even more interesting. When we discussed *OR* gates, we looked at how a gate's output is either high or low, 0 or 1. The tri-state buffer adds a third state—off. In this third state, "floating," no output at all comes from the chip and it will not interfere with other signals on the line.

Examine Figure 3.44 and Table 3.18. You can think of line *G* as a valve that turns on the flow of electricity. So long as G is low (in other words, the flow is turned off), you can put any signal you want on the output lines without harming the chip. This allows us to create circuits such as that in Figure 3.45. Beware, though, if both gate's outputs are turned on at the same time, you'll damage your chips. If you'd like to try wiring some of these yourself, you can use the 74LS367 (see Figure 3.46).

Figure 3.44 A Tri-State Buffer

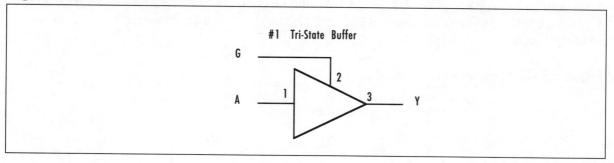

Table 3.18 Tri-State Buffer Truth Table

Input A	Input G	Output Y
0	0	X
0	1	0
1	0	X
1	1	1

Figure 3.45 A Circuit with Tri-State Buffers

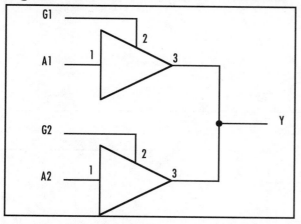

Figure 3.46 A 74LC367 IC

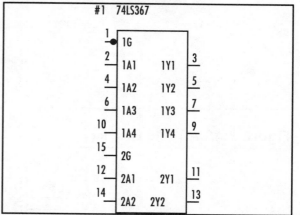

Encoders and Decoders

We have eight inputs. Line six is high. Let's say we want to send the number 6 to our computer or to some output device such as a numeric display. The receiving device is going to expect this data in binary format. If you've paid attention to the patterns in binary digits, a binary encoder is not very difficult to make. To express numbers between 0 and 7 in binary, we need 3 bits. Examine the patterns in Table 3.14 earlier in this chapter and you'll see that the lowest bit (bit 0) alternates between 0 and

1 such that bit 0 is high for 1, 3, 5, and 7. The second lowest bit (bit 1) alternates every two lines between 0 and 1, so it's high for 2, 3, 6, and 7. Finally, bit 3 alternates every four lines, so it's high for 4, 5, 6, and 7. This circuit is expressed in Figure 3.47. The same circuit is shown in Figure 3.48 as an ordinary encoder.

Figure 3.47 Encoder with Gates

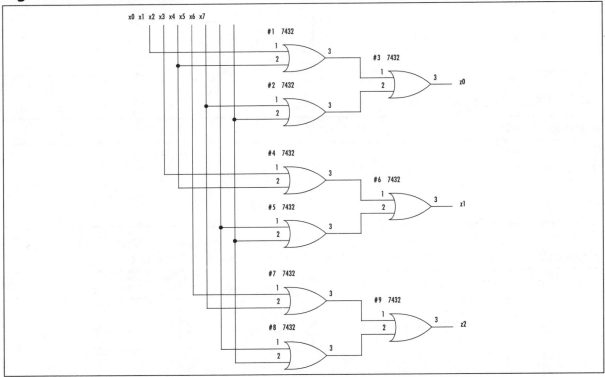

Figure 3.48 A 1-of-8 Encoder

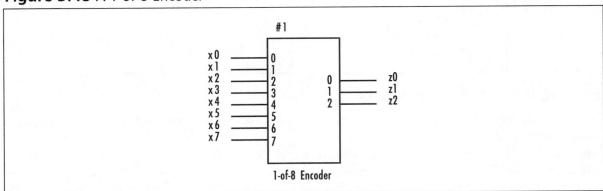

Is it possible to go in the reverse from binary to single-line output? Let's design a 1-of-8 decoder (see Figure 3.49). First step, fill out a truth table (see Table 3.19). Consider writing this out by hand before looking ahead. Remember that your inputs ($x0$, $x1$, $x2$) represent the binary digits and $z0$ through $z7$ are your outputs, so when you're filling out the table, first fill in all the inputs before solving the outputs, line by line.

Figure 3.49 A 1-of-8 Decoder

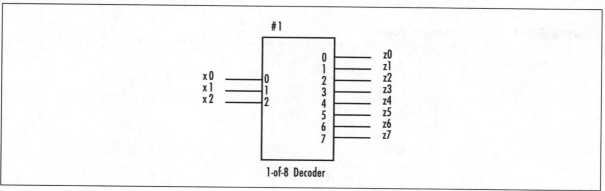

Table 3.19 Decoder Truth Table

x2	x1	x0	z0	z1	z2	z3	z4	z5	z6	z7
0	0	0	1	0	0	0	0	0	0	0
0	0	1	0	1	0	0	0	0	0	0
0	1	0	0	0	1	0	0	0	0	0
0	1	1	0	0	0	1	0	0	0	0
1	0	0	0	0	0	0	1	0	0	0
1	0	1	0	0	0	0	0	1	0	0
1	1	0	0	0	0	0	0	0	1	0
1	1	1	0	0	0	0	0	0	0	1

Next, write logic statements based on this truth table. For example, $z0$ is high only when $x2$ is not high, $x1$ is not high, and $x0$ is not high; hence, we write $z0 = x0' \cdot x1' \cdot x2'$. The complete set of logic statements is:

$z0 = x0' \cdot x1' \cdot x2'$

$z1 = x0 \cdot x1' \cdot x2'$

$z2 = x0' \cdot x1 \cdot x2'$

$z3 = x0 \cdot x1 \cdot x2'$

$z4 = x0' \cdot x1' \cdot x2$

z5 = x0 • x1' • x2

z6 = x0' • x1 • x2

z7 = x0 • x1 • x2

Finally, we draw a circuit based on these logic gates (see Figure 3.50). (You might notice that this circuit uses three more inverters than it needs to. There are two ways to cut the number of inverters in half, by using DeMorgan's law or by simply rearranging some wires.)

Figure 3.50 A Decoder with Gates

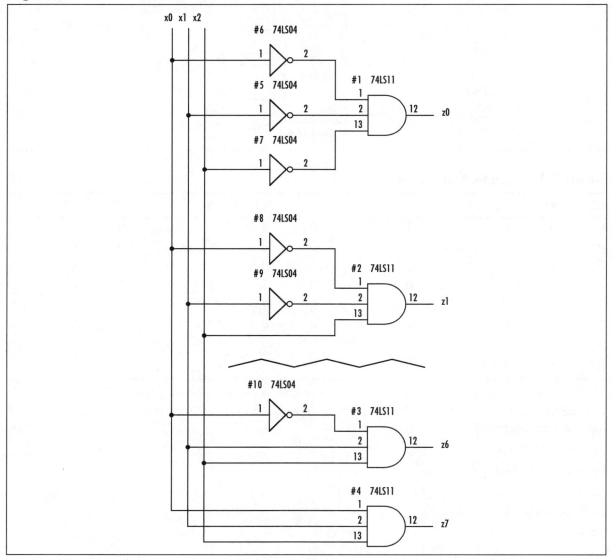

Summary

We've covered a lot of ground in this chapter. Each layer—digital logic, microcomputer, and software—can stand on its own, so there's no need to be too concerned if you didn't grasp everything; that doesn't mean you won't be able to understand the upcoming chapters. If you'd like to learn even more about digital logic, I would encourage you to look at the following list of resources:

Books:

The Art of Electronics, by Horowitz and Hill (Cambridge University Press, 1989)

Hands-On Electronics, by Kaplan and White (Cambridge University Press, 2003)

Web sites:

CAL for Digital Logic: www.ee.surrey.ac.uk/Projects/Labview/

Digital Logic: www.play-hookey.com/digital/

Discover Circuits: www.discovercircuits.com/D/digital.htm

How Electronic Gates Work: http://electronics.howstuffworks.com/digital-electronics.htm

TTL Data Book: http://upgrade.cntc.ac.kr/data/ttl/

Chapter 4

Building the Replica

Topics in this Chapter:

- **Learning to Solder**
- **Assembling the Replica I**
- **Serial I/O Board**
- **Using McCAD EDS SE**
- **Summary**

Introduction

Before learning microcomputer design, it helps to know how to program, and before learning how to program, it's best to have a computer with which you can program. This chapter discusses building the Replica I but with a minimum of theory. An introduction to soldering is followed by step-by-step instructions for assembling the Replica I kit sold by Vince Briel and a discussion of the Serial I/O board. Finally, the McCAD EDS SE package will be introduced for readers interested in making their own boards and then having them fabricated.

Learning to Solder

Soldering is a skill that takes time to learn. If you've never soldered before, we suggest acquiring some practice before attempting to assemble the Replica I. Test your skills on old circuit boards by removing components and putting them back in, or buy a couple of cheap parts from Radio Shack on which to practice.

The first time you use a new soldering iron, you need to tin the tip, which is done by heating the iron and applying a thin coating of solder to the tip. The surface and components you are about to solder must be clean. With a new Replica I board, this is not a concern, but if any of your parts are older or appear dirty, clean them with steel wool or alcohol.

Insert the component you want to solder into the board. In this example we use a resistor (see the section on resistors later in this chapter). Identify the correct location for the part and bend the leads so that it can be inserted, then insert it. Flip the board over and bend the resistor's leads slightly outward so that it will stay in place.

Allow your soldering iron to fully heat up before you start. Place the tip of the iron so it touches both the lead and the hole (see Figure 4.1). Both must be hot for a reliable connection. Hold the solder so that it touches both the lead and the hole, but not the soldering iron. In a second or two, the solder will start to flow. When the hole fills and begins to look like the solder joints you've seen on professionally done boards, stop applying solder. This will probably take no longer than a second.

Figure 4.1 Soldering

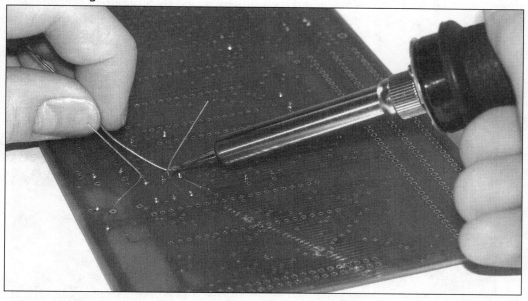

Allow a few seconds for the solder to cool. Then cut the lead (see Figure 4.2). Be careful not to jostle the joint before it is cool or you risk damaging the connection.

Figure 4.2 Cutting the Lead

Figure 4.3 shows some finished solder joints. Your joints should be shaped like these, with a shiny and smooth finish. If your joint is dull and dirty, you have a cold solder joint, possibly because you bumped the joint or because the joint is not getting hot enough. Though the connection might look solid, it is not electrically reliable and should be resoldered.

Figure 4.3 The Finished Joints

Assembling the Replica I

Figure 4.4 shows the unassembled Replica I kit, available from Briel Computers. Included with the kit is all the parts you'll need to build a working Replica I. If you're a more advanced user, Briel also sells components individually, which allows you to mix and match parts or install them on your own printed circuit board (PCB), described later in this chapter. Users who are uncomfortable with soldering can order preassembled kits.

Figure 4.4 The Unassembled Briel Replica I Kit

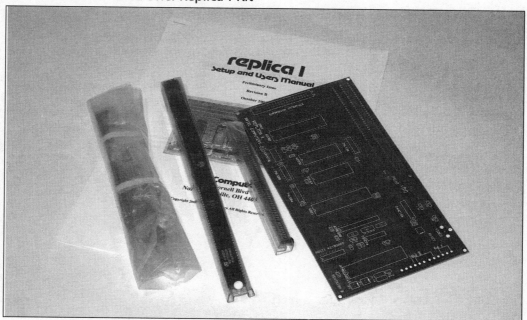

Parts List

Here's what you'll need to build your own Replica I.

- ICs:

    6502 CPU 40-pin IC

    6821 PIA 40-pin IC

    28C64 EEPROM 28-pin IC

    62256 SRAM 28-pin IC

    74LS00 TTL 14-pin IC

    74LS04 TTL 14-pin IC

    74HC74 TTL 14-pin IC

    74LS138 TTL 16-pin IC

    74HC166 TTL 16-pin IC

    ATMEGA8 28-pin IC

    ATMEGA8515 40-pin IC

- Crystals:

  14.31818MHz crystal

  8.0MHz crystal

  1MHz TTL clock

- Sockets:

  Qty 3—40-pin

  Qty 2—28-pin (wide)

  Qty 1—28-pin (narrow)

  Qty 2—16-pin

  Qty 1—16-pin (spring socket, for ASCII keyboard)

  Qty 3—14-pin

- Connectors:

  Qty 1—40-pin expansion header

  Qty 1—DIN PS/2 keyboard connector

  Qty 2—power supply connectors

  Qty 1—video connector

- Resistors:

  R1: 1.5K Ohm (brown, green, red, gold)

  R2: 470 Ohm (yellow, magenta, brown, gold)

  R3: 100 Ohm (brown, black, brown, gold)

  R4, R5: 4.7K Ohm (yellow, magenta, red, gold)

  R6 – R10: 3.3K Ohm (orange, orange, red, gold)

- Capacitors:

  C1, C2, C4, C4: 18pF

  C3: 0.1uF

  C6 – C17: 0.1uF bypass

  C18: 0.01uF

- Diodes:

  D1, D2: 1N4148

- Other:

   Qty 2—button

   Qty 1—jumper pad

Resistors

It's easiest to install smaller components first. This way, when you turn the board over, the component will be held in place between the table and the board. Let's install the resistors first. The 10 resistors on the Replica I board are labeled R1 through R10. These labels are silk-screened onto the Replica I's printed circuit board, making it easy to determine where parts should go. In the case of resistors, the resistor value is shown beneath the label (see Figure 4.5). You can check these values using the table of resistor codes in Chapter 3.

Polarity does not matter for resistors—you can install them in either direction. For the sake of aesthetics, I like to place all of mine in the same direction. With all resistors installed, your board should look like the one shown in Figure 4.6. If you have doubts about the quality of your soldering, use a multimeter and measure across the resistors, solder joint to solder joint.

Figure 4.5 Resistors

Figure 4.6 Installed Resistors

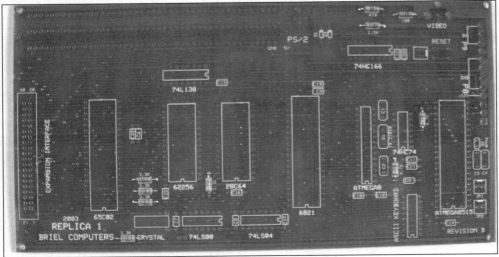

Diodes and Bypass Capacitors

Next install the two diodes at D1 and D2. For diodes, polarity *does* matter. The negative (cathode) end of the diode is indicated by a black ring, and the negative end on the board is indicated by a square pin. Match these up when installing the diodes. You can also refer to the silk-screened image between the pins, which illustrates where the ring should be. Figure 4.7 shows the two diodes properly installed.

Figure 4.7 Installed Diodes

The 11 bypass capacitors (see Figure 4.8) are as easy to install as the resistors. Polarity is unimportant. Bend the leads, solder them into place, and snip the extra length off.

Figure 4.8 The 0.1uF Bypass Capacitor at C6–C17

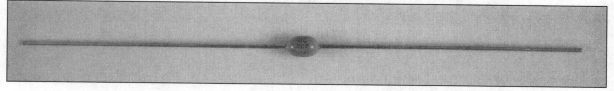

Buttons

There are two buttons on the Replica I motherboard: one for RESET and one for CLEAR (see Figure 4.9). Polarity on these does not matter. Near each button you'll see a pair of holes for connecting an external button. If you're installing your Replica I in a case, you'll probably want to do this. The wires from the external button can be soldered directly to the board, or a socket can be used. Figure out what sort of external button you'll be using before doing anything with these.

Figure 4.9 Motherboard Button

Sockets

Sockets should be installed so that the notch shown in the silkscreen matches the notch in the socket (see Figure 4.10). Pin 1 on the circuit board is also indicated by a square pin. If you have trouble holding the socket in place while you turn the board over to solder, you can tape it down.

Figure 4.10 Socket Orientation

ASCII Keyboard Socket

The ASCII keyboard connects via a spring socket (see Figure 4.11), which looks slightly different than the machined sockets used for the chips. A spring socket is used here because it's easy to connect and disconnect the keyboard connector from it. Machined sockets are generally of higher quality, which is why they're used for the rest of the board. If you're going to be using a PS/2 keyboard exclusively, there's no need to install this part.

Figure 4.11 The ASCII Keyboard Socket

Capacitors

The capacitors are not polarized. Installing them is trivial once you've learned to distinguish one type from another. Figure 4.12 shows the 0.1uF capacitor used in C3. The 18pf capacitor in Figure 4.13 is for locations C1, C2, C4, and C5. Figure 4.14 shows a 0.01uF capacitor, which belongs at C18.

Figure 4.12 The 0.1uF Capacitor for C3

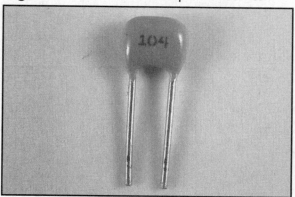

Figure 4.13 The 18pF Capacitor for C1, C2, C4, and C5

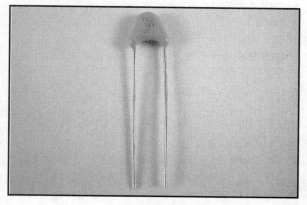

Figure 4.14 The 0.01uF Capacitor at C18

The Header and Jumper

The 40-pin expansion header should be installed so that the single notch faces outward, away from the board, and the double notches face inward, toward the board. The double notches are toward the top in Figure 4.15.

The jumper (see Figure 4.16) has no polarity and should be installed at location JP1. The shorter end of the pin is for soldering. The longer end should be facing up, away from the board. The jumper is used for switching between PS/2 and ASCII keyboard modes. If you're using an ASCII keyboard, a shorting jumper should be placed across the pins. For a PS/2 keyboard, the shorting jumper is not needed.

Figure 4.15 The 40-pin Expansion Header

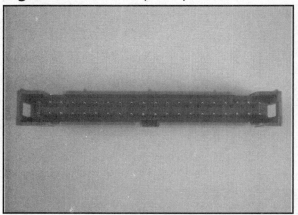

Figure 4.16 The Jumper Pad

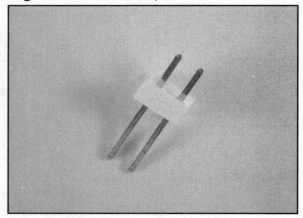

Crystals

The crystals are easy to damage and should be installed with care. The polarity of the 1MHz TTL clock (see Figure 4.17) is critical. Pin 1 on the clock is indicated by a black dot and a squared corner (the rest of the corners are rounded off). In Figure 4.17, pin 1 is in the lower-left corner. On the circuit board, pin 1 is indicated by a square pin, whereas the rest of the pins are round. The 1MHz clock should be installed at the location labeled OSC, for *oscillator*.

For the other two crystals, polarity is not important. The 14MHz crystal (see Figure 4.18) should be installed next to the ATMega8 IC at the location labeled Q1. The 8MHz crystal (see Figure 4.19) should be installed beside the ATMega515 IC at location Q2.

Figure 4.17 The 1MHz TTL Clock

Figure 4.18 The 14MHz Crystal

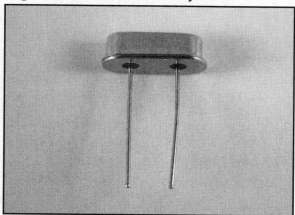

Figure 4.19 The 8MHz Crystal

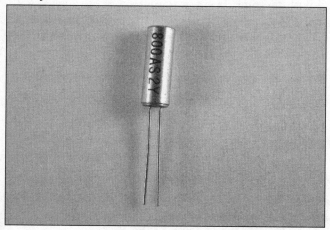

Connectors

Almost done! The PS/2 connector (see Figure 4.20) should be installed at the PS/2 label. Likewise, the video connector (see Figure 4.21) should be installed at the video label. Both of these fit in only one way. The holes for the video connector are large. Be sure the entire hole is filled with solder for a secure electrical connection.

Figure 4.20 The PS/2 Connector

Figure 4.21 The Video Connector

Finally, install the power connectors. The two connectors are identical and therefore interchangeable, but remember that orientation is important. The flat white support edge should be against the edge of the circuit board with the pins on the inside, as shown in Figure 4.22. When soldering these into place, we recommend using tape. The holes for the power connector's pins are large and it's easy for the connectors to slide around. Your finished board will look much nicer if the two connectors are neatly lined up.

Figure 4.22 Power Connectors

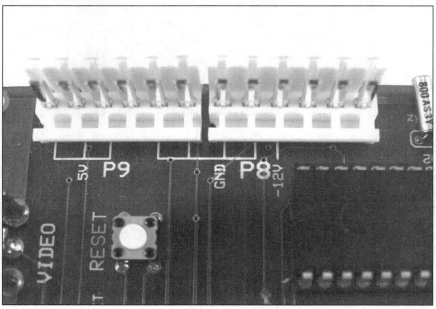

Finishing the Assembly

Congratulations! You've completed all the soldering. Now all that remains is to install the chips. Each chip and each socket is labeled; therefore, it should be evident where the chips belong. Make sure you get the orientation correct. The notch on the chip should match the notch on the socket. Gently press the chips into their sockets and ensure that no pins are bent out of place.

When you've completed the preceding steps, connect the power cables. The black wires should be on the inside to match the silk-screened label of *GND* (see Figure 4.23). Connect a composite monitor and your keyboard. Make sure the keyboard select jumper (*JP1*) is set correctly for your keyboard. Step back and admire your masterpiece (see Figure 4.24). Turn on the power and press **RESET**. A \ prompt should appear on the screen, which means you're ready to move on to start programming.

Figure 4.23 Connected Power

Figure 4.24 Completed Replica I System

ASSEMBLING THE REPLICA I: A NOVICE'S PERSPECTIVE

I first encountered Vince Briel and his Replica I kit in 2003. Building an Apple I replica sounded like fun, as my first childhood computer was an Apple IIe, and the legendary engineer Steve Wozniak is a hero of mine. But growing up in the 1980s meant that I missed out on the real microcomputer revolution. I always felt envious of those who hand-built their machines. Yet for under $200, here was a chance to live the past for myself! Considering that real Apple I systems are very rarely available for purchase, and when they are for sale the price usually exceeds $10,000, the value here is obvious.

Unfortunately, my electrical engineering skills are very rudimentary. The last time I soldered anything substantial was in the early 1990s, and that was just thick battery wire on 1/10-scale electric racing cars. Over e-mail, Vince assured me I had enough talent to build his kit, but still I hesitated.

Then in July 2004, at the Vintage Computer Festival East 2.0 outside Boston, luck intervened: My own exhibit table was directly adjacent to Vince's. We spent much of the weekend talking about his replica and how even an entry-level technician like me could assemble it. We worked out a deal: He'd send me a kit and I would review it for my weekly e-publication, the *Computer Collector Newsletter*. He promised to give me unlimited telephone technical support, and a few weeks later, my kit arrived in the mail.

The replica came in simple but functional packaging. It had plenty of heavy-duty bubble wrap for cushioning, the motherboard was in an antistatic bag, and a sandwich baggy protected the electronics. Every capacitor, diode, and resistor had a sticky label. I stretched a clean white towel over the work table, neatly laid out all the parts, kept a small cup nearby for the extra bits of wire and such, and plugged in a brand-new soldering iron.

The first problem arose immediately. The soldering iron, bought just one day earlier, didn't work at all. Its tip remained ice cold. I drove back to the local electronics supply shop where the elder guru proclaimed, "That almost never happens!" Great. Solution: they replaced the tool. On Vince's suggestion, I also bought a new roll of extra-thin solder.

I read the manual cover to cover, plugged in the new soldering iron, and started by installing the resistors. Another problem: the manual stated that resistor 1 is 470 Ohms and resistor 2 is 1.5K Ohms, and the actual resistors were labeled the same. But the motherboard was labeled the opposite. Solution: I called Vince a second time, and we determined that he made a typing error long ago, which he since had fixed. That's understandable, since the manual I had was an outdated version. So we made sure there were no other errors, and I soldered in the first two resistors properly and moved on. Installing the rest of the resistors and diodes was easy.

I wasn't clear about where all the sockets go, so I moved on again while pondering it. Apparently I didn't pay enough attention to detail, and I accidentally soldered the first major IC chip directly into the circuit board. That was a huge mistake! All the chips are supposed to go into the sockets, not directly into the board. Any experienced electronics assembler would know that. (I made a mental note at that point: How much should the instruction manual "dummy-down" these concepts for people like me? Probably just a little bit. On the other hand, considering that the kit is from one man and not a big company, the manual is quite good, given the limited resources available to produce it.)

Regardless, Vince assured me (in a third phone call) that the circuit works either way, even if my approach did make the kit a little bit less attractive. Also, the process of desoldering the chip's 40 precision pins would have been a major task for a rookie like me. So instead of worrying about it, Vince emphasized to me where all the other sockets and chips belong, and yet again, I continued.

Still another problem arose: One socket seemed to be missing from my kit. Eventually I found it, but unfortunately I'd already soldered it to the board, where the ASCII keyboard adapter goes. Unlike with the integrated circuits, you're supposed to attach the keyboard adapter directly. But a socket fit there, so I put one in—just more ignorance on my part. Luckily this problem also turned out to be moot, since Vince said I could just pick another chip with the same number of pins as the "missing" socket and solder that one directly to the board as well. So, the result is that I had three parts incorrectly attached, but except for aesthetics and convenience, it didn't really matter. (I didn't even use the ASCII keyboard adapter, choosing to go with the option for a modern PS/2 keyboard instead.)

My series of mistakes led to a nice touch: I was officially left with an extra part (the ASCII adapter). My father taught me as a boy that no good project ever uses all the parts. He failed to mention that good projects also work the first time but I will address that topic later.

Everything else progressed nicely. I installed the expansion interface connector, capacitors, crystals, keyboard jumper, reset switch, video connector, and power adapters. I installed a small part called "OSC"—I think that's a crystal, but am not sure and probably am better off that way. I also installed the PS/2 adapter and the "clear screen" button. Those weren't covered in the manual, but they were both clearly labeled on the board.

But still another problem: About halfway through the installation, my nice shiny silver solder connections started to become ugly, dull, and black. [Author's note: This sounds like a dirty, cold solder joint, which can result in a poor electrical connection.] Vince previously suggested using a damp towel to clean the tip of the soldering iron. I finally took his advice, and it made a big difference.

After a couple of hours, I suddenly realized there were no parts left to install, and the project was complete. I double- and triple-checked all the solder connections, made sure everything was in tight and nothing was short-circuited, and went to power it up.

I plugged in a brand-new LCD screen, a PS/2 keyboard, and a standard AT-style power supply … but nothing appeared on the screen. I thought, perhaps, that I incorrectly installed the ground wire, but I checked with the screen manufacturer and they said it was correct. What was the problem? Eventually I figured out that I installed two of the integrated circuits in the wrong direction. I removed them, taking extra patience to avoid bending the pins, and reinserted them into the sockets. It still didn't work. Days passed, then weeks, and I couldn't figure it out by myself. Finally I surrendered my nerd pride and mailed the replica back to Vince, who of course figured out the problem at first sight! It turned out to be something incredibly dumb: Despite my two checks of every solder connection, followed by two more checks of every connection after I reversed and fixed the two backward chips, I still somehow managed to install the two power adapters backward.

That is the latest news about my kit before this book's deadline approached. I hope that I did not fry my board by applying the power in the wrong direction!

Regardless of whatever damage I inflicted to my board and my pride, I can safely conclude that the overall Replica I kit is extremely easy to assemble, just as Vince told me from the very beginning. Every problem I encountered was reasonably attributable to my own impatience and inexperience. Of course, any instruction manual can always be one step clearer, but considering the audience for this product, how much explaining should the authors really have to do? If a major corporation ever reproduces the kit, then it would be fair to demand a colorful, detailed, glossy manual. However, that is beside the point. I rightfully accept 99 percent of the blame for marring this project entirely on my own, and I thoroughly endorse the replica to anyone who shares even my own inexperience. Just bring your concentration hat.

Evan Koblentz is a freelance technology editor in the New York City area. He plans to build a highly custom outer case for his Replica I after fixing the power adapter mistake. An article about the finished computer and a review of its software aspects will be posted at his Computer Collector Newsletter web site, http://news.computercollector.com. He can be reached by e-mail at news@computercollector.com.

Serial I/O Board

The Serial I/O board by Briel Computers (see Figure 4.25) provides an easy way to interface the Apple I to a modern computer. The I/O board allows emulation of the keyboard and mouse using a terminal program on your modern computer. The board plugs into the 6821 socket and provides a standard nine-pin serial interface. Sending data to this serial port is the same as typing it on the keyboard. All data that is sent to the video section is also sent out the serial interface.

Figure 4.25 The Serial I/O Board

To connect the I/O board, first disconnect all power. Next, use a small screwdriver to gently pry the 6821 out of its socket (see Figure 4.26). Alternate between gently prying each side so as not to bend any pins. Do not use an IC puller to remove the chip, because this will put stress on the socket connections. Next, gently insert the Serial I/O board into the socket. In the Replica I, the nine-pin serial port should face the same direction as the video and PS/2 ports. The installed board is shown in Figure 4.27.

Figure 4.26 Removal of the 6821

Figure 4.27 The Serial I/O Board Installed

If you ever need to remove the Serial board, be very careful. Its pins are brittle and will easily snap off if bent too far. It is very easy to end up with a pin stuck in your socket that will be extremely difficult to remove.

If you have a PC or an older Mac, the Serial I/O board can be connected directly to your computer's serial port via a straight serial cable (not null-modem cable). New Macs require a serial-to-USB adapter. I'm using a Keyspan USB Serial Adapter (#USA-19). The communication needs of the Apple I are very basic; consequently, any USB adapter that isn't special-purpose should work.

Windows users can use Hyper Terminal, which is included with the operating system as the terminal. Macintosh users will want to look at ZTerm by Dave Alverson. When launching ZTerm, hold down the **Shift** key. This will produce a menu where you can choose the serial port to use. If you're using the internal serial port on an older machine, you'll want to select "printer" or "modem" port. With a USB adapter, the name will be something obscure, such as USA19191P1.1.

Once the program is launched, choose **Connection** from the **Settings** menu and confirm that all your settings match those shown in Table 4.1. All other settings can be left at their defaults. Make sure your replica is running and has been reset. Now text you type in the terminal will be sent to the Apple I, and video output will be sent to the terminal. Programs, available from the Apple I Owners Club on Applefritter, can be entered merely by using cut and paste in the terminal or by going to the **File** menu, selecting **Send Text**, and choosing the file that contains the program.

Table 4.1 Connection Settings

Label	Setting
Data Rate	2400 bps
Data Bits	8
Parity	None
Stop Bits	1
Echo	Off
Xon/Xoff	Off
Hardware Handshake	Off

NEED TO KNOW

Nonvolatile RAM (NVRAM) can be used in lieu of static RAM in your replica. NVRAM preserves the contents of memory, even when the computer is turned off. This means that programs you enter by hand will still be accessible the next time you use your replica. NVRAM is implemented either by placing a battery inside the IC to provide constant power to standard SRAM or by using an EEPROM. The DS130Y-120 is an equivalent replacement for the 32KB SRAM IC that is used standard in the Replica I. It's available from Digikey and others for about $20.

Using McCAD EDS SE

McCAD EDS SE is an electronic design system that includes all the tools you need to take a design from idea to production. McCAD EDS SE is a package that includes Schematics, PCB-ST, and Gerber Translator. McCAD Schematics is a very easy-to-use program. The schematics it generates can be used with McCAD PCB-ST, a PCB layout design environment, to design a printed circuit board based on the schematic. McCAD Gerber Translator will convert the PCB-ST document to a standard Gerber photo-plotting text command file that can be read by PCB manufacturers anywhere.

If you are new to circuit design, the circuits shown in this section will probably look foreign to you until you read the later chapters. McCAD EDS SE is included with this book primarily for readers interested in modifying the Replica I circuit to suit their own needs and interests. If you plan on using the McCAD Tools which have been provided, be sure that you fill out the Registration Card included with this book and mail it in to VAMP Inc. In return they will send you an authorization code which will enable you to unlock the full capabilities of the SE versions. One should not be fooled by the simple appearance of the McCAD interface. This is a very capable tool set configured in such a way that it is easy to master yet very robust in its capabilities. Those of you who wish to modify the Replica I design will find it very easy to use.

All the schematics you see in this book were drawn using McCAD EDS SE. Documentation for McCAD EDS in PDF can be found on the included CD. You are encouraged to read through the documentation before attempting a new design or modifying the files which have been provided on the CD. A brief tutorial training video is available on the CD or from the McCAD website at www.McCAD.com. If you run into difficulty, visit the McCAD EDS peer support forum on Applefritter at www.applefritter.com/forum.

McCAD Schematics

Figure 4.28 shows the Replica I circuit opened in McCAD Schematic. The circuit can be modified using the tools on the left of the screen. Components selected from the Library Menu can be placed and new components can be created using the online library editor. A separate library of Apple I components (6502, 6821, etc.) was created for inclusion with this book.

Figure 4.28 McCAD Schematics

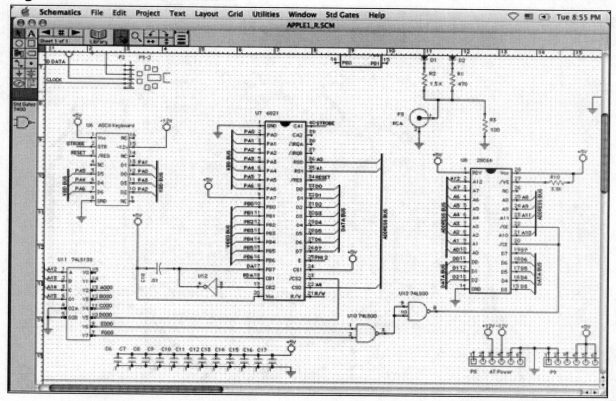

McCAD PCB-ST

Figure 4.29 shows the Replica I PCB open in McCAD PCB-ST. When you import a McCAD Schematic file to PCB-ST it will automatically collect the needed parts and allow you to place them and route the interconnecting traces. If you are happy with the Replica I circuit design but perhaps wanted to change the component layout or board shape, you could do so with this software. The standard Gerber file generated by PCB-ST can be sent to any PCB manufacturer to be fabricated.

Figure 4.29 McCAD PCB-ST

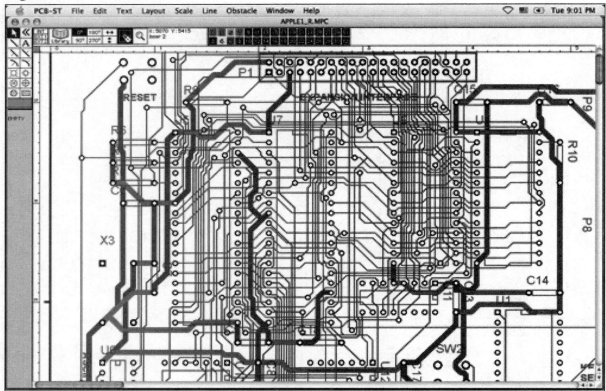

Summary

Whether you assembled the Replica I kit or used McCAD EDS SE to make your own board, having concluded this chapter you should now have a working Apple I replica. The next two chapters will address programming the Apple I, which will be of great aid in understanding the system. In the final chapter, we will take an indepth look at the design of the Apple I. Replica I kit builders who have familiarized themselves with the design of the Apple I may later wish to return to this chapter and use McCAD EDS SE to build their own customized Apple I computer.

Chapter 5

Programming in BASIC

Topics in this Chapter:

- Setting Up BASIC
- Hello World
- Input, Variables, Strings
- Math
- FOR/NEXT
- IF/THEN
- GOSUB
- Arrays
- Richard III: Interactive Fiction
- Summary

Introduction

As its name suggests, Beginner's All Purpose Symbolic Instruction Code (BASIC) is a great high-level programming language for beginners. BASIC was developed at Dartmouth College in 1964 and became the dominant programming language on microcomputers in the 1970s and '80s. If you visit your local library, you'll probably find dozens of books devoted to programming in BASIC, whether for the Apple II, Commodore 64, or IBM PC. All these variations of BASIC have the same base syntax, but they differ in more advanced features. Apple I BASIC is among the simplest of the variations. In this chapter, you'll learn how to set up BASIC on the Apple I and write some simple programs.

Setting Up BASIC

The original Apple I did not have BASIC in ROM. Instead, users had to either load it into RAM using an optional cassette interface or, even worse, type the entire program in by hand. If you're using a Replica I ROM, you already have BASIC ready to run. Power the system up and press **RESET**. At the / prompt, type:

```
E000R
```

This means "run the code, starting at address $E000." Press **Return** and a > prompt will appear. You're now running BASIC.

NEED TO KNOW...

The Apple I supports only uppercase type. However, if you're using a PS/2 keyboard, it will probably be possible for you to input lowercase text. The Replica I video section will properly display lowercase, but BASIC and Apple I software will not recognize it. Keep the Caps Lock on to avoid entering any lowercase letters.

Hello World

First, we'll discuss a few steps to take when you're loading BASIC for Apple 1.

The *PRINT* Command

We'll start at the same place at which every programming introduction starts: "Hello World." Load BASIC and type the following at the prompt:

```
10 PRINT "HELLO WORLD"
20 END
```

Type **RUN** followed by pressing **Return**, and the program will display:

```
HELLO WORLD
```

In the aforementioned example, note the line numbers down the left column of the code. The processor executes statements in numerical order. If, later on, you came back and added the line:

```
15 PRINT "GOODBYE WORLD"
```

line 15 would execute before line 20, even though line 20 was typed in first. If you ran the program, the result would be:

```
HELLO WORLD
GOODBYE WORLD
```

To see a list of all your code, type:

```
LIST
```

The program you entered will be printed to screen, line by line. If you were to type:

```
10 PRINT "GOODBYE WORLD"
```

your original line 10 would be overwritten with the new line 10. This is especially useful when you discover a typo.

As you've probably guessed, the *PRINT* command prints to screen. The *END* command tells the processor when to stop executing.

Multiple strings can be printed with one *PRINT*. Separating strings with a semicolon will cause them to be printed without any space between them:

```
>PRINT "HELLO";"WORLD"

HELLOWORLD
```

Using commas will insert spaces so that the strings line up in columns:

```
10 PRINT "1","2"
20 PRINT "428","84"
30 END


>RUN
1        2
428      84
```

The *TAB* Command

TAB is used to insert spaces before the next *PRINT*. This is useful for formatting. For example, *TAB 15* indents a line 15 spaces; *TAB 20* indents 20 spaces.

```
10 TAB 15: PRINT "HELLO"
20 TAB 20: PRINT "WORLD"
30 END
```

```
>RUN

            HELLO

                WORLD
```

A colon : is used to place two instructions on the same line and can be used with any BASIC instruction, not just with *TAB*.

The *GOTO* Command

Suppose we want to write a really obnoxious program that says "Hello World" over and over again. This is where the *GOTO* command comes into play:

```
10 PRINT "HELLO WORLD"

20 GOTO 10

30 END
```

The program loops infinitely, printing "HELLO WORLD" each time, and never reaches line 30.

Input, Variables, Strings

In this section, we'll look at inputting data and storing it in variables. Variables can be one of two types, either integer strings or character strings. An integer may be named with a letter or a letter and a digit (for example, *A, N, A1, B8*). A character string must be named with a letter and a dollar sign $ (for example, *A$, R$, Z$*).

Characters are ASCII; therefore, each character in a string occupies 1 byte of memory. BASIC needs to be told how many bytes to allocate to a string, a process called *dimensioning*. The maximum string length is 255 characters (or bytes). For example:

```
10 PRINT "WELCOME TO THE APPLE I!"

20 DIM N$(20)

30 INPUT "WHAT IS YOUR NAME", N$

40 INPUT "PICK A NUMBER",A

50 PRINT "YOUR NAME IS "; N$

60 PRINT "YOU PICKED "; A

70 END
```

The output of this code will look like this:

```
>RUN

WELCOME TO THE APPLE I!

WHAT IS YOUR NAME?TOM

PICK A NUMBER?5
```

```
YOUR NAME IS TOM
YOU PICKED 5


>
```

You'll see that there is a question mark added after *WHAT IS YOUR NAME.* A question mark is automatically inserted after each *INPUT* statement. Unfortunately, there is no way to turn it off.

Let's examine the importance of quotation marks in statements. Note the difference between lines 30 and 40 in this code:

```
10 DIM N$(2)
20 N$="HI"
30 PRINT N$
40 PRINT "N$"
50 END


>RUN
HI
N$
```

The first line prints the string contained in the variable *N$.* The second line, because of the quotes, literally prints *"N$."*

Math

Apple I BASIC allows simple mathematical functions to be performed directly from the command line. Without writing a program, you can simply type:

```
>PRINT 8+3
11
>PRINT 3-7
-4
>PRINT (8+3)*4
44
>A=12
>PRINT A-7
5
>B = A*3
>PRINT B
36
>
```

Apple I BASIC only supports integers; so, if you do division, you'll get results like this:

```
>PRINT 38/9
4
```

You can, however, use *MOD* (modulus) to calculate the remainder.

```
>PRINT 38 MOD 9
2
```

From these two commands, we can ascertain that 38/9 is equal to 4 2/9.

Here's a simple program to add two numbers:

```
10 INPUT "FIRST NUM",A
20 INPUT "SECOND NUM",B
30 PRINT A+B
40 END
>RUN
FIRST NUM?9872
SECOND NUM?1111
10983
```

BASIC supports integers in the range of −32,767 to 32,767 (2 bytes). There are several mathematical functions built into BASIC (see Table 5.1).

Table 5.1 BASIC's Built-in Mathematical Functions

Function	Description
ABS(N)	Returns the absolute value of *N*. If *N* is positive, *N* will be returned. If *N* is negative, −*N* will be returned.
SGN(N)	Returns 1 if *N* is positive, 0 if *N* is 0, and −1 if *N* is negative.
RND(N)	Returns a random number between 0 and *N* - 1 if *N* is positive. Returns a random number between *N* + 1 and 0 if *N* is negative.

Here's a quick example of the functions in action:

```
10 A= RND (-10000)
20 PRINT "RANDOM INT IS: ";A
30 PRINT "SIGN OF INT IS: "; SGN (A)
40 PRINT "ABSOLUTE VALUE OF INT IS: "; ABS (A)
50 END

>RUN
```

```
RANDOM INT IS: -9758
SIGN OF INT IS: -1
ABSOLUTE VALUE OF INT IS: 9758
```

Each time you run this program, *RND* will generate a new random number.

FOR/NEXT

The *FOR* and *NEXT* commands create a loop that runs a set number of times:

```
FOR I=a TO b STEP c
instructions here
NEXT I
```

In a simple example, $a = 1$, $b = 10$, and $c = 1$. For the first iteration of the loop, $a = 0$. Then, the *NEXT* I instruction is reached, and a is incremented by c (in this case, 1). The program continues to loop until $b = c$. Here's an example:

```
10 INPUT "ENTER INCREMENT",I
20 INPUT "START WHERE",S
30 FOR V=S TO 0 STEP -I
40 PRINT V
50 NEXT V
60 END

20000
25000

>RUN
ENTER INCREMENT?3
START WHERE?27
27
24
21
18
15
12
9
6
3
0
```

If *STEP* is left off the *FOR* statement, *STEP* will default to +1.

IF/THEN

IF/THEN is a very powerful tool that allows the program to branch in two directions. Look at this sample:

```
10 DIM N$(20)
20 INPUT "WHAT IS YOUR NAME", N$
30 IF N$ = "TOM" THEN 100
40 PRINT "HELLO, STRANGER!"
50 END
100 PRINT "WELCOME BACK, TOM!"
110 END
```

If the user's name is Tom, the program issues a *GOTO* that jumps execution to line 100. If it's not Tom, the program continues executing at the next line, which is 40. *IF/THEN* statements can be used with an instruction. Here's a sample using *PRINT*:

```
10 DIM N$(20)
20 INPUT "WHAT IS YOUR NAME", N$
30 IF N$ = "SECRETAGENT" THEN PRINT "THE CROW FLIES AT MIDNIGHT."
40 PRINT "WELCOME TO THE APPLE I, "; N$; "!"
50 END

>RUN
WHAT IS YOUR NAME?TOM
WELCOME TO THE APPLE I, TOM!

>RUN
WHAT IS YOUR NAME?SECRETAGENT
THE CROW FLIES AT MIDNIGHT.
WELCOME TO THE APPLE I, SECRETAGENT!
```

If you've programmed in other languages, you're used to having an *else* statement, such as "If *a* then *b* else *c*". Unfortunately, *else* is not provided by Apple I BASIC.

Expressions

Apple I BASIC supports the following types of expressions:

A = B

A > B

A < B

A > = B

A < = B

A < > B (A does not equal B)

A # B (same as A < > B)

Only = and # may be used with strings. These expressions evaluate to 1 if true and 0 if false. For example:

```
>PRINT 5=5
1
>PRINT 5=6
0
```

The *IF/THEN* statement bases its operation on the resulting 1 or 0. In fact, from the command line you can even type:

```
>IF 1 THEN PRINT "HI"
HI
```

It's possible to combine multiple statements with the *AND* and *OR* commands:

```
40 IF A=5 AND B=12 THEN PRINT "WINNER!"
50 IF A=7 OR B=19 OR N$="TOM" OR I$="HELLO" THEN PRINT "WHAT AN ODD COMBINATION."
```

Parentheses can be used for nesting statements, which are useful for ordinary algebra:

```
>PRINT (5+2)*8
56
```

More interestingly, parentheticals can also be used with *AND/OR* statements:

```
10 A=5
20 B=8
30 C=11
40 IF A=5 AND (B=927 OR C=11) THEN PRINT "CLOSE ENOUGH"
50 END

>RUN
CLOSE ENOUGH!
```

Finally, we have *NOT*. *NOT* allows us to get the BASIC-equivalent of *NAND* and *NOR* logic gates. With it, we can write statements such as:

```
IF NOT (A=5 AND B=7) THEN PRINT "NOT BOTH, BUT POSSIBLY ONE"
IF NOT (A=9 OR B=2) THEN PRINT "NEITHER"
```

GOSUB

GOSUB, which is short for "go to subroutine," is like a more advanced *GOTO* command. Whereas *GOTO* permanently branches off to a new location, *GOSUB* lets the user branch off, run a few lines of code, then *RETURN* where the program left off before branching. It works like this:

```
10 GOSUB 100
20 GOSUB 100
30 END


100 PRINT "HELLO"
110 RETURN


>RUN
HELLO
HELLO
```

Here's another example using nested subroutines:

```
10 PRINT "START"
20 GOSUB 100
30 PRINT "FINISH"
40 END


100 PRINT "SUBROUTINE 1"
110 GOSUB 200
120 RETURN


200 PRINT "SUBROUTINE 2"
220 RETURN


>RUN
START
SUBROUTINE 1
SUBROUTINE 2
FINISH
```

When *GOSUB* is called, BASIC records the line number of origin. *RETURN* is like a *GOTO*, which goes back to that original point and begins executing at the next line. Up to eight subroutines can be nested. The program just cited uses two nested subroutines.

GOSUB is a vital tool for structuring programs. It allows us to establish subroutines, which we can repeatedly use within our program. A well-written subroutine may even be worth saving to use in future programs. In the next example, the sample program illustrates the uses of GOSUB and GOTO. It's more complex than the previous programs we've looked at, so I've included REMs (remarks). The REM statements are not executed by BASIC. They are only displayed when the program is LISTed and exist only to provide guidance to those reading the code.

This program is similar to the battle scenes in a traditional text adventure or dungeon game:

```
10 REM DUNGEON BATTLE
20 DIM I$ (1)


30 REM HEALTH OF MONSTER M AND YOU Y
40 M = RND(1000)
45 PRINT "MONSTER'S HEALTH: ";M
50 Y = RND(1000)
55 PRINT "YOUR HEALTH: ";Y


60 REM WEAPON STRENGTHS OF MONSTER M1 AND YOU Y1
70 M1 = 250
80 Y1 = 250


100 REM USE A GOTO TO MAKE A LOOP.
101 REM IF/THEN'S ARE USED TO BREAK OUT OF THE LOOP.
120 INPUT "DO YOU WANT TO FIGHT OR RUN (F/R)", I$
130 IF I$ = "R" THEN GOTO 200
140 GOSUB 500
150 IF Y < 1 THEN GOTO 400
160 IF M < 1 THEN GOTO 300
170 GOTO 100


200 PRINT "YOU FLEE IN COWARDLY TERROR. "
210 GOTO 1000


300 PRINT "YOU HAVE VANQUISHED THE MONSTER!"
310 GOTO 1000


400 PRINT "THE MONSTER HAS EATEN YOU."
410 GOTO 1000
```

```
500 REM ATTACK
510 M = M-RND(Y1)
520 Y = Y-RND(M1)
530 PRINT "MONSTER HEALTH: "; M
540 PRINT "YOUR HEALTH: "; Y
550 RETURN

1000 END
```

Here are two sample runs of the game:

```
>RUN
MONSTERS HEALTH: 466
YOUR HEALTH: 758
DO YOU WANT TO FIGHT OR RUN (F/R)?F

MONSTER HEALTH: 335
YOUR HEALTH: 558
DO YOU WANT TO FIGHT OR RUN (F/R)?F

MONSTER HEALTH: 164
YOUR HEALTH: 474
DO YOU WANT TO FIGHT OR RUN (F/R)?F

MONSTER HEALTH: -21
YOUR HEALTH: 408
YOU HAVE VANQUISHED THE MONSTER!

>RUN
MONSTERS HEALTH: 326
YOUR HEALTH: 69
DO YOU WANT TO FIGHT OR RUN (F/R)?F

MONSTER HEALTH: 312
YOUR HEALTH: -20
THE MONSTER HAS EATEN YOU.
```

Arrays

An *array* is a collection of variables stored consecutively in memory. They are accessed by a single variable name followed by their array location in parentheses (as a subscript). Table 5.2 shows a sample array named *A*.

Table 5.2 Sample Array *A*

Location	Value
1	89
2	7
3	123
4	2
5	1015
6	42
7	123

In this example, 89 would be accessed with *A(1)*, 42 with *A(6)*, and so on. An attempt to access a value outside 1 to 7 will produce an out-of-range error (*RANGE ERR*).

Like a string, which is actually an array of characters, an array needs to be dimensioned with DIM. Here's a program to create an array similar to the one shown in Table 5.1 and then print all the values:

```
10 REM  DETERMINE ARRAY LENGTH
20 C = RND(20)
30 DIM A(C)

100 REM LOAD VALUES
110 FOR I = 1 TO C
120 A(I) = RND(32767)
130 NEXT I

200 REM  PRINT VALUES
210 FOR I=1 TO C
220 PRINT A(I)
230 NEXT I
500 END

>RUN
10411
```

```
26608
8259
785
5324
30034
32729
428
```

Arrays are a useful means of organizing data and are especially well suited to use with *FOR/NEXT* loops. They also provide the ability to work with a varying number of variables. The execution of the program just shown would not be possible using ordinary variables. When each variable has its own name (for example, *A, B*), there is no way to loop through them, let alone declare a random number of variables.

Strings, In Depth

Apple I BASIC has considerably advanced string manipulation, given its other limitations. Extracting substrings is simple. A string's length can be retrieved with a single function call. Comparing two strings to see if they're equal is trivial.

Substrings

It is possible to select a substring by specifying the start and end points in a subscript. Suppose we have the string:

```
T$ = "APPLE I REPLICA CREATION"
```

This string has 24 characters, which are numbered 1 through 24. Substrings are specified in the form of *T$(I,J)*, where *I* is the location of the first character to be printed and *J* is the location of the last:

```
>PRINT T$(1,5)
APPLE
>PRINT T$(7,9)
I R
>PRINT T$(21,21)
T
>PRINT T$(1,24)
APPLE I REPLICA CREATION
```

It is also possible to specify only the starting point. In which case, all characters from that point on are returned:

```
>PRINT T$(11)
PLICA CREATION
```

The *LEN* Function

The *LEN* function returns the number of characters in a string. For example:

```
>DIM R$(20)
>R$ = "REPLICA"
>PRINT LEN(R$)
7
```

This is useful when you're using a *FOR/NEXT* statement to cycle through each character in a string. *LEN* can be used to tell the *FOR/NEXT* when to stop. *LEN* also makes it easy to combine strings, as shown in the next section.

Appending Strings

It's easy to overwrite a string, using a command such as:

```
DIM $S(20)
$S = "ORIGINAL STRING"
$S = "NEW STRING"
```

It is also possible to append one string to the end of another. To do this, specify the location where the appended string should start. For example:

```
>DIM A$(30)
>DIM B$(30)
>A$ = "ABCDEFG"
>B$ = "HIJKLMNOP"
>A$(LEN(A$)+1) = B$
>PRINT A$
ABCDEFGHIJKLMNOP
```

If the location specified is before the end of the string, the rest of the string will be overwritten. Continuing from the previous example:

```
>DIM C$(30)
>C$ = "123"
>A$(4) = C$
>PRINT A$
ABC123
```

Conditionals

The = symbol can also be used to compare two strings. This works for simple comparisons of entire strings:

```
>DIM A$(30)
>DIM B$(30)
>DIM C$(30)
>A$ = "HELLO"
>B$ = "HELLO"
>C$ = "WORLD"
>PRINT (A$ = B$)
1
>PRINT (A$ = C$)
0
```

A 1 means that the strings are equal. A 0 means they are different. These comparisons can also be used in *IF/THEN* statements.

It is also possible to compare any two substrings:

```
>DIM A$(30)
>DIM B$(30)
>A$ = "NONETHELESS"
>B$ = "JOHANN THEILE"
>PRINT (A$(5,7) = B$(8,10))
1
```

Sample String Program

This simple program combines substrings, the *LEN* function, and string comparisons to reverse the order of a name. Here is a sample run of the program:

```
>RUN
ENTER YOUR FULL NAME?JAMES CONNOLLY
YOUR NAME IS: CONNOLLY, JAMES
```

The program in full is as follows:

```
10 REM FULL NAME, FIRST NAME, LAST NAME
15 DIM N$(50)
20 DIM F$(50)
25 DIM L$(50)
30 REM REVERSED NAME
```

```
35 DIM R$(50)


50 REM LOAD FULL NAME
55 INPUT "ENTER YOUR FULL NAME", N$


100 REM FIND FIRST NAME BY SEARCH FOR SPACE
105 FOR I = 1 TO LEN(N$)
110 IF N$(I,I) = " " THEN F$ = N$(1,I-1)
115 NEXT I


150 REM LAST NAME STARTS ONE CHAR AFTER THE
155 REM END OF THE FIRST NAME AND ENDS AT
160 REM END OF THE FULL NAME
165 L$ = N$(LEN(F$)+2, LEN(N$))


200 REM REARRANGE NAMES
205 R$ = L$
210 R$(LEN(R$)+1) = ", "
215 R$(LEN(R$)+1) = F$


250 PRINT "YOUR NAME IS: "; R$


300 REM WERE THOSE REALLY DIFFEENT NAMES?
305 IF F$ = L$ THEN PRINT "ARE YOU TELLING THE TRUTH?"


350 END
```

You might have noticed that the loop at lines 100–115 searches the entire string, even though there's no reason for it to continue after finding the space. Here's an alternative that breaks out of the loop once the space is found:

```
100 REM FIND FIRST NAME BY SEARCH FOR SPACE
105 FOR I = 1 TO LEN(N$)
110 IF N$(I,I) = " " THEN F$ = N$(1,I-1)
112 IF N$(I,I) = " " THEN 150
115 NEXT I
```

PEEK and POKE

PEEK and *POKE* are used for manually accessing memory locations. This is useful if you're interfacing with an in/out device or writing part of your program in assembly. Inconveniently, BASIC uses decimal for *PEEKs* and *POKEs*; as a result, you'll have to covert your address from hexadecimal to decimal (discussed in Chapter 3) before poking or peeking.

To place the value 42 in location 9000, type:

```
POKE 9000,42
```

To read it back and print it to the screen, type:

```
PRINT PEEK (9000)
```

The Apple I has 65,535 memory locations. Apple I BASIC allows for integers in the range of −32,767 to 32,767. Memory locations 0 through 32767 are accessed directly. Addresses above 32,767 are accessed using two's complement notation (see Table 5.3).

To get the two's complement notation for −2:

1. Convert +2 to binary.

   ```
   0000 0000 0000 0010
   ```

2. Take the complement.

   ```
   1111 1111 1111 1101
   ```

3. Add 1.
   ```
   1111 1111 1111 1110
   ```

4. Convert to hexadecimal, for ease of use.

   ```
   $FFFE
   ```

Table 5.3 Two's Complement Notations and Hexadecimal Values

Two's Complement Notation	Hexadecimal Value
+32,767	$7FFF
+32,766	$7FFE
…	…
+1	$0001
0	$0000
-1	$FFFF
-2	$FFFE
…	…

Continued

Table 5.3 Two's Complement Notations and Hexadecimal Values

Two's Complement Notation	Hexadecimal Value
-32,767	$8001
-32,768	$8000

Since location $8000 is represented by a value less than −32,767, it cannot be reached with BASIC.

The CALL Command

CALL is used to access a subroutine written in assembly. It is used in the manner:

```
CALL  n
```

Here, *n* is the memory location of the subroutine, which is represented in decimal format. In your assembly subroutine, use an *RTS* to return control to the BASIC program.

CALL is useful if you want to write most of your program in BASIC but occasionally need a fast assembly-language subroutine.

Commands

Table 5.4 lists *CALL* commands and their meanings.

Table 5.4 *CALL* Commands and Explanations

Command	Explanation
AUTO a, b	AUTO automatically numbers lines for you as they are typed. a is the first line number. b is the increment between lines. If b is not specified, it defaults to 10. **Ctrl-D** terminates AUTO mode.
CLR	CLR resets all variables, FOR loops, GOSUBs, arrays, and strings. It does not delete the program in memory.
DEL a, b	DEL deletes all lines of code between a and b, inclusive. If b is omitted, only line a is deleted.
LIST a, b	LIST displays all lines of code between a and b inclusive. If b is omitted, only line a is displayed. If both are omitted, all lines are displayed.
RUN a	RUN does a CLR and then begins executing code starting at line a. If a is omitted, the program begins executing at the first line.
SCR	SCR scratches (deletes) the entire program and clears memory.
LOMEM = n	LOMEM sets the memory floor for user programs. It is initialized to 2048. LOMEM clears all user programs and values.

Continued

Table 5.4 *CALL* Commands and Explanations

Command	Explanation
HIMEM = n	*HIMEM* sets the memory ceiling for user programs. It is initialized to 4096. Replica I users can increase this value to 32767 to take advantage of the Replica I's extended memory. *HIMEM* clears all user programs and values.

Error Codes

Table 5.5 lists *CALL* error codes and their meanings.

Table 5.5 *CALL* Error Codes and Explanations

Error Code	Explanation
>256 ERR	A value restricted to one byte was outside the allowed range of 0 to 255.
>32767 ERR	The value entered or calculated was outside the range of (–32767, 32767).
>8 FORS ERR	There are more than eight nested *FOR* loops.
>8 GOSUBS ERR	There are more than eight nested subroutines.
BAD BRANCH ERR	There is an attempt to branch to a line number that does not exist.
BAD NEXT ERR	A *NEXT* statement is encountered without a corresponding *FOR*.
BAD RETURN ERR	A *RETURN* statement is encountered without a corresponding *GOSUB*.
DIM ERR	There is an attempt to dimension a character string that has already been dimensioned.
END ERR	There is no *END* command at the end of the program.
MEM FULL ERR	Occurs when the size of an array exceeds the amount of space available in memory.
RANGE ERR	The requested value is smaller than 1 or larger than the maximum value of the array or string.
RETYPE LINE	Data entered for an *INPUT* is not of the correct type.
STR OVFL ERR	The maximum length of the string is exceeded.
STRING ERR	The attempted string operation was illegal.
SYNTAX ERR	The line is not properly formatted or it contains some typo.
TOO LONG ERR	There are too many nested parentheses in a statement.

Richard III: Interactive Fiction

Richard III is a piece of interactive fiction based on Shakespeare's play of the same name. It is presented here to give you an example of how a small program might be constructed. The story was written by Sarah McMenomy.

Walkthrough

Before writing any code, it's necessary to figure out the basics of how the game is going to work. Sarah wrote a walkthrough of *Richard III*. Let's look at her original design:

```
Intro:


King Richard: Is thy name Tyrrel?
Tyrrel: James Tyrrel, and your most obedient subject.
King Richard: Art thou indeed?
Tyrrel: Prove me, my gracious lord.
King Richard: Dar'st' thou resolve to kill a friend of mine?
Tyrrel: Please you;
But I had rather kill two enemies.
King Richard: Why, then thou hast it! Two deep enemies,
Foes to my rest and my sweet sleep's disturbers,
Are they that I would have thee deal upon:
Tyrrel, I mean those bastards in the Tower.
Tyrrel: Let me have open means to come to them,
And soon I'll rid you from the fear of them.
King Richard: Thou sing'st sweet music. Hark, come hither, Tyrrel.
Go, by this token. Rise, and lend thine ear.
There is no more but so: say it is done,
And I will love thee and prefer thee for it.
Tyrrel: I will dispatch it straight.


Outside Tower.
Ravens are flying around your head as you stand outside the tower.
There are two spigots on the wall; one says "Haute," and the other,
"Caulde." "Caulde" is on.


 >N
The Ravens swoop down and peck at you, blocking your entrance.


 >Turn Haute on
"Haute" is now on.


 >Turn Caulde off
```

"Caulde" is now off. The ravens are happily bathing in the hot water.

```
 >N
You enter the tower.

Bottom of tower.
You are at the bottom of the tower. There is a dagger on the floor and
a slip of paper underneath it. There is a guard on the stairs.

 >Take dagger and paper
Taken.

 >Read paper
The paper says "1483."

 >Up
The guard blocks your ascent.

 >Kill/stab guard
The guard crumples to the floor, falling on the dagger.

 >Up
You ascend the stairs.

Middle of Tower.
You are in the middle of the tower. There is a key in the corner. There
are four number dials on the door to the north.

 >Take key
Taken.

 >N
The door is closed.

 >Open door
You can't.
```

```
 >Read dials
The dials read "0000."

 >Turn first dial to 1
The dial clicks.

 >Turn second dial to 4
The dial makes a whir.

 >Turn third dial to 8
The dial squeaks.

 >Turn fourth dial to 3
The dial whines.

 >Open door
The door opens.

 >N
You are so close...


Top of tower.
You are at the top of the tower. There is a door to the north.

 >Unlock door
You push the key into the door and it swings open; you can see shapes
silhouetted in the moonlight.

 >N
You enter the chamber of the sleeping princes...

Tyrrel: The tyrannous and bloody act is done,
The most arch deed of piteous massacre
That ever yet this land was guilty of.
Dighton and Forrest, who I did suborn
To do this piece of ruthless butchery,
Albeit they were fleshed villains, bloody dogs,
```

```
Melted with tenderness and mild compassion,
Wept like to children in their deaths' sad story.
'O, thus,' quoth Dighton, 'lay the gentle babes.'
'Thus, thus,' quoth Forrest, 'girdling one another
Within their alabaster innocent arms.
Their lips were four red roses on a stalk,
And in their summer beauty kissed each other.
A book of prayers on their pillow lay,
Which once,' quoth Forrest, 'almost changed my mind;
But, O! The devil' - there the villain stopped;
When Dighton thus told on - 'We smothered
The most replenished sweet work of nature
That from the prime creation e'er she framed.'
Hence both are gone with conscience and remorse:
They could not speak; and so I left them both,
To bear this tidings to the bloody king.

Your villainous task is done; long live King Richard!
***You have won***
```

I originally wanted to implement a command parser, but the complexity of writing this in BASIC would have made for a very poor beginner's example. To simplify things, I decided to make the options multiple choice. The game is less interesting this way, but it also makes for an easier demonstration.

Structure

Now that we know what the game should look like from the user's perspective, let's examine the structures needed to implement it.

Each room will be a subroutine; consequently, we can allocate each a range of lines (see Table 5.6).

Table 5.6 Line Allocations for Interactive *Richard III*

Room	Line Allocation
Outside Tower	1,000–1,999
Bottom of Tower	2,000–2,999
Middle of Tower	3,000–3,999
Top of Tower	4,000–4,999

Most of the game will take place within the code allocated for the rooms shown in Table 5.6. However, we can make things simpler by using a couple of other subroutines. The Intro and Conclusion speeches can each be their own subroutines. Likewise, we can use a single subroutine to print the room descriptions. The description will be stored in a string by the room and then used by the subroutine. This will allow us to change the layout for all descriptions by simply modifying one subroutine (see Table 5.7).

Table 5.7 Subroutines for Interactive *Richard III*

Subroutine	Line Allocation
Introduction	30,000–30,499
Conclusion	30,500–30,999
Initialize	31,000–31,999
Print Room	32,000–32,499

Variables

Next, let's look at the variables we'll need. Ideally, each string of text would be stored in its own variable, making it easy to update and access data. Unfortunately, Apple I BASIC only allows 26 string variables, so the less commonly used strings will have to be stored directly in *PRINT* statements (see Tables 5.8–5.12).

Table 5.8 Variables for All Rooms

Object	Variable Name	Description
Room title	R$	These variables will be overwritten at the beginning of each room and then used by the *Print Room* subroutine to display the room's information.
Room description	D$	
Temporary	T$	A temporary variable, which can be used for any purpose.
Choice	Y	The user's input at the multiple choice.
Increment variable	I	This variable is used by the *FOR/NEXT* loops.

Table 5.9 Variables for Hot and Cold Spigots

Object	Variable Name	Description
Haute spigot	H1	The haute and caulde spigots are either on (1) or off (0). By default, haute is off and caulde is on.
Caulde spigot	C1	

Table 5.10 Variables for Bottom of Tower

Object	Variable Name	Description
Dagger	D2	The dagger is either in the player's possession (1) or not (0).
Paper	P2	The paper is either in the player's possession (1) or not (0).
Guard	G2	The guard is either alive (1) or dead (0).

Table 5.11 Variables for Middle of Tower

Object	Variable Name	Description
Key	K3	The key is either in the player's possession (1) or not (0).
Door	D3	The door is either in the open (1) or closed (0) position.
Lock	L3	An array of four integers hold the lock combinations. Each value is initialized to 0.

Table 5.12 Variables for Top of Tower

Object	Variable Name	Description
Door	D4	The door is either in the unlocked (1) or locked (0).

Skeleton

Each phase of the game is its own subroutine. Rooms can easily be rearranged. Adding another room simply requires adding another subroutine. Italicized names are used in place of line numbers. Omitting line numbers in the program's rough draft will make it easier to make changes along the way.

```
GOSUB initialize
GOSUB introduction
GOSUB outside_tower
GOSUB bottom_tower
GOSUB middle_tower
GOSUB top_tower
GOSUB conclusion
END
```

Initialization

The program should start by initializing all the variables we're going to use.

```
initialize:
DIM R$(255)
R$ = "X" : REM ROOM TITLE
DIM D$(255)
D$ = "X" : REM ROOM DESCRIPTION
DIM T$(255)
T$ = "X" : REM TEMPORARY  VARIABLE
DIM L3(4) : REM LOCK COMBINATION
FOR I = 1 TO 4
L3(I) = 0 : REM LOCK COMBINATION   SET TO 0000
NEXT I
H1 = 0 : REM HAUTE IS OFF
C1 = 1 : REM CAULDE IS ON
D2 = 0 : REM NO DAGGER
P2 = 0 : REM NO PAPER
G2 = 1 : REM GUARD ALIVE
K3 = 0 : REM NO KEY
D3 = 0 : REM DOOR CLOSED
D4 = 0 : REM DOOR LOCKED

RETURN
```

Intro and *Conclusion* Subroutines

We can address the subroutines for the introduction and conclusion next because they are extremely basic. These two methods consist of nothing more than a series of *PRINT* statements followed by a *RETURN* to give back control to the calling routine.

An *INPUT* line half way through pauses the scrolling text so that the user has time to read it. The user need not enter any data but only presses keys for the program to continue.

When a line of poetry exceeds 40 characters, it is manually divided into two lines. The second line is indented four spaces using *TABs*.

```
PRINT "KING RICHARD: IS THY NAME TYRREL?"
PRINT "TYRREL: JAMES TYRREL, AND YOUR MOST"
TAB 4: PRINT "OBEDIENT SUBJECT."
PRINT "KING RICHARD: ART THOU INDEED?"
```

```
PRINT "TYRREL: PROVE ME, MY GRACIOUS LORD."
PRINT "KING RICHARD: DAR'ST' THOU RESOLVE TO"
TAB 4: PRINT "KILL A FRIEND OF MINE?"
PRINT "TYRREL: PLEASE YOU;"
TAB 4: PRINT "BUT I HAD RATHER KILL TWO ENEMIES."
PRINT "KING RICHARD: WHY, THEN THOU HAST IT!"
TAB 4: PRINT "TWO DEEP ENEMIES,"
PRINT "FOES TO MY REST AND MY SWEET SLEEP'S"
TAB 4: PRINT "DISTURBERS,"
PRINT "ARE THEY THAT I WOULD HAVE THEE DEAL"
TAB 4: PRINT "UPON:"
PRINT "TYRREL, I MEAN THOSE BASTARDS IN THE"
TAB 4: PRINT "TOWER."
PRINT "TYRREL: LET ME HAVE OPEN MEANS TO COME"
TAB 4: PRINT "TO THEM,"
PRINT "AND SOON I'LL RID YOU FROM THE FEAR OF"
TAB 4: PRINT "THEM."
PRINT "KING RICHARD: THOU SING'ST SWEET MUSIC."
TAB 4: PRINT "HARK, COME HITHER, TYRREL."
INPUT "CONTINUE",T$
PRINT "GO, BY THIS TOKEN. RISE, AND LEND THINE"
TAB 4: PRINT "EAR."
PRINT "THERE IS NO MORE BUT SO: SAY IT IS DONE,"
PRINT "AND I WILL LOVE THEE AND PREFER THEE FOR"
TAB 4: PRINT "IT."
PRINT "TYRREL: I WILL DISPATCH IT STRAIGHT."
RETURN
```

The conclusion is nearly identical:

```
PRINT "TYRREL: THE TYRANNOUS AND BLOODY ACT IS"
TAB 4: PRINT "DONE,"
PRINT "THE MOST ARCH DEED OF PITEOUS MASSACRE"
PRINT "THAT EVER YET THIS LAND WAS GUILTY OF."
PRINT "DIGHTON AND FORREST, WHO I DID SUBORN"
PRINT "TO DO THIS PIECE OF RUTHLESS BUTCHERY,"
PRINT "ALBEIT THEY WERE FLESHED VILLAINS,"
TAB 4: PRINT "BLOODY DOGS,"
```

```
PRINT "MELTED WITH TENDERNESS AND MILD"
TAB 4: PRINT "COMPASSION,"
PRINT "WEPT LIKE TO CHILDREN IN THEIR DEATHS'"
TAB 4: PRINT "SAD STORY."
PRINT "'O, THUS,' QUOTH DIGHTON, 'LAY THE"
TAB 4: PRINT "GENTLE BABES.'"
PRINT "'THUS, THUS,' QUOTH FORREST,"
TAB 4: PRINT "'GIRDLING ONE ANOTHER"
PRINT "WITHIN THEIR ALABASTER INNOCENT ARMS."
PRINT "THEIR LIPS WERE FOUR RED ROSES ON A"
TAB 4: PRINT "STALK,"
INPUT "CONTINUE", T$
PRINT "AND IN THEIR SUMMER BEAUTY KISSED EACH"
TAB 4: PRINT "OTHER."
PRINT "A BOOK OF PRAYERS ON THEIR PILLOW LAY,"
PRINT "WHICH ONCE,' QUOTH FORREST, 'ALMOST"
TAB 4: PRINT "CHANGED MY MIND;"
PRINT "BUT, O! THE DEVIL' - THERE THE"
TAB 4: PRINT "VILLAIN STOPPED;"
PRINT "WHEN DIGHTON THUS TOLD ON - 'WE"
TAB 4: PRINT "SMOTHERED"
PRINT "THE MOST REPLENISHED SWEET WORK OF NATURE"
PRINT "THAT FROM THE PRIME CREATION E'ER SHE"
TAB 4: PRINT "FRAMED.'"
PRINT "HENCE BOTH ARE GONE WITH CONSCIENCE AND"
TAB 4: PRINT "REMORSE:"
PRINT "THEY COULD NOT SPEAK; AND SO I LEFT THEM"
TAB 4: PRINT "BOTH,"
PRINT "TO BEAR THIS TIDINGS TO THE BLOODY KING."
INPUT "CONTINUE", T$
PRINT "YOUR VILLAINOUS TASK IS DONE."
PRINT "LONG LIVE KING RICHARD!"
PRINT
PRINT "***YOU HAVE WON***"
RETURN
```

Print Room Subroutine

Print Room is so simple it barely deserves its own subroutine. I wrote it this way to allow for customization. Only one line of code has to be changed to modify the display of every room title or description.

```
TAB 10: PRINT T$
PRINT D$
INPUT "CONTINUE",T$
RETURN
```

Outside Tower

Let's examine the first room. The title and description variables are set and the *Print Room* subroutine is called. Next, the program enters the *CHOICE* loop. The options are printed and *IF* statements are used to choose where to go next. Some options will print a message and return the user to the loop. Others will enter a subroutine. The *haute* and *caulde* subroutines allow the user to use the *H1* and *C1* variables. When *H1* and *C1* are set correctly, the *CHOICE* loop jumps to *NEXT_LEVEL* and then returns from the subroutine.

The *Haute* and *Caulde* subroutines take their variables, *H1* and *C1* respectively, and invert their values from 0 to 1 or 1 to 0. (Though they are technically integers, we're using them as Boolean—true or false—variables.) In some languages there is an instruction for this, but in Apple I BASIC there is not. Instead, the *haute* and *caulde* subroutines demonstrate two different methods for inverting a Boolean variable.

```
T$ = "OUTSIDE THE TOWER"
D$ = " RAVENS ARE FLYING AROUND YOUR HEAD AS YOU STAND OUTSIDE THE TOWER.
THERE ARE TWO SPIGOTS ON THE WALL; ONE SAYS 'HAUTE,' AND THE OTHER,
'CAULDE.' 'CAULDE' IS ON."

GOSUB print_room

choose:
PRINT "1) ENTER THE TOWER"
PRINT "2) TURN HAUTE SPIGOT"
PRINT "3) TURN CAULDE SPIGOT"

INPUT "CHOICE", Y
IF Y = 1 AND H1 = 1 AND C1 = 0 THEN next_level
IF Y = 1 THEN PRINT "THE RAVENS SWOOP DOWN AND PECK AT YOU, BLOCKING YOUR ENTRANCE."
IF Y = 2 THEN GOSUB haute
```

```
IF Y = 3 THEN GOSUB caulde
INPUT "CONTINUE",T$
GOTO choose


next_level:
PRINT "YOU ENTER THE TOWER."
RETURN


haute:
H1 = H1 + 1
IF H1 = 2 THEN H1 = 0
IF H1 = O THEN PRINT "HAUTE IS NOW OFF."
IF H1 = 1 THEN PRINT "HAUTE IS NOW ON."
RETURN



caulde:
C1 = 1 - C1
IF C1 = O THEN PRINT "CAULDE IS NOW OFF."
IF C1 = 1 THEN PRINT "CAULDE IS NOW ON."
RETURN
```

Bottom of the Tower

The most interesting feature in this room is the behavior of the paper. The option *READ PAPER* is displayed only and works only if the paper is in the player's possession.

```
T$ = "BOTTOM OF THE TOWER"
D$ = "YOU ARE AT THE BOTTOM OF THE TOWER. THERE IS A DAGGER ON THE FLOOR, AND A SLIP
OF PAPER UNDERNEATH IT. THERE IS A GUARD ON THE STAIRS."


print_room


choose:
PRINT 1)  "ATTACK GUARD"
PRINT 2)  "GO UP STAIRS"
PRINT 3)  "PICK UP PAPER"
PRINT 4)  "PICK UP DAGGER"
```

```
IF P2 = 1 THEN PRINT "5) READ PAPER"

INPUT "CHOICE", Y
IF Y = 1 THEN GOSUB attack_guard
IF Y = 2 AND G2 = 0 THEN GOTO next_level
IF Y = 2 THEN PRINT "THE GUARD BLOCKS YOUR ASCENT."
IF Y = 3 THEN GOSUB get_paper
IF Y = 4 THEN GOSUB get_dagger
IF Y = 5 AND P2 = 1 THEN PRINT "THE PAPER SAYS '1482'."
INPUT "CONTINUE",T$
GOTO choose

next_level:
PRINT "YOU ASCEND THE STAIRS."
RETURN

get_paper:
IF P2 = 1 THEN PRINT "YOU ALREADY HAVE THE PAPER."
IF P2 = 1 THEN RETURN

P2 = 1
PRINT "YOU TAKE THE PAPER."
RETURN

get_dagger:
IF D2 = 1 THEN PRINT "YOU ALREADY HAVE THE DAGGER."
IF D2 = 1 THEN RETURN

D2 = 1
PRINT "YOU TAKE THE DAGGER."
RETURN

attack_guard:
IF D2 = 1 THEN PRINT "THE GUARD KNOCKS YOU TO THE GROUND."
IF D2 = 1 THEN RETURN

G2 = 0
```

```
PRINT "THE GUARD CRUMPLES TO THE FLOOR, FALLING ON THE DAGGER."
RETURN
```

Middle of the Tower

The "combination lock" in this room is a four-integer array. Only when all four values are correctly set via the *ENTER_COMBINATION* subroutine can the player continue to the next room.

```
T$ = "MIDDLE OF THE TOWER"

D$ = "YOU ARE IN THE MIDDLE OF THE TOWER.   THERE IS A KEY IN THE CORNER.   THERE ARE
FOUR NUMBER DIALS ON THE DOOR TO THE NORTH."
```

print_room

choose:
```
PRINT "1) PICK UP KEY"
PRINT "2) OPEN DOOR"
PRINT "3) ENTER COMBINATION"
PRINT "4) ENTER ROOM"
```

```
INPUT "CHOICE", Y
IF Y = 1 THEN GOSUB get_key
IF Y = 2 AND L3(1) = 1 AND L3(2) = 4 AND L3(3) = 8 AND L3(4) = 3 THEN GOSUB open_door
IF Y = 2 THEN PRINT "THE COMBINATION IS NOT CORRECT."
IF Y = 3 THEN GOSUB enter_combination
IF Y = 4 AND D3 = 1 THEN next_level
IF Y = 4 THEN PRINT "THE DOOR IS CLOSED."
INPUT "CONTINUE",T$
GOTO choose
```

next_level:
```
PRINT "YOU ARE SO CLOSE..."
RETURN
```

get_key:
```
IF K3 = 1 THEN PRINT "YOU ALREADY HAVE THE KEY."
IF K3 = 1 THEN RETURN
```

```
K3 = 1
PRINT "YOU TAKE THE KEY."
RETURN


enter_combination:
INPUT "TURN FIRST DIAL TO", L3(1)
PRINT "THE DIAL CLICKS."
INPUT "TURN SECOND DIAL TO", L3(2)
PRINT "THE DIAL WHIRRS."
INPUT "TURN THE THIRD DIAL TO", L3(3)
PRINT "THE DIAL SQUEAKS."
INPUT "TURN THE FOURTH DIAL TO", L3(4)
PRINT "THE DIAL WHINES. "
RETURN


open_door:
IF D3 = 0 THEN PRINT "THE DOOR IS LOCKED."
IF D3 = 0 THEN RETURN
PRINT "THE DOOR OPENS."
D3 = 1
RETURN
```

Top of the Tower

The final room is trivial. The door is unlocked with the key from the previous room—but only if the player picked it up! If you're considering expanding this game, the option to move freely between rooms, picking up and dropping objects, would surely be a welcome feature.

```
T$ = "TOP OF THE TOWER"
D$ = "YOU ARE AT THE TOP OF THE TOWER.  THERE IS A DOOR TO THE NORTH."


print_room


choose:
PRINT "1) UNLOCK THE DOOR"
PRINT "2) ENTER THE CHAMBER."


INPUT "CHOICE", Y
```

```
IF Y = 1 THEN GOSUB unlock_door
IF Y = 2 AND D4 = 1 THEN next_level
IF Y = 2 THEN PRINT "THE DOOR IS LOCKED."
INPUT "CONTINUE",T$
GOTO choose


next_level:
PRINT "YOU ENTER THE CHAMBER OF THE SLEEPING PRINCES... "
RETURN


unlock_door:
IF D4 = 1 THEN PRINT "THE DOOR IS ALREADY UNLOCKED"
IF D4 = 1 THEN RETURN


D4 = 1
PRINT "YOU PUSH THE KEY INTO THE DOOR AND IT SWINGS OPEN; YOU CAN SEE SHAPES
SILHOUETTED IN THE MOONLIGHT."
RETURN
```

Richard III Code

Here is the complete code for *Richard III*. It can also be found on the included CD, so those with a serial I/O board from Briel Computers will be able to transfer it to their replica via the terminal.

The italicized headers from earlier sections have been replaced with *REM* lines to allow them to be stored in the program. Before you begin entering lines, be sure to increase *HIMEM* to 32767. This program is too large to run in the standard 8K.

```
10 REM RICHARD III: (BARELY) INTERACTIVE FICTION
30 GOSUB 31000 : REM INITIALIZE
40 GOSUB 30000 : REM INTRODUCTION
50 GOSUB 1000 : REM OUTSIDE OF TOWER
60 GOSUB 2000 : REM BOTTOM OF TOWER
70 GOSUB 3000 : REM MIDDLE OF TOWER
80 GOSUB 4000 : REM TOP OF TOWER
90 GOSUB 30500 : REM CONCLUSION
100 END
```

```
31000 REM INITIALIZE
31010 DIM R$(255)
31015 R$ = "X" : REM ROOM TITLE
31020 DIM D$(255)
31025 D$ = "X" : REM ROOM DESCRIPTION
31030 DIM T$(255)
31035 T$ = "X" : REM TEMPORARY  VARIABLE
31040 DIM L3(4) : REM LOCK COMBINATION
31045 FOR I = 1 TO 4
31050 L3(I) = 0 : REM LOCK COMBINATION  SET TO 0000
31055 NEXT I
31060 H1 = 0 : REM HAUTE IS OFF
31065 C1 = 1 : REM CAULDE IS ON
31070 D2 = 0 : REM NO DAGGER
31075 P2 = 0 : REM NO PAPER
31080 G2 = 1 : REM GUARD ALIVE
31085 K3 = 0 : REM NO KEY
31090 D3 = 0 : REM DOOR CLOSED
31095 D4 = 0 : REM DOOR LOCKED
31100 RETURN


30000 REM INTRODUCTION
30010 PRINT "KING RICHARD: IS THY NAME TYRREL?"
30015 PRINT "TYRREL: JAMES TYRREL, AND YOUR MOST"
30020 TAB 4: PRINT "OBEDIENT SUBJECT."
30025 PRINT "KING RICHARD: ART THOU INDEED?"
30030 PRINT "TYRREL: PROVE ME, MY GRACIOUS LORD."
30035 PRINT "KING RICHARD: DAR'ST' THOU RESOLVE TO"
30040 TAB 4: PRINT "KILL A FRIEND OF MINE?"
30045 PRINT "TYRREL: PLEASE YOU;"
30050 TAB 4: PRINT "BUT I HAD RATHER KILL TWO ENEMIES."
30055 PRINT "KING RICHARD: WHY, THEN THOU HAST IT!"
30060 TAB 4: PRINT "TWO DEEP ENEMIES,"
30065 PRINT "FOES TO MY REST AND MY SWEET SLEEP'S"
```

```
30070 TAB 4: PRINT "DISTURBERS,"
30075 PRINT "ARE THEY THAT I WOULD HAVE THEE DEAL"
30080 TAB 4: PRINT "UPON:"
30085 PRINT "TYRREL, I MEAN THOSE BASTARDS IN THE"
30090 TAB 4: PRINT "TOWER."
30095 PRINT "TYRREL: LET ME HAVE OPEN MEANS TO COME"
30100 TAB 4: PRINT "TO THEM,"
30105 PRINT "AND SOON I'LL RID YOU FROM THE FEAR OF"
30110 TAB 4: PRINT "THEM."
30115 PRINT "KING RICHARD: THOU SING'ST SWEET MUSIC."
30120 TAB 4: PRINT "HARK, COME HITHER, TYRREL."
30125 INPUT "CONTINUE",T$
30130 PRINT "GO, BY THIS TOKEN. RISE, AND LEND THINE"
30135 TAB 4: PRINT "EAR."
30140 PRINT "THERE IS NO MORE BUT SO: SAY IT IS DONE,"
30145 PRINT "AND I WILL LOVE THEE AND PREFER THEE FOR"
30150 TAB 4: PRINT "IT."
30155 PRINT "TYRREL: I WILL DISPATCH IT STRAIGHT."
30160 INPUT "CONTINUE",T$
30165 RETURN


30500 REM CONCLUSION
30505 PRINT "TYRREL: THE TYRANNOUS AND BLOODY ACT IS"
30510 TAB 4: PRINT "DONE,"
30515 PRINT "THE MOST ARCH DEED OF PITEOUS MASSACRE"
30520 PRINT "THAT EVER YET THIS LAND WAS GUILTY OF."
30525 PRINT "DIGHTON AND FORREST, WHO I DID SUBORN"
30530 PRINT "TO DO THIS PIECE OF RUTHLESS BUTCHERY,"
30535 PRINT "ALBEIT THEY WERE FLESHED VILLAINS,"
30540 TAB 4: PRINT "BLOODY DOGS,"
30545 PRINT "MELTED WITH TENDERNESS AND MILD"
30550 TAB 4: PRINT "COMPASSION,"
30555 PRINT "WEPT LIKE TO CHILDREN IN THEIR DEATHS'"
30560 TAB 4: PRINT "SAD STORY."
30565 PRINT "'O, THUS,' QUOTH DIGHTON, 'LAY THE"
```

```
30570 TAB 4: PRINT "GENTLE BABES.'"
30575 PRINT "'THUS, THUS,' QUOTH FORREST,"
30580 TAB 4: PRINT "'GIRDLING ONE ANOTHER"
30585 PRINT "WITHIN THEIR ALABASTER INNOCENT ARMS."
30590 PRINT "THEIR LIPS WERE FOUR RED ROSES ON A"
30595 TAB 4: PRINT "STALK,"
30600 INPUT "CONTINUE", T$
30605 PRINT "AND IN THEIR SUMMER BEAUTY KISSED EACH"
30610 TAB 4: PRINT "OTHER."
30615 PRINT "A BOOK OF PRAYERS ON THEIR PILLOW LAY,"
30620 PRINT "WHICH ONCE,' QUOTH FORREST, 'ALMOST"
30625 TAB 4: PRINT "CHANGED MY MIND;"
30630 PRINT "BUT, O! THE DEVIL' - THERE THE"
30635 TAB 4: PRINT "VILLAIN STOPPED;"
30640 PRINT "WHEN DIGHTON THUS TOLD ON - 'WE"
30645 TAB 4: PRINT "SMOTHERED"
30650 PRINT "THE MOST REPLENISHED SWEET WORK OF NATURE"
30655 PRINT "THAT FROM THE PRIME CREATION E'ER SHE"
30660 TAB 4: PRINT "FRAMED.'"
30665 PRINT "HENCE BOTH ARE GONE WITH CONSCIENCE AND"
30670 TAB 4: PRINT "REMORSE:"
30675 PRINT "THEY COULD NOT SPEAK; AND SO I LEFT THEM"
30680 TAB 4: PRINT "BOTH,"
30685 PRINT "TO BEAR THIS TIDINGS TO THE BLOODY KING."
30690 INPUT "CONTINUE", T$
30700 PRINT "YOUR VILLAINOUS TASK IS DONE."
30705 PRINT "LONG LIVE KING RICHARD!"
30710 PRINT
30715 PRINT "***YOU HAVE WON***"
30720 INPUT "CONTINUE",T$
30725 RETURN


32000 REM PRINT ROOM
32010 TAB 10: PRINT T$
32015 PRINT D$
```

```
32020 INPUT "CONTINUE",T$
32025 RETURN



1000 REM OUTSIDE THE TOWER
1010 T$ = "OUTSIDE THE TOWER"
1015 D$ = "RAVENS ARE FLYING AROUND YOUR HEAD AS YOU STAND OUTSIDE THE TOWER. THERE
ARE TWO SPIGOTS ON THE WALL; "1016 D$(LEN(D$)+1) = "ONE SAYS 'HAUTE,' AND THE OTHER,
'CAULDE.' 'CAULDE' IS ON."


1020 GOSUB 32000


1025 PRINT "1) ENTER THE TOWER"
1030 PRINT "2) TURN HAUTE SPIGOT"
1035 PRINT "3) TURN CAULDE SPIGOT"


1040 INPUT "CHOICE", Y
1045 IF Y = 1 AND H1 = 1 AND C1 = 0 THEN 1200
1050 IF Y = 1 THEN PRINT "THE RAVENS SWOOP DOWN AND PECK AT YOU, BLOCKING YOUR
ENTRANCE."
1060 IF Y = 2 THEN GOSUB 1300
1065 IF Y = 3 THEN GOSUB 1400
1070 INPUT "CONTINUE",T$
1075 GOTO 1025


1200 REM NEXT LEVEL
1205 PRINT "YOU ENTER THE TOWER."
1210 RETURN


1300 REM HAUTE
1305 H1 = H1 + 1
1310 IF H1 = 2 THEN H1 = 0
1315 IF H1 = O THEN PRINT "HAUTE IS NOW OFF."
1320 IF H1 = 1 THEN PRINT "HAUTE IS NOW ON."
1325 RETURN
```

```
1400 REM CAULDE
1405 C1 = C1 - 1
1410 C1 = ABS(C1)
1415 IF C1 = O THEN PRINT "CAULDE IS NOW OFF."
1420 IF C1 = 1 THEN PRINT "CAULDE IS NOW ON."
1425 RETURN


2000 REM BOTTOM OF THE TOWER
2010 T$ = "BOTTOM OF THE TOWER"
2015 D$ = "YOU ARE AT THE BOTTOM OF THE TOWER. THERE IS A DAGGER ON THE FLOOR, AND A
SLIP OF PAPER UNDERNEATH IT."
2016 D$(LEN(D$)+1) = "THERE IS A GUARD ON THE STAIRS."

2020 GOSUB 32000

2025 PRINT "1) ATTACK GUARD"
2030 PRINT "2) GO UP STAIRS"
2035 PRINT "3) PICK UP PAPER"
2040 PRINT "4) PICK UP DAGGER"
2045 IF P2 = 1 THEN PRINT "5) READ PAPER"

2050 INPUT "CHOICE", Y
2055 IF Y = 1 THEN GOSUB 2500
2060 IF Y = 2 AND G2 = 0 THEN GOTO 2200
2065 IF Y = 2 THEN PRINT "THE GUARD BLOCKS YOUR ASCENT."
2070 IF Y = 3 THEN GOSUB 2300
2075 IF Y = 4 THEN GOSUB 2400
2080 IF Y = 5 AND P2 = 1 THEN PRINT "THE PAPER SAYS '1482'."
2085 INPUT "CONTINUE",T$
2090 GOTO 2025

2200 REM NEXT LEVEL
2205 PRINT "YOU ASCEND THE STAIRS."
2210 RETURN
```

```
2300 REM GET PAPER
2305 IF P2 = 1 THEN PRINT "YOU ALREADY HAVE THE PAPER."
2310 IF P2 = 1 THEN RETURN
2315 P2 = 1
2320 PRINT "YOU TAKE THE PAPER."
2325 RETURN


2400 REM GET DAGGER
2405 IF D2 = 1 THEN PRINT "YOU ALREADY HAVE THE DAGGER."
2410 IF D2 = 1 THEN RETURN
2415 D2 = 1
2420 PRINT "YOU TAKE THE DAGGER."
2425 RETURN


2500 REM ATTACK GUARD
2505 IF D2 = 0 THEN PRINT "THE GUARD KNOCKS YOU TO THE GROUND."
2510 IF D2 = 0 THEN RETURN
2515 G2 = 0
2520 PRINT "THE GUARD CRUMPLES TO THE FLOOR, FALLING ON THE DAGGER."
2525 RETURN



3000 REM MIDDLE OF THE TOWER
3010 T$ = "MIDDLE OF THE TOWER"
3015 D$ = "YOU ARE IN THE MIDDLE OF THE TOWER.  THERE IS A KEY IN THE CORNER."
3016 D$(LEN(D$)+1) = "THERE ARE FOUR NUMBER DIALS ON THE DOOR TO THE NORTH."

3020 GOSUB 32000

3025 PRINT "1) PICK UP KEY"
3030 PRINT "2) OPEN DOOR"
3035 PRINT "3) ENTER COMBINATION"
3040 PRINT "4) ENTER ROOM"

3045 INPUT "CHOICE", Y
3050 IF Y = 1 THEN GOSUB 3200
```

```
3055 IF Y = 2 AND L3(1) = 1 AND L3(2) = 4 AND L3(3) = 8 AND L3(4) = 3 THEN GOSUB 3400
3060 IF Y = 2 AND D3 = 0 THEN PRINT "THE COMBINATION IS NOT CORRECT."
3065 IF Y = 3 THEN GOSUB 3300
3070 IF Y = 4 AND D3 = 1 THEN 3100
3075 IF Y = 4 THEN PRINT "THE DOOR IS CLOSED."
3080 INPUT "CONTINUE",T$
3085 GOTO 3025

3100 REM NEXT LEVEL
3105 PRINT "YOU ARE SO CLOSE..."
3110 RETURN

3200 REM GET KEY
3205 IF K3 = 1 THEN PRINT "YOU ALREADY HAVE THE KEY."
3210 IF K3 = 1 THEN RETURN
3215 K3 = 1
3220 PRINT "YOU TAKE THE KEY."
3225 RETURN

3300 REM ENTER COMBINATION
3305 INPUT "TURN FIRST DIAL TO", L3(1)
3310 PRINT "THE DIAL CLICKS."
3315 INPUT "TURN SECOND DIAL TO", L3(2)
3320 PRINT "THE DIAL WHIRRS."
3325 INPUT "TURN THE THIRD DIAL TO", L3(3)
3330 PRINT "THE DIAL SQUEAKS."
3335 INPUT "TURN THE FOURTH DIAL TO", L3(4)
3340 PRINT "THE DIAL WHINES."
3345 RETURN

3400 REM OPEN DOOR
3405 PRINT "THE DOOR OPENS."
3410 D3 = 1
3415 RETURN
```

```
4000 REM TOP OF THE TOWER
4010 T$ = "TOP OF THE TOWER"
4015 D$ = "YOU ARE AT THE TOP OF THE TOWER.  THERE IS A DOOR TO THE NORTH."

4020 GOSUB 32000

4025 PRINT "1) UNLOCK THE DOOR"
4030 PRINT "2) ENTER THE CHAMBER."4035 INPUT "CHOICE", Y
4040 IF Y = 1 THEN GOSUB 4200
4045 IF Y = 2 AND D4 = 1 THEN 4100
4050 IF Y = 2 THEN PRINT "THE DOOR IS LOCKED."
4055 INPUT "CONTINUE",T$
4060 GOTO 4025

4100 REM NEXT LEVEL
4105 PRINT "YOU ENTER THE CHAMBER OF THE SLEEPING PRINCES..."
4110 RETURN

4200 REM UNLOCK DOOR
4205 IF K3 = 0 THEN PRINT "YOU DO NOT HAVE A KEY"
4210 IF K3 = 0 THEN RETURN
4215 IF D4 = 1 THEN PRINT "THE DOOR IS ALREADY UNLOCKED"
4220 IF D4 = 1 THEN RETURN
4225 D4 = 1
4230 PRINT "YOU PUSH THE KEY INTO THE DOOR AND IT SWINGS OPEN; YOU CAN SEE SHAPES
SILHOUETTED IN THE MOONLIGHT."
4235 RETURN
```

Summary

This chapter has attempted to provide a reasonable introduction to programming the Apple I in BASIC. Particular emphasis has been placed on the pecularities of the Apple I's version of BASIC. For more sample programs written in Apple I BASIC, visit the Apple I Owners Club on Applefritter. If you'd like a more in-depth guide to programming BASIC in general, most public libraries will have countless books on the subject.

Chapter 6

Programming in Assembly

Topics in this Chapter:

151

Introduction

Programming in Assembly, a low-level programming language, can be difficult, but it is also a very rewarding process that allows you to get to the core of how the processor interacts with other components. The programmer issues arcane instructions to the processor, and those instructions are exactly what the processor does. BASIC, by contrast, is a high-level language. Instructions in BASIC are translated into a series of Assembly instructions. Thus, with BASIC, it's difficult to know precisely what the processor is doing, whereas with Assembly, you directly control the processor.

Using the Monitor

Power on your Apple I replica and press **Reset**. The \ prompt tells you that you've entered the monitor. In the monitor, it's possible to read and write data to and from memory. Everything is presented in hexadecimal format. To view the contents of location *$FFEF*, for example, type:

```
FFEF
```

The output will be:

```
FFEF: 2C
```

It is also possible to view a range of addresses by specifying the beginning and end addresses with a period between them, such as:

```
FFF0.FFFF
```

```
FFF0: 12 D0 30 FB 8D 12 D0 60
FFF8: 00 00 00 0F 00 FF 00 01
```

Note that only the address for the first value of each line is given. *$FFF0* contains *$12, $FFF1* contains *$D0,* and so on. Each line displays the contents of 8 bytes.

Nonconsecutive memory locations can be viewed by separating addresses with a space:

```
EFA1 FFEF FFFF
```

```
FFA1: CA
FFEF: 2C
FFFF: 01
```

All the addresses we've been looking at are in the *$FFxx* range. This range was chosen because $FFxx contains the monitor, which guarantees we'll be looking at known values. From here onward, you'll be working in main memory. If you're using your own replica with the traditional 8 KB of RAM, you have 4 KB of main memory, located at *$0000.0FFF*. If you're using a Replica I, you have *$0000.7FFF* available.

You can edit data in a manner similar to the way you view it. To insert *$AA* in *$0000*, type:

```
0000:AA
```

The output will be the previous content of *$0000*:

```
0000: 02
```

Now examine *$0000* to view the new contents:

```
0000
```

```
0000: AA
```

It is also possible to enter multiple bytes of data at one time. For example:

```
0000: 01 02 03 04 05 06 07 08 09 0A 0B 0C 0D 0E 0F 10 11 12 13 14
```

```
0000: AA
```

```
0000.0017
```

```
0000: 01 02 03 04 05 06 07 08
0008: 09 0A 0B 0C 0D 0E 0F 10
0010: 11 12 13 14 68 FF 02 FF
```

Finally, to begin running a program, specify the line number and append an **R** for *RUN*. To run the program we just reviewed, for example, you would type:

```
0000R
```

If you try this right now, the system will hang because the program is meaningless. Press **RESET** to recover. You should now have a basic working understanding of the monitor, which will allow you to enter programs. If you'd like to learn more, see the *Apple I Operations Manual* found at the Apple I Owners Club.

Setting Up the Assembler

Assembly code is written using mnemonics such as LDA and JMP. An assembler translates these mnemonics into hexadecimal codes, which can be understood by the processor. The conversion can be done by hand. (Appendix B shows the conversions to opcodes.) Assemble a program by hand, and you can type it directly into the Apple I monitor and run it. The conversion is simple but very tedious. A much easier method is to use an assembler program such as xa65 by Andre Fachat and Cameron Kaiser.

xa65 is released under the GNU General Public License. Source code is included on the CD that accompanies this book, as is a compiled version for Mac OS X. If you're running Mac OS X, copy the application's directory to your hard drive. Open **Terminal** (in Applications/Utilities) and navigate to the xa65's folder. Your command will look something like this, depending upon where you copied the folder to:

```
cd /Users/owad/xa-2.1.4h
```

Here, *cd* stands for "change directory." To run the program, type:

```
./xa
```

This will present the Help screen:

```
Cross-Assembler 65xx V2.1.4h 12dec1998 (c) 1989-98 by A.Fachat
usage : xa { option | sourcefile }
options:
 -v          = verbose output
 -x          = old filename behaviour (overrides -o, -e, -l)
 -C          = no CMOS-opcodes
 -B          = show lines with block open/close
 -c          = produce o65 object instead of executable files (i.e. do not link)
 -o filename = sets output filename, default is 'a.o65'
                    A filename of '-' sets stdout as output file
 -e filename = sets errorlog filename, default is none
 -l filename = sets labellist filename, default is none
 -r          = adds crossreference list to labellist (if -l given)
 -M          = allow ":" to appear in comments, for MASM compatibility
 -R          = start assembler in relocating mode
 -Llabel     = defines 'label' as absolute, undefined label even when linking
 -b? adr     = set segment base address to integer value adr.
                  '?' stands for t(ext), d(ata), b(ss) and z(ero) segment
                  (address can be given more than once, latest is taken)
 -A adr      = make text segment start at an address that when the _file_
                  starts at adr, relocation is not necessary. Overrides -bt
                  Other segments have to be take care of with -b?
 -G          = suppress list of exported globals
 -DDEF=TEXT  = defines a preprocessor replacement
 -Idir       = add directory 'dir' to include path (before XAINPUT)
Environment:
 XAINPUT = include file path; components divided by ','
 XAOUTPUT= output file path
```

At the moment, we're concerned with only a couple of options: *-v, -o, -bt,* and *-C. -v* turns on verbose output. This provides more error messages, more detailed descriptions, and a better idea of what's going on. If something's not working right, turn on this option to get more details on the problem. *-o* lets you specify what the output file will be called. *-bt* allows you to specify the starting address of the code. Note that to avoid modifying blocks used by the monitor, your programs will start at location *$0280* (decimal 640). *-C* turns off support for opcodes that were added in the 65c02. Since you won't be using these opcodes, this isn't necessary at the present time, but if you're assembling someone else's code, turning on this options will warn you if they've used any opcodes that your processor doesn't support.

Your typical assembler command will look like this:

```
./xa -o samplefile.hex —bt640 samplefile
```

Samplefile is the input; *samplefile.hex* is the output. Hex files, such as samplefile.hex, can be viewed using HexEdit, which is included on this book's accompanying CD.

Need to Know

The Apple I monitor uses memory locations *$0024* through *$002B* as index pointers and locations *$0200* through *$027F* as input buffer storage. The monitor will not let you edit these locations. It will let you try, and it won't give you any error message, but when you go to examine the contents you'll find them unchanged.

Registers

You're going to find that moving data around consumes a massive portion of the Apple I's processor time. There are three general-purpose registers in the 6502, each of which holds 1 byte of data. These are the Accumulator, X, and Y. The Accumulator is the register that handles all arithmetic operations and is the one through which most data passes. X and Y are generic registers for temporarily storing data that you want to keep close to the processor. Additional registers are discussed in Chapter 7.

Hello World

Your first Assembly program, like your first BASIC program, is "Hello World." You'll need three instructions for this program: *LDA, JSR,* and *JMP.*

JMP is the mnemonic for "jump." It's the equivalent of the *GOTO* instruction in BASIC. Instead of specifying line numbers, however, you specify memory addresses. When your program is finished running, you want to return control to the monitor. You do this by jumping to location *$FFIF.* To jump to the monitor, you would type:

```
JMP $FFIF
```

The xa65 assembler allows us to use labels to represent physical addresses so that at the start of the file you could state:

```
Monitor = $FF1F
```

and then later in the code, you should include the instruction:

```
JMP Monitor
```

JSR stands for "jump subroutine." It is the equivalent of BASIC's *GOSUB* instruction. The Apple I monitor has a subroutine called *Echo* that sends whatever value is in the accumulator to the display. First you load an ASCII value (see the chart in Appendix A). Then you call the *Echo* subroutine. The character is printed, and control returns to the main program. To jump to the *Echo* subroutine, you would type:

```
JSR $FFEF
```

LDA is the mnemonic for "load accumulator." The # symbol is used to indicate Immediate Addressing mode. This means that the actual value specified—as opposed to the value stored at that address in memory—is loaded into the accumulator. For example, to load the value *$3B* into the accumulator, you would type:

```
LDA #$3B
```

Your "Hello World" program should load *H* into the accumulator, jump to the *Echo* subroutine, and then move on to the next letter. When it's done, control should be returned to the monitor. Since all these letters could get a bit tedious, let's make it "HI W!" instead of "HELLO WORLD":

```
Echo = $FFEF
Monitor = $FF1F


   LDA #$48     ;  H in ASCII is $48
   JSR Echo
   LDA #$49     ;  I
   JSR Echo
   LDA #$20     ;  SPC
   JSR Echo
   LDA #$57     ;  W
   JSR Echo
   LDA #$21     ;  !
   JSR Echo


   JMP Monitor  ;  Return to Monitor
```

Save this file in the same directory as xa65 with the name "hiw." In Terminal, navigate to that directory and run the line:

```
./xa -o hiw.hex -bt640 hiw
```

Now open hiw.hex in HexEdit (see Figure 6.1). If you're using a Serial I/O card on your Apple I, select all the text and copy it into your text editor, such as SubEthaEdit or BBEdit. In your text editor, select the line break and copy it into the **Clipboard**. Paste the line break into the **Find** field of your Find/Replace window and replace all line breaks with a single space. This will place the entire program on a single line, which is what you'll need when you attempt to send it to the Apple I. If you don't have a Serial I/O card, you'll have to type the program in by hand.

Figure 6.1 Hexadecimal Codes in HexEdit

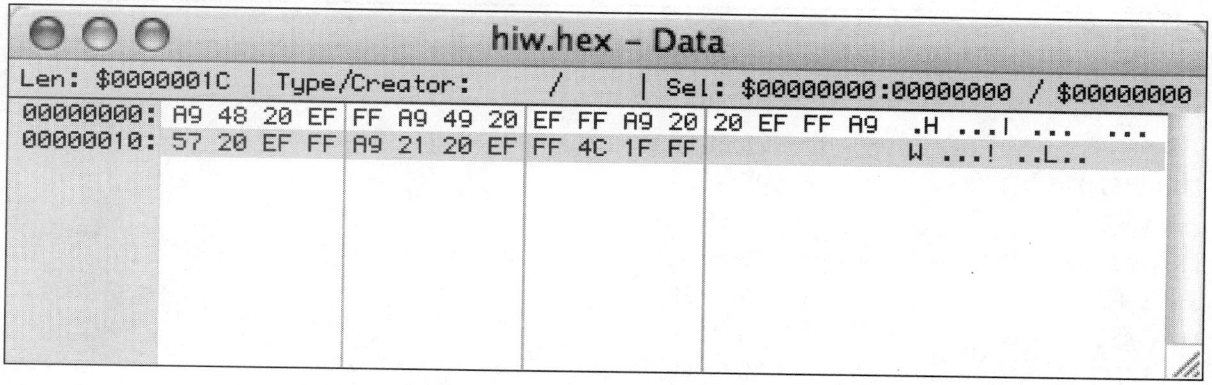

The assembled machine code for hiw is:

```
A9 48 20 EF FF A9 49 20 EF FF A9 20 20 EF FF A9 57 20 EF FF A9 21 20 EF FF 4C 1F FF
```

You want to load this into the memory, starting at location *$0280*; therefore, you need to enter the line:

```
0280: A9 48 20 EF FF A9 49 20 EF FF A9 20 20 EF FF A9 57 20 EF FF A9 21 20 EF FF 4C
1F FF
```

Type **R** to begin running at the most recently examined location (*$0280*) or specify a particular line:

```
0280R
```

The program will output:

```
HI W!
```

and return control to the monitor. If the program doesn't run correctly, examine it in memory. You should get:

```
0280.029D
```

```
0280: A9 48 20 EF FF A9 49 20
0288: EF FF A9 20 20 EF FF A9
```

```
0290: 57 20 EF FF A9 21 20 EF
0298: FF 4C 1F FF E4 FF
```

How do those assembly instructions translate into machine code? Table 6.1 presents a line-by-line comparison.

Table 6.1 Machine Code

Assembly Code	Machine Code
LDA #$48	A9 48
JSR $FFEF	20 EF FF
LDA #$49	A9 49
JSR $FFEF	20 EF FF
LDA #$20	A9 20
JSR $FFEF	20 EF FF
LDA #$57	A9 57
JSR $FFEF	20 EF FF
LDA #$21	A9 21
JSR $FFEF	20 EF FF
JMP $FF1F	4C 1F FF

From this table, we can ascertain that *$A9* is the opcode for *LDA* (when using immediate addressing). *$A9* is followed by the value being loaded into the accumulator. The opcode for *JSR* is *$20*. It's followed by the address of the subroutine in reverse order—low byte first, then high byte. *JMP's* opcode is *$4C*, and it uses the same addressing method as *JSR*.

TV Typewriter

Hello World demonstrated how to output text to the screen. The next program, TV Typewriter, illustrates how to read text from the keyboard. First, you need to introduce two new assembly instructions: *RTS* and *BPL*.

RTS is short for "Return from Subroutine." It is the equivalent of *RETURN* in BASIC. *JSR* (jump to subroutine) is used to enter a subroutine; *RTS* is used to return from it.

BPL is the mnemonic for "Branch on Plus." It is similar to an *IF* and *GOTO* statement in BASIC. *BPL* appears in the form:

```
BPL addr
```

If the value in the accumulator is positive or zero, *BPL* branches to the location specified by *addr*. If the value in the accumulator is negative, *BPL* does not branch but continues execution at the next line.

There are also two new memory addresses that you need to acquaint yourself with. They are *KbdRdy* (*$D011*) and *Kbd* (*$D010*). These addresses are both on the 6821 PIA. The value at *KeyboardRdy* is negative when there is data waiting to be read from the keyboard. When there is no data waiting, it is positive. The location *Kbd* contains the value of the character read in from the keyboard.

A subroutine to read data from the keyboard should loop (wait) until a character is available and then load that character into the accumulator and return:

```
KbdRdy = $D011
Kbd = $D010


GetChar:

    LDA  KbdRdy       ;  Key ready?

    BPL  GetChar      ;  Loop until ready

    LDA  Kbd          ;  Load character

    RTS               ;  Return
```

Note the use of the *GetChar* label in this example. *BPL* branches to whatever address *GetChar* is. *GetChar* is whatever address at which *LDA KbdRdy* begins. The assembler will figure out these actual addresses and insert numbers.

Configure your TV Typewriter program so that it reads a character from the keyboard, echoes that character to the screen, and repeats this loop indefinitely:

```
Begin:

    JSR  GetChar      ;  Read character from keyboard and store in accumulator

    JSR  Echo         ;  Echo value in accumulator  to screen

    JMP  Begin        ;  Loop forever
```

The completed program might look like this:

```
Echo = $FFEF
KbdRdy = $D011
Kbd = $D010


Begin:

    JSR  GetChar      ;  Read character from keyboard and store in accumulator

    JSR  Echo         ;  Echo value in accumulator  to screen

    JMP  Begin        ;  Loop forever


GetChar:

    LDA  KbdRdy       ;  Key ready?
```

```
BPL GetChar      ;  Loop until ready
LDA Kbd          ;  Load character
RTS              ;  Return
```

Assemble the program with the instruction:

```
./xa -o tvtypewriter.hex -bt640 tvtypewriter
```

This will produce the machine code:

```
20 89 02 20 EF FF 4C 80 02 AD 11 D0 10 FB AD 10 D0 60
```

Precede that with the starting memory location (0280:) and copy the whole string into the Apple I monitor, just as you did for Hello World. Press **R** and **Return** to start the programming running. Your Apple I will now allow you to display whatever you can type. To clear the screen without halting the program, press the **CLEAR** button on the motherboard. To halt execution, press **RESET**.

X and Y

The X and Y registers are very similar to the Accumulator, but without the additional mathematical abilities. One mathematical function X and Y *can* perform is increment. The *INX* and *INY* instructions increment X and Y, respectively, by one. The converse is also available: *DEX* and *DEY* are used to decrement.

X and Y support the basic memory-addressing operations supported by the Accumulator (see Appendix C for specific addressing modes). Several instructions allow you to transfer values between the Accumulator and the X and Y registers (see Table 6.2).

Table 6.2 Transfer Instructions

Instruction	Description
TAX	Transfer Accumulator to X
TAY	Transfer Accumulator to Y
TXA	Transfer X to Accumulator
TYA	Transfer Y to Accumulator

Note that it is not possible to transfer directly between X and Y without first going through the Accumulator.

In the sample program that follows, *$00* is loaded into X. X is incremented and then transferred to the Accumulator. The Accumulator is echoed to the screen. The loop is repeated. This will print every value from 0 through 255 and then loop around again. Since your display interprets all values as ASCII codes, you won't see the numbers 0 through 255. Instead, you'll see all the symbols those values represent.

```
Echo = $FFEF
```

```
Begin:
  LDX #$00       ;  Load 0 into X


Loop:
  INX            ;  Increment X
  TXA            ;  Transfer X to A
  JSR Echo       ;  Echo A to screen
  JMP Loop       ;  Repeat loop
```

To run the program, assemble it with xa65 and copy the hexadecimal code to the Apple I monitor, as you did in the Hello World and TV Typewriter samples.

Memory Addressing

The 6502 has myriad addressing techniques used for moving data between memory and the processor's registers. The most basic of these are used constantly. Some of the more complex modes will seem almost esoteric, but they're invaluable under the right circumstances. The examples in this section refer to the data in Table 6.3.

Table 6.3 Memory Location and Contents

Location	Contents
X (register)	$02
Y (register)	$03
PC (register)	$C100
$0000	$00
$0001	$00
$0002	$B3
$0003	$5A
$0004	$EF
$0017	$10
$0018	$D0
$002A	$35
$002B	$C2
$D010	$33
$C238	$2F

Accumulator: *A*

The Accumulator is implied as the operand in Accumulator addressing, and thus no address needs to be specified. An example is the *ASL* (arithmetic shift left) instruction, covered later in this chapter. It is understood that the value in the Accumulator is always the value being shifted left.

Implied: *i*

With implied addressing, the operand is implied and therefore does not need to be specified. An example is the *TXA* instruction.

Immediate: *#*

Immediate addressing loads the operand directly into the Accumulator. In this example:

```
LDA #$22
```

the Accumulator now contains the value *$22*.

Absolute *a*

Absolute addressing specifies a full 16-bit address. For example:

```
LDA $D010
```

The Accumulator now contains *$33*, the value stored at location *$D010*.

Zero Page: *zp*

Zero page addressing uses a single byte to specify an address on the first page of memory (*$00xx*). Thus, in the example:

```
LDA $02
```

the value *$B3* at location *$0002* is loaded into the Accumulator.

Relative: *r*

Relative addressing specifies memory locations relative to the present address. The current address is stored in the Program Counter (PC). Relative addressing adds the address in PC to the specified offset. In this example:

```
BPL $2D
```

PC is *$C100* and the offset is *$2D*, so the new address is *$C12D*.

Absolute Indexed with X: *a,x*

With absolute indexed addressing with X, the value stored in X is added to the specified address. In this example:

```
LDA $0001,X
```

the value in X is *$02.* The sum of *$0001* and *$02* is *$0003*; therefore, the value at location *$0003*, which is *$5A,* is loaded into the Accumulator.

Absolute Indexed with Y: *a,y*

Absolute indexed addressing with Y works the same as it does with X. In this example:

```
LDA $0001,Y
```

The value in Y is *$03.* The sum of *$0001* and *$03* is *$0003,* so the value at location *$0004,* which is *$EF,* is loaded into the Accumulator.

Zero Page Indexed with X: *zp,x*

Zero page indexed addressing is like absolute indexed addressing but limited to the zero page. In the example:

```
LDA $01,X
```

X contains *$02,* which is added to *$01* to present the zero page address *$03* and is equivalent to the absolute address *$0003. $0003* contains *$5A,* which is loaded into the Accumulator.

Zero Page Indexed with Y: *zp,y*

Zero page indexed addressing with Y works the same as it does with X. In the example:

```
LDA $01,Y
```

Y contains *$03,* which is added to *$01* to present the zero page address *$04* and is equivalent to the absolute address *$0004. $0004* contains *$EF,* which is loaded into the Accumulator.

Absolute Indexed Indirect: *(a,x)*

With absolute indexed indirect addressing, the value stored in X is added to the specified address. In this example:

```
JMP ($0001,X)
```

the value of X is *$02;* so the processor loads the address stored in locations *$0003* and *$0004* and jumps to that address. This mode of addressing is only supported by the *JMP* instruction.

Zero Page Indexed Indirect: *(zp,x)*

Zero page indexed indirect addressing first adds X to the zero page address, such as in this example:

```
LDA ($15,X)
```

X contains *$02,* so the address $0017 is generated. Zero page indexed indirect addressing next goes to that address and the following address (*$0017* and *$0018*) and loads the values contained there as an address. *$0017* contains *$10* and *$0018* contains *$D0*; consequently, the address *$D010* is loaded. Finally, the processor goes to this address and loads the value it contains, *$33*, into the Accumulator.

Zero Page Indirect Indexed with Y: *(zp),y*

Zero page indirect indexed addressing with Y begins by fetching the value at the zero page address and the zero page address plus one. In our example:

```
LDA ($2A),Y
```

the values at locations *$2A* and *$2B* would be fetched. *$2A* contains *$35*, and *$2B* contains *$C2*. This gives you the address *$C235*. Next, the value of Y, which is *$03,* is added to this address to create the address *$C238*. Location *$C238* contains the value *$2F*, which is loaded into the Accumulator.

Interacting with Memory

We used *LDA* as our sample instruction for memory addressing to load the Accumulator, but the same can be done with *LDX* and *LDY* to load the X and Y registers. Data can be transferred from the registers to memory using the store instructions: *STA, STX,* and *STY.* A few of the more esoteric addressing modes are supported only by particular instructions. See Appendix C for details.

The following program demonstrates some simple memory interactions, in which you store three variables in memory and then later retrieve them. Tables 6.4 and 6.5 show the contents of the registers before and after running the program.

Table 6.4 Register Contents Before Running

Register	Value
A	*$73*
X	*$E2*
Y	*$90*

```
STA $05      ;   Store $73 at $0005
STX $1023    ;   Store $E2 at $1023
STY $00FF    ;   Store $90 at $00FF

LDA $1023    ;   Load $E2 from $1023
LDX $FF      ;   Load $90 from $00FF
LDY $0005    ;   Load $73 from $0005
```

Table 6.5 Register Contents After Running

Register	Value
A	$E2
X	$90
Y	$73

Printing Strings

The program described in this section will introduce two new functions: the ability to assemble strings of characters and the ability to branch on a condition. ASCII characters can be stored in memory just like instructions, and by using the ASCII table in Appendix A, you could manually enter the hexadecimal values into the Apple I's memory, just as you entered the instructions. The xa65 assembler provides a pseudo-opcode, *.asc,* that automatically converts a string of characters to hex-adecimal. The statement:

```
.asc "HELLO WORLD"
```

will enter *"HELLO WORLD"* as ASCII wherever the statement is placed.

The Branch on Result Zero instruction (*BEQ*) branches (jumps) to a new memory location whenever the *Z* (*Zero*) flag is high. *BEQ* uses relative addressing, so the value following the *BEQ* instruction is added to the current address (in the program counter) to get the new address.

The *N* flag can be set using the *Compare* (*CMP*) instruction. *CMP* compares the value in the Accumulator to the value specified after *CMP*. If the value in the Accumulator is less than the value in memory, $\underline{N}$ equals 1. If the values are equal, *Z* and *C* equal 1. If the value in the Accumulator is greater than the value in memory, *C* equals 1. In the following example, *$AA* is compared with the value in the Accumulator:

```
0000: CMP #$AA

0002: BEQ $05

0004: INX
```

If the Accumulator does not contain *$AA,* the *Z* flag is reset to 0 and *BEQ* does not cause a branch. If the Accumulator does contain *$AA, Z* is set to 1 and *BEQ* causes a branch to *$05* + PC. The PC is at *$0004* (the next instruction); therefore, the program branches to *$0009* and continues execution at that location.

CPX and *CPY* work the same as *CMP* but use the X and Y registers instead of the Accumulator.

The program displayed later uses branching to print an array of characters. The characters begin at the label string, such that the instruction:

```
LDA string
```

will load the first value at string, in this case *H*, represented by an ASCII *$48.* The instruction:

```
LDA string + 1
```

will load the second value in the array, which is *E*, or *$45* in ASCII.

With this strategy, your program can use absolute indexed addressing to specify the offset (i.e., which character to load). This instruction:

```
LDA string,X
```

loads the value at string + X into the Accumulator. By starting X at zero and repeatedly incrementing it, every character in the array can be reached.

How do you know when to stop incrementing? The *NULL* character, *$00,* can be appended to the end of the string:

```
.asc "HELLO WORLD",$00
```

After loading the character into the Accumulator, you can compare it with the *NULL* character. If it is the *NULL* character, you know that you have reached the end of the string and can branch to done:

```
CMP #$00          ;  Compare char to NULL ($00)
BEQ done          ;  If NULL break out of loop
```

The following program uses these methods to print to screen a character array of undetermined length:

```
Echo = $FFEF
Monitor = $FF1F


Begin:
  LDX #$00               ;  Our loop expects X to start at 0

print:
  LDA string,X           ;  Load the next character
  CMP #$00               ;  Compare char to NULL ($00)
  BEQ done               ;  If NULL break out of loop
  JSR Echo               ;  If not NULL, print the character
  INX                    ;  Increment X, so we can get at the next character
  JMP print              ;  Loop again

done:
  JMP Monitor            ;  Return to Monitor

string:
  .asc "HELLO WORLD",$00     ;  ASCII string, $00 is NULL
```

Assemble this program and examine it in HexEdit. You will see your string displayed in ASCII on the right side of the window. Highlight the string, and the corresponding ASCII values will be boxed (see Figure 6.2). You can see *NULL ($00)* following immediately after the string. Preceding the character string is the rest of the program.

Figure 6.2 ASCII in HexEdit

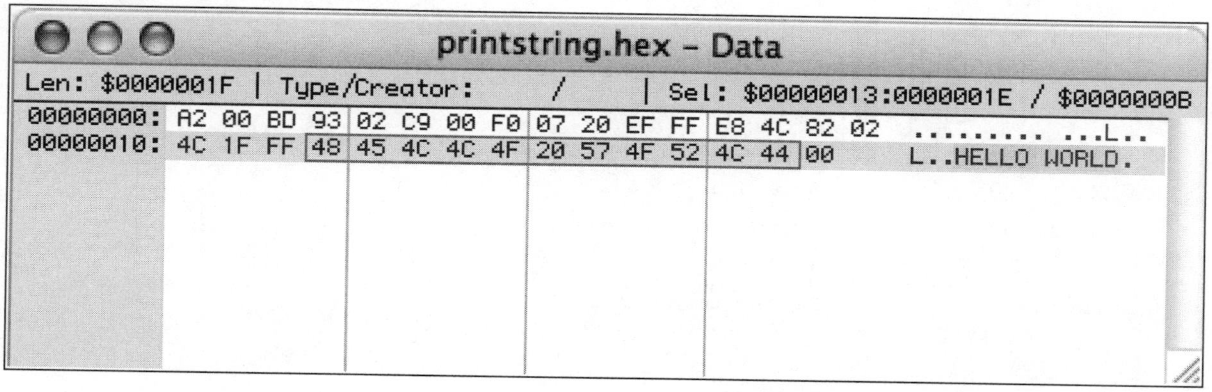

```
                    printstring.hex – Data
Len: $0000001F | Type/Creator:      /     | Sel: $00000013:0000001E / $0000000B
00000000: A2 00 BD 93 02 C9 00 F0 07 20 EF FF E8 4C 82 02    ......... ...L..
00000010: 4C 1F FF 48 45 4C 4C 4F 20 57 4F 52 4C 44 00       L..HELLO WORLD.
```

String Subroutines

The objective in this section is to develop a subroutine that can be used by any program to print any string. This subroutine draws heavily from the program developed in the previous section. The primary difference is that instead of hardcoding the location of the string, you want it to be able to load characters from any address. Since the Accumulator, X, and Y registers are only 8-bit, passing a 16-bit address is rather tricky.

One possible workaround is to store the string's address in a predefined memory location and then have the subroutine load it from that location. This can be done with zero page indirect indexed addressing. This addressing mode is only supported by Y; as a result, all our previous uses of the X register must be changed to Y.

If you load the string's address into *$00* and *$01*, you can access the characters in the string with the command:

```
LDY ($00),Y
```

The following program and subroutine demonstrate this method. This subroutine could be assembled separately and stored in ROM for use with any program. If you want to use this subroutine frequently but don't have the tools to program a ROM, you can load it into a high location of memory. Since memory is preserved through resets, you'll lose the code only when power is turned off.

```
Echo = $FFEF
Monitor = $FF1F
```

```
Begin:
  LDA #<welcome        ;  Load low byte of string's addr (indicated by <)
  STA $00              ;  Save addr to $00
  LDA #>welcome        ;  Load high byte of string's addr (indicated by >)
  STA $01              ;  Save addr to $01
  JSR printsub         ;  Print the string

  LDA #<goodbye        ;  Load low byte of string's addr
  STA $00              ;  Save addr to $00
  LDA #>goodbye        ;  Load high byte of string's addr
  STA $01              ;  Save addr to $01
  JSR printsub         ;  Print the string


  JMP Monitor          ;  Return to Monitor



/* Strings */


welcome:
  .asc "Welcome to the Apple I",$0D,$00      ; $0D is carriage return
                                             ; $00 is NULL


goodbye:
  .asc "That was a short demo.",$00



/*
Name:               PrintSub
Precondtions:       Address of string to print is stored at $00,$01.
Postcondtions:      The string is printed to screen.
Destroys:           A, Y, Flags.
Description:        Prints the string at the address at $00,$01.
*/


printsub:
  LDY #$00             ;  Our loop expects Y to start at 0
print:
```

```
    LDA ($00),Y         ;  Load the next character
    CMP #$00            ;  Compare char to NULL ($00)
    BEQ done            ;  If NULL break out of loop
    JSR Echo            ;  If not NULL, print the character
    INY                 ;  Increment X, so we can get at the next character
    JMP print           ;  Loop again
done:
    RTS
```

This program exceeds the monitor's maximum line length; thus, the simplest way to transfer it is to enter one line at a time. Each line in HexEdit contains 16 (*$10*) bytes, so you'll need to increment the memory address by *$10* with each line you copy. Your entry will look like this:

```
280:  A9 99 85 00 A9 02 85 01 20 C8 02 A9 B1 85 00 A9
290:  02 85 01 20 C8 02 4C 1F FF 57 65 6C 63 6F 6D 65
2A0:  20 74 6F 20 74 68 65 20 41 70 70 6C 65 20 49 0D
2B0:  00 54 68 61 74 20 77 61 73 20 61 20 73 68 6F 72
2C0:  74 20 64 65 6D 6F 2E 00 A0 00 B1 00 C9 00 F0 07
2D0:  20 EF FF C8 4C CA 02 60
```

Bit Representation

Your video section can print only ASCII characters, but the processor instructions are geared primarily toward integer operations. The subroutine presented in this section will print the Accumulator's contents in its binary representation. For example, if *$05* is in the Accumulator, this subroutine will print *00000101*.

There are many possible ways to approach writing this subroutine. One way is to use the negative (*N*) flag. This flag is used in two's complement notation to indicate that the highest bit (bit 7) is a 1. By rotating the byte so that each value has its turn in the bit 7 position, *N* will be reset after each rotation. By branching whenever *N* is 1 to print an ASCII 1 and not branching whenever it is 0 to print an ASCII 0, you can print a 1 or 0 for each bit.

Five new instructions are used in this subroutine: *CPY, ROL, ROR, BMI,* and *BNE*.

Compare Y (CPY) is the equivalent of *CMP* for the Y register. The instruction:

```
CPY #$08
```

compares the value in the Y register with the value *$08*. If they are equal, the *Zero (Z)* flag is set. *Branch on Result Not Zero (BNE)* branches whenever *Z* equals 0. We can use this combination of instructions to create a loop:

```
LDY #$00        ;  Initialize Y to 0
loop:
```

```
INY                ;   Increment Y
CPY #$08           ;   Compare Y to $08
BNE loop           ;   If Y != $08 then loop
```

The aforementioned program initializes Y to *$00* and then loops, incrementing Y until it equals *$08.*

Branch on Minus (BMI) branches when *N* equals 1. The *N* flag is set whenever bit 7 is high, by numerous instructions (see Appendix D), such as *LDA* and *CMP*. For example:

```
loop:
  LDA #$80
  BMI loop
```

will load the value *$80 (1000 0000b)* into the Accumulator and set *N* to 1, since bit 7 is high. Because *N* is high, *BMI* will branch to loop, and the program will run indefinitely.

Rotate Right (ROR) and *Rotate Left (ROL)* rotate the contents of the Accumulator or a memory address. The *Carry (C)* is included in the rotation such that if you did a *ROL* on the value:

```
0000 1111 C=1
```

the result would be:

```
0001 1111 C=0
```

It takes nine rotations to return the memory or Accumulator contents to their original value. Each time a rotation is done, the *N* flag responds to the new bit 7.

The *PrintBin* subroutine that follows uses these new instructions to print the binary representation of whatever value is passed to it in the Accumulator:

```
Echo = $FFEF
Monitor = $FF1F


Begin:
  LDA #$00
  JSR printbin       ;   Print $00 in binary
  LDA #$FF
  JSR printbin       ;   Print $FF in binary
  LDA #$AA
  JSR printbin       ;   Print $AA in binary
  JMP Monitor


/*
```

```
Name:              PrintBin
Precondtions:      Byte to print is in Accumulator.
Postcondtions:     The string is printed to screen.
Destroys:          A, X, Y, Flags.
Description:       Prints the binary representation of the value in A.
*/


printbin:
  LDY #$00          ;  Initialize counter to 0
  ROR               ;  ROR once so initial setup will mesh with the loop
  TAX               ;  Loop expects value to be in X register

begin:
  TXA               ;  Restore value to Accumulator
  ROL               ;  Rotate next bit into bit 7's location
  BMI neg           ;  If that bit is a 1, then branch to neg
  TAX               ;  The bit is 0; save byte to X
  LDA #$30          ;  Load ASCII '0' for printing
  JSR Echo          ;  Print 0
  JMP continue      ;  Skip over code for printing a 1
neg:
  TAX               ;  Save byte to X
  LDA #$31          ;  Load ASCII '1' for printing
  JSR Echo          ;  Print 1

continue:
  INY               ;  Increment counter
  CPY #$08          ;  Compare counter to 8 (number of bits to print)
  BNE begin         ;  If counter != 8, then not all bits have been printed,
                    ;  so loop again, otherwise continue

  LDA #$0D          ;  Load ASCII Carriage Return (CR)
  JSR Echo          ;  Print CR to screen
  RTS               ;  Exit subroutine
```

Using the Stack

A great feature of the *Echo* subroutine is that it doesn't destroy the contents of any registers; you can call *Echo* and pick up right where you left off without worrying about the contents of the Accumulator or the X and Y registers being any different. The *PrintBin* subroutine, by contrast, destroys the contents of all three. We can preserve the contents of these registers by saving them to the stack.

The *stack* is a data structure that only allows data to be added or removed at the topmost location. Data is either "pushed" onto the top of the stack or "popped" (sometimes called "pulled") off the top of the stack. Figure 6.3 shows data being pushed and popped.

Figure 6.3 ASCII in HexEdit

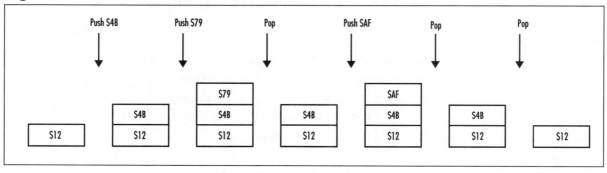

The 6502 uses the stack to store the return address when jumping to a subroutine (*JSR*). When returning from a subroutine (*RTS*), the address is popped from the stack and loaded into the PC so the processor can continue operation where it left off. The stack is allocated the addresses between *$0100* and *$01FF*. Overwrite data within this range and you risk corrupting the contents of the stack.

You can also use the stack for our own purposes, using the commands *PHA, PLA, PHP, PLP, TSX,* and *TXS.*

Push Accumulator on Stack (PHA) pushes the value in the Accumulator onto the top of the stack. *Pull Accumulator from Stack (PLA)* pops the top value off the stack and places it in the Accumulator. If you were to put the actions in Figure 6.3 into code, it would look like this:

```
LDA #$4B
PHA          ; Push $4B
LDA #$79
PHA          ; Push $79
PLA          ; Pull $79
LDA #$AF
PHA          ; Push $AF
```

```
PLA            ; Pull $AF
PLA            ; Pull $4B
```

In this example, every time a PLA instruction is issued, the contents of the Accumulator are over-written. Normally, something would be done with the data after popping it.

The stack pointer is the address of the top of the stack. The value is stored in its own register, S. The address changes every time you push or pop a byte. If you want to manipulate this address, you can copy it into the X register using the *Transfer Stack Pointer to Index X (TSX)* instruction. You can copy your own stack pointer into S using the *Transfer Index X to Stack Register (TSX)* instruction.

Push Processor Status on Stack (PHP) and *Pull Processor Status from Stack (PLP)* are used to preserve the contents of processor flags (for example, N, V, and so on). This is particularly useful when you don't want a subroutine to destroy your flags. Using *PHP* before the subroutine is called and *PLP* after it returns will ensure that they are not lost. You can use this concept to preserve all your register contents when calling a subroutine.

Suppose you want to print the binary representation of every integer from 0 to 255. This is best done with a loop:

```
LDX #$00            ; Initialize counter to 0
  JMP start         ; Skip over increment first time through the loop


next:
  INX               ; Increment the counter
start:
  TXA               ; printbin2 requires the value be in the accumulator
  JSR printbin2     ; print the value as binary
  CPX #$FF          ; If we've reached 255 ($FF), we're done
  BNE next          ; If not, loop again


  JMP Monitor
```

There's just one problem: The X register is overwritten each time the *printbin* subroutine is called, destroying our counter. A possible fix for this is to push X onto the stack before calling the subroutine, then pop it after the subroutine returns, which could be done like this:

```
LDX #$00            ; Initialize counter to 0
  JMP start         ; Skip over increment first time through the loop


next:
  INX               ; Increment the counter
start:
  TXA               ; printbin2 requires the value be in the accumulator
```

```
PHA                     ;   Save X (already in the accumulator), before subroutine
JSR printbin            ;   print the value as binary
PLA                     ;   Retreive X from Stack, place it in the accumulator
TAX                     ;   Copy X from accumulator to X register
CPX #$FF                ;   If we've reached 255 ($FF), we're done
BNE next                ;   If not, loop again


JMP Monitor
```

Another possibility is to modify the *PrintBin* subroutine so that it does not destroy the registers. You can do this by pushing all registers onto the stack at the start of the program and popping them at the end:

```
/*
Name:                   PrintBin2
Precondtions:           Byte to print is in Accumulator.
Postcondtions:          The string is printed to screen.
Destroys:               Flags
Description:             Prints the binary representation of the value in A.
*/


printbin2:

  STA temp              ;   Save Accumulator for later
  PHA                   ;   Push Accumulator
  TXA
  PHA                   ;   Push X (via A)
  TYA                   ;   Push Y (via Y)
  PHA
  LDA temp              ;   Restore the Accumulator

  LDY #$00              ;   Initialize counter to 0
  ROR                   ;   ROR once so initial setup will mesh with the loop
  TAX                   ;   Loop expects value to be in X register

  JSR PrintBin          ;   Now that registers are saved, call the ordinary
                        ;   PrinBin subroutine
```

```
      PLA
      TAY                    ;   Recover Y
      PLA
      TAX                    ;   Recover X
      PLA                    ;   Recover Accumulator


      RTS                    ;   Exit subroutine


temp:
      .asc $00               ;   Temporary storage location for Accumulator value
```

Which method is better? It depends on the application. If it doesn't matter that your subroutine destroys the registers, there's no point in wasting time and space in the subroutine to preserve them. On the rare occasions when you do want to preserve the registers, it would be more efficient to do so in the calling program. On the other hand, some subroutines, such as *Echo*, are called very frequently. Imagine having to first push and then pop the contents of all the registers each time *Echo* is called. In such a case, it's much less frustrating and more space-efficient to put the stack operations inside the subroutine.

Bit Manipulation

The instructions *AND Memory with Accumulator (AND), OR Memory with Accumulator (ORA),* and *Exclusive-OR Memory with Accumulator (EOR)* are used to perform bit-by-bit operations on data. These are the same operations discussed in Chapter 2, but whereas there you applied them to single bits, here you apply them on a bit-by-bit basis to bytes. To *AND $AC* with *$E6*, for example, produces *$A5*:

```
      1010 1100 = $AC
AND   1110 0110 = $E6
      1010 0101 = $A5
```

In an *AND* operation, each resulting bit is high only if both bits in that column are high. This is very useful for masking. Suppose you want to isolate the lower 4 bits from the upper—that is, you want to change *$B6* into just *$06*. Use *$0F* as a mask:

```
      1011 0110 = $B6
AND   0000 1111 = $0F
      0000 0110 = $06
```

To turn *$B6* into just *$0B*, use *$F0* as a mask and then *ROR* four times.

Suppose that, by some terrible calamity, you come upon a string of text that contains lowercase characters. You can use masking to make these uppercase. Uppercase ASCII characters have hex values in the range of *$41* (*0100 0001b*) for *A* to *$5A* (*0101 1010b*) for *Z*. Lowercase characters are in the range *$61* (*0110 0001b*) for *a* to *$7A* (*0111 1010b*) for *z*. You'll note that the values for *A* and *a* are identical, except for bit 5. The same applies to *Z* and *z*, as well as every other letter. To change a character from lowercase to uppercase, you only need to change bit 5 from a one to a zero.

This can be done by masking the ASCII value with *1101 1111b*. This passes through every bit except bit 5, which is forced to a 0. Here are some examples:

```
        0110 0001 = $61 = 'a'
AND     1101 1111 = $DF
        0100 0001 = $41 = 'A'


        0100 0001 = $41 = 'A'
AND     1101 1111 = $DF
        0100 0001 = $41 = 'A'


        0111 0011 = $73 = 's'
AND     1101 1111 = $DF
        0101 0011 = $53 = 'S'
```

The following program uses a mask with *$DF* to convert all letters in a string from lowercase to uppercase; it will leave uppercase letters untouched but will affect a few nonletter characters above *$5A*:

```
Echo = $FFEF
Monitor = $FF1F


    LDY #$00             ;   Initialize counter to 0


caps:
    LDA string,Y         ;   Load in first character
    CMP #$00             ;   Is this character null?
    BEQ done             ;   If so, we're done converting
    CMP #$41             ;   Is this character a letter?
    BMI skip             ;   If not, skip it
    AND #$DF             ;   Mask with $DF to convert to uppercase
    STA string,Y         ;   Overwrite original character with the new
skip:
    INY                  ;   Increment the counter
```

```
    JMP caps              ;  Loop to the next character


done:
  LDA #<string           ;  Save memory address of string for access by PrintSub
  STA $00
  LDA #>string
  STA $01
  JSR printsub           ;  Print the new uppercase string


  JMP Monitor


string:
  .asc "lowercase string, MOSTLY",$00


/* Append PrintSub subroutine here */
```

Although *AND* is useful for clearing bits to 0, *OR* can be used to set them to 1. Suppose, for example, that contrary to the last example, you now want to convert all letters from uppercase to lowercase. Bit 5 would then need to be set high. You can do this with an *OR* operation:

```
     0100 0001 = $41 = 'A'
OR   0010 0000 = $20
     0110 0001 = $61 = 'a'


     0110 0001 = $61 = 'a'
OR   0010 0000 = $20
     0110 0001 = $61 = 'a'


     0101 0011 = $53 = 'S'
OR   0010 0000 = $20
     0111 0011 = $73 = 's'
```

To modify this program so that it converts uppercase to lowercase instead of vice-versa, you need to change only one line:

```
AND #$DF               ;  Mask with $DF to convert to uppercase
```

so that it reads:

```
ORA #$20               ;  Set bit 5 to convert to lowercase
```

Finally, the *Exclusive-OR* command is useful for flipping bits:

```
    0010 1010 = $2A
XOR 1111 1111 = $FF
    1101 0101 = $D5


    1111 0000 = $F0
XOR 1111 1111 = $FF
    0000 1111 = $0F
```

One particularly interesting feature of *Exclusive-OR* is that it can be used to swap two values without using a temporary variable. Under normal circumstances, if we were trying to swap two values stored in memory, the code would look something like this:

```
LDA $00     ;  Load both values into registers
LDX $01
STA $01     ;  Store both values to memory
STX $00
```

But what if only one register is available? The following code will swap the contents of *$00* and *$01* using only the Accumulator:

```
LDA $00     ;  Load v1
EOR $01     ;  v1 xor v2 = v1
STA $00     ;  Store in v1
EOR $01     ;  v1 xor v2 = v2
STA $01     ;  Store in v2
EOR $00     ;  v1 xor v2 = v1
STA $00     ;  Store in v1
```

AND, OR., and *EOR* are powerful tools for bit manipulation. Most of the examples in this chapter deal with ASCII manipulation, where these tools are of limited usefulness, but for other applications, such as interacting with peripherals, they are invaluable.

Math Calculations

The 6502 has instructions for both addition and subtraction and can work in both a binary and a decimal mode. The examples in this section use binary mode, but you can find many examples of decimal mode and *Binary Coded Decimal (BCD)* online.

Add Memory to Accumulator with Carry (ADC) is the instruction for addition. The *carry* bit is a flag in the Processor Status Register that indicates there is a bit to carry beyond the eighth place. Here are a few examples of simple arithmetic, with *carry* first reset to 0:

```
  0000 0001 = $01
+ 0000 0001 = $01
```

```
  0000 0010 = $02


  0000 0001 = $01
+ 0000 0011 = $03
  0000 0100 = $04


  0000 0011 = $03
+ 0000 0011 = $03
  0000 0110 = $06


  0000 1111 = $0F
+ 0000 1111 = $0F
  0001 1110 = $1E


  0110 1110 = $6E
+ 0001 1111 = $1F
  1000 1101 = $8D


  1001 1101 = $9D
+ 0110 0001 = $61
  1111 1110 = $FE
```

The last example came dangerously close to overflowing the available 8 bits. The largest value a single byte can hold is 255. To calculate values larger than this, the *carry* flag is needed. The *carry* flag allows us to continue our operation into the next byte, with a carry, so that no part of the value is lost. For example:

```
c             1
  0000 0000 = $00              1000 0100 = $84
+ 0000 0000 = $00            + 1001 0010 = $92
  0000 0001 = $01      C=1     0001 0110 = $16
```

The sum of *$84* and *$92* exceeds *$FF*, and our byte overflows. This overflow sets the *carry* flag, and we can continue our addition in the next byte with a sum of *$01*. Putting the bytes together, we get the grand sum of *$0116*.

Using two bytes, we can address values up to 65,535. Suppose we were to add *$42A5* to *$15D2*. The same layout can be used:

```
c             1
  0100 0010 = $42              1010 0101 = $A5
```

```
 +  0001 0101 = $15              +  1101 0010 = $D2
    0101 1000 = $58       C=1       0111 0111 = $77
```

The method is equally effective when no *carry* flag is necessary, such as in the case of adding *$3E1F* to *$1A73*:

```
C           0
   0011 1110 = $3E                 0001 1111 = $1F
 + 0001 1010 = $1A               + 0111 0011 = $73
   0101 1000 = $58       C=0       1001 0010 = $92
```

The *carry* flag can be manually set or cleared using the *Set Carry Flag (SEC)* and *Clear Carry Flag (CLC)* instructions, respectively. Many instructions set the *carry* flag; subsequently, it is important to clear the flag before performing addition. The following is the code for adding *$61* to *$9D*:

```
LDA #$9D            ;   $9D + ...
CLC                 ;   Make sure Carry is not already set
ADC #$61            ;   $9D + $61
JSR printbin        ;   Print the result in binary
```

Sixteen-bit addition is only slightly more complex. Suppose we want to add the value in the locations *$00,$01* to *$02,$03* and store the result in *$04,$05*. First the low bits are added and then the high bits, with *carry*:

```
CLC                 ;   Make sure Carry is not already set
LDA $00
ADC $02             ;   Add the low bytes
STA $04             ;   And save sum to memory
LDA $01
ADC $03             ;   Add the high bytes (note that Carry was NOT cleared)
STA $05             ;   And save sum to memory


LDA $04
JSR printbin        ;   Print low byte
LDA $05
JSR printbin        ;   Print high byte
JMP Monitor
```

Subtraction is handled just like addition, except it expects the *carry* flag to be high when it starts. Before issuing the first *SBC* instruction, you always need to set the *carry* flag using *SEC*.

You might have noticed by now that there is no instruction for multiplication. There are many techniques for multiplying two numbers. The simplest is to place the first value in the Accumulator and the second in Y, then decrement Y each time you add the value in the Accumulator to its original value. In this manner, 5 × 4 becomes 5 + 5 + 5 + 5.

Since we're working in base 2, multiplying or dividing by powers of two stands out as particularly easy. To multiply by two, simply shift once to the left; to multiply by 4, shift twice to the left, and so on. The same technique applies to division. Shift once to the right to divide by two, twice to the right to divide by four, and so on. Here are some examples:

```
  0110 1100 = $6C
x _____2        (shift left 1 bit)
  11011000  = $D8


  0000 0110 = $06
x _____16        (shift left 4 bits)
  0110 0000 = $60


  1110 1000 = $E8
÷ _____8        (shift right 3 bits)
  0001 1101 = $1D
```

These multiplication and division operations can be performed with the *Accumulator Shift Left (ASL)* and the *Logical Shift Right (LSR)* instructions. *ASL* shifts the value in the Accumulator (or memory) left by one bit. Bit 7 is shifted into the *carry* flag. A zero is shifted into bit 0. *LSR* shifts the value in the Accumulator (or memory) left by one bit. A zero is shifted into bit 7, and bit 0 is shifted into the *carry* flag. The following program multiplies the value in the accumulator by 8:

```
ASL
ASL
ASL
```

This program divides the value in the accumulator by 4:

```
LSR
LSR
```

Obviously, this method has its limitations. When multiplying, it is easy to exceed 255, and when dividing to generate a fraction. Checking the *carry* flag after each shift will alert you if this occurs.

It is possible to use *ASL* and *LSR* to multiply by values that are not powers of two. To multiply by 10, for example, multiply by 2, multiply by 8, and add the results together.

Summary

This chapter has attempted to give a basic overview of the instructions for programming in Assembly and their practical applications. Some instructions, which are similar to those covered here, have been passed over. For a complete list of instructions and their uses, see Appendix D. For a more thorough look at programming in assembly, visit the Apple I Owners Club's Web site on applefritter.com or Mike Naberezny's site at 6502.org. There you'll find a wealth of data sheets, tutorials, and source code.

## Chapter 7

Understanding
the Apple I

Topics in this Chapter:

- Bus
- Clock
- Processor
- Memory
- Keyboard In
- Video Out

Introduction

The design of the Apple I is as simple and straightforward as any computer you'll find. To see what we mean, look at the block diagram in Figure 7.1. At the center of the design is the processor, the brains of the operation. All data passes through it, and it controls what data is transmitted, and when. The ROM contains the *monitor*, which you can think of as a very simple operating system. When the computer is first turned on, the processor immediately goes to the ROM and runs the monitor program. The RAM is used to store user programs and data. You'll note that there is no mass storage device (hard drive, floppy drive, or the like) in this diagram or in the Apple I, though it would be possible to add one.

Once the computer boots, it outputs a command-line prompt (a slash, or /) to the screen. The processor sends the character to the in/out (I/O) chip. The I/O chip waits until the video section is ready for the next character, then sends it off. The video section converts the character from digital data to an analog signal suitable for a video monitor. Input comes from the keyboard, where it is stored in the I/O chip, and is then transferred to the processor. It's very important to understand that the processor does all the work and directs all operations.

In this chapter, we discuss the workings of the processor, RAM, ROM, and I/O. The video section is addressed briefly, but we will not cover the complexities of adapting the data for output to a CRT. Our emphasis is on the digital workings of the computer.

Figure 7.1 An Apple I Block Diagram

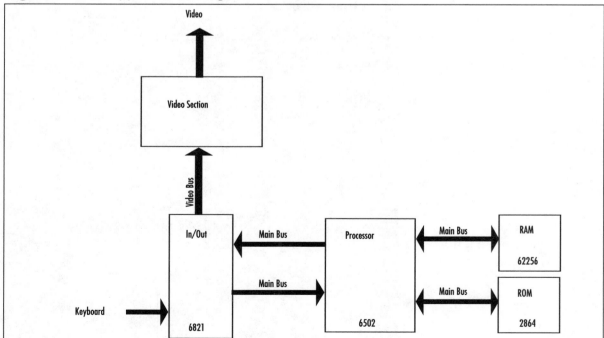

Bus

This section discusses two types of bus: the *bidirectional* data bus and the *unidirectional* address bus.

Data Bus

The Apple I's main components are all attached to the 8-bit data bus (see Figure 7.2). All the data the processor sends or receives travels over this bus. The individual components cannot communicate with one another; all data must pass through the processor.

Let's say that we have a character (we'll make it *J*) in RAM and we want to send it to the display. An ASCII character is a single byte, so it fits perfectly on our 8-bit data bus. Our first step is to get the data out of RAM and load it into the processor. We know the location (the address) of the character; therefore, we put that location on the address bus. If the address were *$2100*, for example, the instruction would be *LDA $2100*.

Each device on the bus sees that address. The ROM and I/O chips look at the address and see that it's not for them. The RAM chip recognizes the address as its own and knows exactly to which location in its memory that address refers. The RAM chip looks at the Read/Write line to see whether the processor wants to read a byte from this address or write a byte to it (in other words, whether it should load the *J* into the processor or overwrite the *J* with some other letter). The Read line is high; consequently, the RAM chip places the *J* on the data bus, where it's then loaded into the processor.

Next, we want to send the data from the processor to video-out via the I/O chip. A specific address on the I/O chip is associated with sending data to video-out. The processor puts that address on the address bus. The I/O chip recognizes that address as its own, the one intended for video-out data. The other chips don't recognize the address and so ignore it. The Read line goes low (which means *write*); subsequently, the I/O chip knows it will be receiving data, and the character *J* is placed on the data bus. At the clock pulse, the I/O chip reads the data off the data bus. Then the I/O chip sends it off to the video circuitry.

Figure 7.2 Data Flow

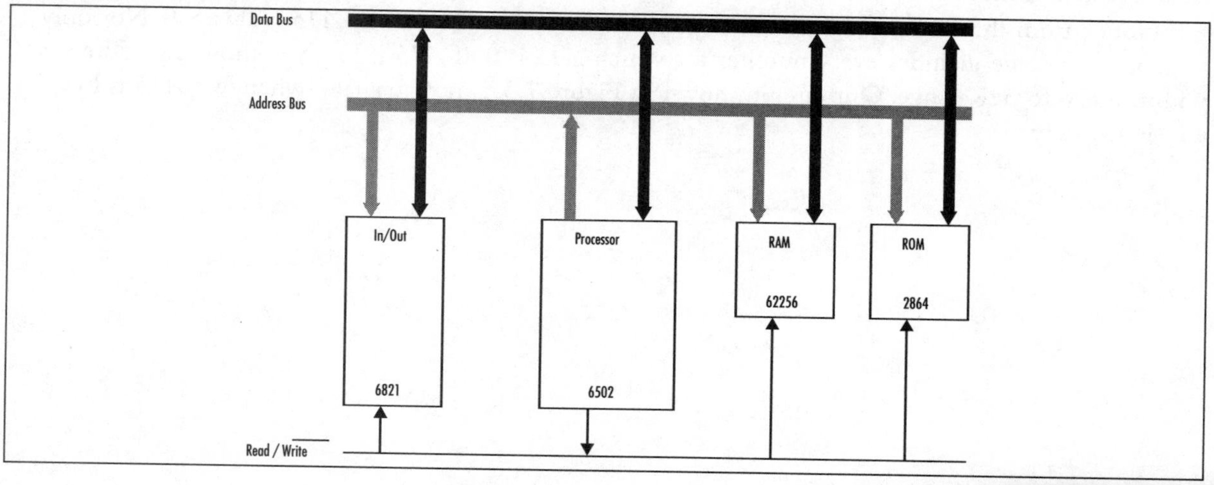

Address Bus

The address bus is 16 bits wide, which means it provides enough addresses for 65,536 (64K, or 2^{16}) unique locations. Usually, these locations are memory addresses (RAM), but they could range anywhere from light-emitting diodes (LEDs) to sensors or I/O chips. Let's say we have a 32-kilobyte RAM chip. Half our available addresses is 32K; accordingly, let's make this chip occupy the lower half of the address space, addresses 0 through 32,767. Whenever the address is 32,767 or less, we want to enable the chip. How can we check for numbers in this range?

One very complex possibility is to check each possible combination. For example, to check for 1, which is within our range, we would write:

```
Enabled for 1 = A15' · A14' · A13' · A12' · A11' · A10' · A9' · A8' · A7' · A6' · A5'
· A4' · A3' · A2' · A1' · A0
```

Or to check for 14,287, which is also within our desired range, we would write:

```
Enabled for 14287 = A15' · A14' · A13 · A12 · A11' · A10 · A9 · A8 · A7 · A6 · A5' ·
A4' · A3 · A2 · A1 · A0
```

And we would end up doing this 32,767 times, once for each address. This approach would certainly work, but the amount of work and time needed to complete the task would be so enormous that it would be terribly impractical. Let's try to find a simpler method by examining the relevance of each bit. The lowest bit, *A0*, alternates high and low with each number; so it's no good for determining whether a number is larger or smaller than 32K. The same applies to bit *A1*, which alternates high and low with every second number. Let's look at the range of numbers we have to cover (see Table 7.1).

Table 7.1 A 32KB Address Range

Decimal	Binary
0	0000 0000 0000 0000b
32,767	0111 1111 1111 1111b

Notice from this table that although bits *A14* through *A0* change, bit *A15* is always 0. Not only that, but our range includes every number for which *A15* is 0. If *A15* is low, we know the address is within our 0 to 32K range. Our circuit, shown in Figure 7.3, is now trivial—whenever *A15* is low, enable the chip.

Figure 7.3 32KB Enable

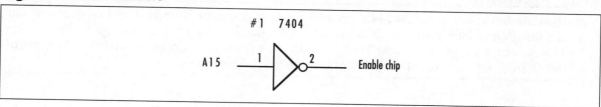

You might be thinking that this example was contrived to work out easily, and it certainly was, however, that doesn't make it unrealistic. Any memory chip you find is going to be based on a power of two, and when you're designing a computer, it certainly behooves you to use start and end points that are easily defined in logic.

Let's take a harder example. Suppose we have 16 kilobytes of RAM and we want to locate this memory at addresses 32K through 48K. Our table would then look like Table 7.2.

Table 7.2 A 16KB Address Range

Decimal	Binary
32,768	1000 0000 0000 0000b
49,151	1011 1111 1111 1111b

Bits $A0$ through $A13$ will vary, so we can disregard those for now. $A14$ must be 0, because if it were 1, the value would be larger than 48K. $A15$ must be 1, because if it were 0, the value would be smaller than 32K. Thus, we want to enable our chip whenever $A15$ is high and $A14$ is low (see Figure 7.4).

Figure 7.4 A 16KB Enable

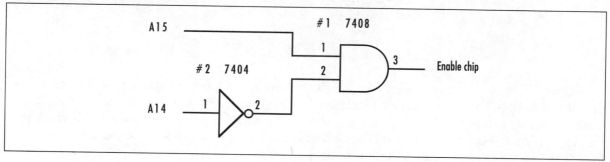

Now that we've enabled the chip we want to use, we need to identify the location on that chip. This is where the rest of the address lines on the address bus come into play. Bits $A0$ through $A13$ can express our entire range of locations. These lines are connected directly to the address lines on the chip so that it can find the internal location on the requested data.

The data bus is a *bidirectional* bus, meaning that data can be both sent and received over it. The Read/Write line is used to determine the direction in which the data is going. The address bus, by contrast, is *unidirectional*. Only the processor can send data to it. The rest of the chips (RAM and so on) can read only what's on the address bus.

Clock

Everything happens at the clock pulse. New values are waiting at the register inputs. When the clock pulses, the new values are loaded into the registers over the course of a couple nanoseconds, then become present at the output of the registers. The output signal propagates through the circuit, each logic gate taking a few more nanoseconds. Eventually, all is updated and the lines stabilize. At this point, the clock pulses and the cycle repeats. Figure 7.5 shows a MHz TTL crystal oscillator, which we will use for our clock.

Figure 7.5 A 1MHz TTL Crystal Oscillator

Figure 7.6 shows a timing diagram for the clock pulse. At each rising edge, indicated by an arrow, the circuit updates. The Apple I uses a 1MHz clock. Compare that frequency with the multigigahertz clocks in today's computers, and that's glacially slow. What would happen if we put a 1GHz clock in the Apple I? At 1GHz, the circuit would not have time to fully propagate after each clock pulse, leaving the circuit partially updated and in an uncertain state.

Figure 7.6 Timing Diagram

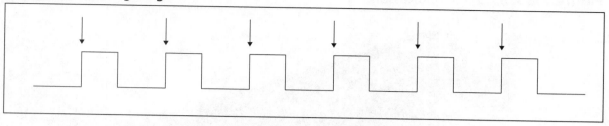

Figure 7.7 shows the pinout for a 1MHz TTL crystal oscillator. Pin 1 is not used. Pins 7 and 14 are ground and power, respectively. Pin 8 is our clock output. The output is low for 0.5MHz, then high for 0.5MHz. Our circuitry triggers on the rising edge.

Figure 7.7 A 1MHz TTL Crystal Oscillator Pinout

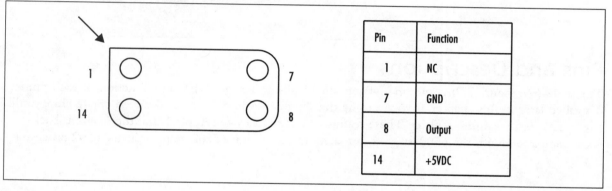

Processor

Fully understanding the operations of the 6502 processor (shown in Figure 7.8) sounds daunting, and it certainly would be. However, we're going to concentrate on understanding the processor from the user's perspective, which simplifies our cause. You won't learn how to build a processor from scratch (that's another book in itself), but you will learn how to design basic circuits that interact with the processor. In Chapter 6, we discussed how to write programs in machine language that can be directly understood by the 6502. This chapter goes into more depth, looking at what happens when you run those programs.

Figure 7.8 A 6502 Microprocessor

Pins and Descriptions

The 6502 (see Figure 7.9) comes in a 40-pin dual in-line package (DIP). The function of each pin is described later in this chapter. If you're using the slightly newer and more advanced 65c02 chip, you'll have a few extra features available. These features aren't used by the Apple I, and the 65c02 is backward compatible with the 6502, so, you can safely think of your 65c02 as an ordinary 6502 processor.

Figure 7.9 A 6502 Pinout

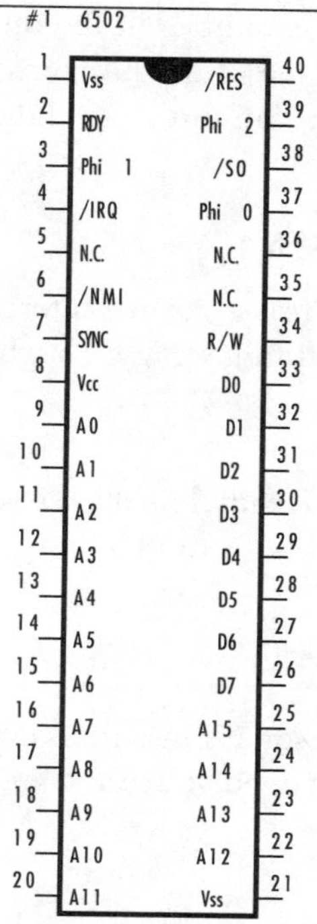

```
              #1    6502
         1  ┌──────────────┐ 40
         ───┤ Vss      /RES ├───
         2  │               │ 39
         ───┤ RDY     Phi 2 ├───
         3  │               │ 38
         ───┤ Phi 1    /SO  ├───
         4  │               │ 37
         ───┤ /IRQ    Phi 0 ├───
         5  │               │ 36
         ───┤ N.C.     N.C. ├───
         6  │               │ 35
         ───┤ /NMI     N.C. ├───
         7  │               │ 34
         ───┤ SYNC     R/W  ├───
         8  │               │ 33
         ───┤ Vcc       D0  ├───
         9  │               │ 32
         ───┤ A0        D1  ├───
        10  │               │ 31
         ───┤ A1        D2  ├───
        11  │               │ 30
         ───┤ A2        D3  ├───
        12  │               │ 29
         ───┤ A3        D4  ├───
        13  │               │ 28
         ───┤ A4        D5  ├───
        14  │               │ 27
         ───┤ A5        D6  ├───
        15  │               │ 26
         ───┤ A6        D7  ├───
        16  │               │ 25
         ───┤ A7        A15 ├───
        17  │               │ 24
         ───┤ A8        A14 ├───
        18  │               │ 23
         ───┤ A9        A13 ├───
        19  │               │ 22
         ───┤ A10       A12 ├───
        20  │               │ 21
         ───┤ A11       Vss ├───
            └──────────────┘
```

Address Bus (*A0–A15*)

The address bus is a 16-bit bus capable of addressing 64 kilobytes. Those bytes could be locations in memory or on in/out devices. For a more in-depth discussion of the address bus, see the bus section of this chapter.

Clock (*ϕ0, ϕ1, ϕ2*)

The symbol *ϕ0* stands for the oscillator input. Connect the output of your 1MHz clock to this line. Symbols *ϕ1* and *ϕ2* are outputs that are offset from this clock line, and *ϕ1* is not used by the Apple I. The *ϕ2* output is used when writing to the 6821 PIA and the RAM.

Data Bus (*D0–D8*)

The 8-bit data bus allows bidirectional communication between the processor and memory or other peripheral devices. The data bus is discussed in more depth in the bus section of this chapter.

Interrupt Request (IRQ)

This line is not used by the Apple I. A pulse on the interrupt line tells the processor to stop what it's doing and to process data from another location.

No Connection (NC)

There is no signal on this line; as a result, it can be left disconnected. If you're using the later 65c02 instead of the original 6502, you'll find some of the NC pins have been replaced with actual signals. The 65c02 is backward compatible, so you can just leave these lines disconnected as you would on the 6502.

Nonmaskable Interrupt (NMI)

This line is not used by the Apple I. Whereas a normal interrupt (IRQ) can be blocked by software, a nonmaskable interrupt will always succeed in getting through and interrupting the system.

Ready (RDY)

This line is not used by the Apple I. The Ready line allows you to halt or single-step the processor. This can be especially handy if you're trying to troubleshoot your design and you want to see what the system is doing, one step at a time.

Reset (RES)

When power is first applied to the processor, it's in an unknown state. Pressing the Reset button tells it to load the program at the address contained at $FFFC$ and $FFFD$ and to start executing.

Read/Write (R/W)

The Read/Write line is used in conjunction with the data bus. When Read is high, the processor is reading data from the data bus. When Read is low, the processor is writing data to the data bus.

Set Overflow Flag (SO)

This line is not used by the Apple I. Its function is to manually set the overflow flag in the processor. The overflow flag is used to indicate that a number is larger than can be contained.

SYNC

This line is not used by the Apple I. SYNC can be used in combination with RDY to single-step the processor.

Voltage Common Collector (VCC)

VCC is the positive voltage line. It provides power for the chip and connects to the five-volt signal.

Voltage Source (VSS)

VSS is the ground line. The 6502 has two VSS lines, probably for additional current-handling.

   With this knowledge, we can draw the schematic for the processor (see Figure 7.10). The address lines go to the address bus and the data lines to the data bus. The Read/Write, Phi 0, and Phi 2 pins are all wired to their respective lines. /SO is disabled by being tied to High. *RDY, /IRQ,* and */NMI* are tied to High with current-limiting resistors. *RESET* is connected to the reset circuitry, which is high until the switch is depressed.

Figure 7.10 A Processor Schematic

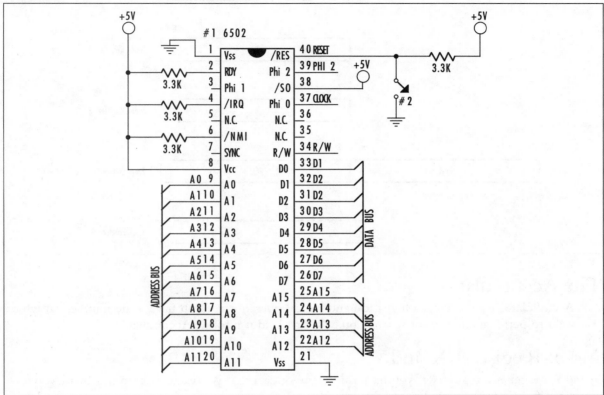

Registers

Registers, discussed in Chapter 5, are a fundamental part of the microprocessor. Each data register in the 6502 has an 8-bit storage capacity and can therefore store an entire byte of data. The Program Counter (PC) has a 16-bit storage capacity. Registers allow the processor easy access to the data it needs to operate. Figure 7.11 shows the five registers that are most important to us; they are described in more detail in the following sections.

Figure 7.11 6502 Registers

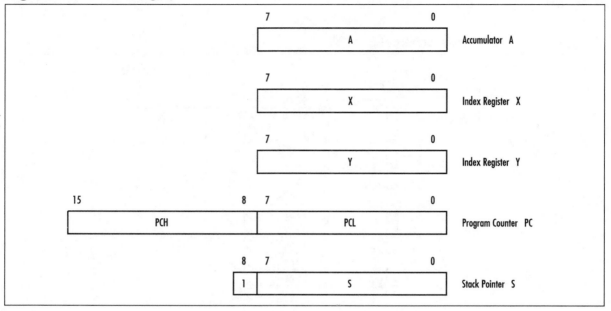

The Accumulator

The Accumulator is used for mathematical and logical operations. If you have some number on which you want to perform addition or subtraction, you first load it into the Accumulator.

Index Registers X and Y

X and Y are generic registers. If you have some byte of data that you want to keep nearby or you're moving it from one peripheral to another, the X and Y registers are convenient nearby storage places. It's also very easy to move data between various registers; hence, if you have a byte in X on which you want to do some mathematical operation, you can easily transfer it to the Accumulator.

The Program Counter (PC)

The PC is a 16-bit register used for keeping track of the address of the current instruction. It is incremented each time an instruction or data is fetched from memory. The processor looks at the PC to see from where it should fetch the next instruction.

The Stack Pointer

The stack pointer points to (gives the address of) the current top of the stack. This address changes every time a byte is added or removed from the stack. The function of the stack is described later in this chapter.

The Processor Status Register

The processor status register (see Figure 7.12) is a collection of individual flags that serve as indicators for various instructions. For example, if you do perform a subtraction and the answer is negative, the negative flag will be set. Then the next instruction can check that flag, see that the answer was negative, and report back to your program. See the instruction table (section XX) for a list of instructions that can read data from this register.

Figure 7.12 The Processor Status Register

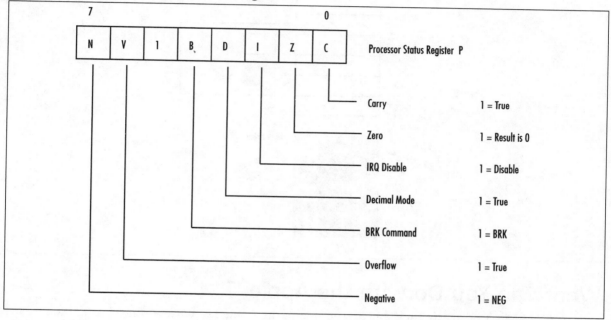

The Arithmetic and Logic Unit

The arithmetic and logic unit (ALU) is at the heart of the microprocessor. You can think of the ALU as a processing machine. Put the numbers you want to work on at the entry, choose the function you want, and let it run. The answer comes out the other end and is stored in the Accumulator.

The Stack

The stack lets us save data for future use. Access to data on the stack is limited. Only the topmost value can be read. Data is either "pushed" onto the stack or "popped" off the stack. The stack pointer remembers the current location of the top of the stack. When data is pushed, the stack grows and the stack pointer is incremented. When data is popped, the stack shrinks and the stack pointer is decremented. Chapter 6 discusses how to program with the stack.

The stack uses memory from *$0100* to *$01FF* (see Figure 7.13). *$01FF* is the base address. As data is pushed onto the stack, the stack grows toward *$0100*. The size of the stack cannot exceed the 255 bytes allocated to it.

Figure 7.13 A 6502 Stack

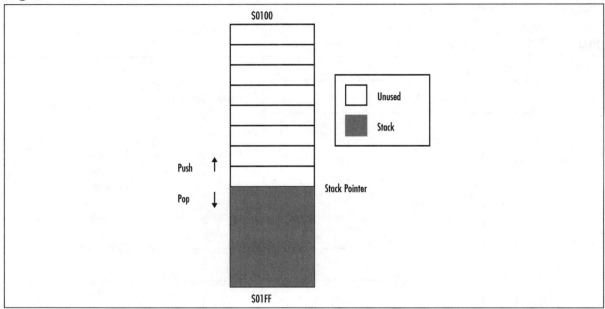

What Can You Do with the Apple I?

This section focuses primarily on the hardware side of the Apple I,—what you need to know to wire it up and create a functioning system. Instructions on how to program and use the microprocessor once you have a functioning system are covered in the second part of the book. You will find a detailed description of the 6502 instruction set and an introduction to assembly language programming in Chapter 6 and in the appendices.

Memory

Let's now take a look at the way memory is used in the Apple I.

Where Is It?

The Apple I has 64KB of addressable space. The monitor ROM occupies 256 bytes. The original Apple I also had 8KB of RAM. Of the 64K addresses (*$0000* through *$FFFF*), where should this memory be located? Deciding on a location for the ROM is easy. The 6502 microprocessor requires that a memory address be stored at addresses *$FFFE* and *$FFFF* (the address is 16-bit, so it takes two bytes). When the 6502 is reset, it immediately loads the address at *$FFEF* and *$FFFF* into its program counter and begins executing that address. Thus, you need to have a ROM at *$FFFE–$FFFF*, and if you need to have it there, you might as well keep the ROM in a solid block. The monitor ROM, therefore, starts at *$FF00* and ends at *$FFFF*.

The memory, by contrast, is divided into two parts. Four kilobytes are for system and user access. These 4KB are located at *$000–$0FFF*. The other 4KB, which are intended for Apple's Integer BASIC, are located at *$E000–$EFFF.* You'll note that *$E000–$EFFF* are RAM, not ROM. Every time the original Apple I was powered up, the code for BASIC would either have to be loaded from cassette or typed in by hand. If the user did not need BASIC, he or she could refrain from loading it and just use that memory as generic memory space.

Figure 7.14 shows the memory map for the Apple I, as designed by Steve Wozniak.

Figure 7.14 Apple I Memory Map

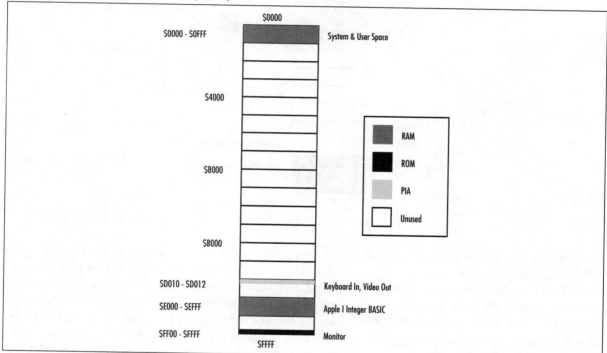

You'll note that the vast majority of this address space is unused. If the user wanted, he could expand the RAM in some of these blocks or use it for other peripheral devices. Joe Torzewski, who started the Apple I Owners Club in 1977, upgraded his Apple I to 16KB. It would be possible to fill the entire unused memory with additional RAM.

Why did Apple include so little memory? Back in 1976, that 8KB of RAM was prohibitely expensive. Today, by contrast, the price of RAM has plummeted, and the difference in cost between

8KB and a hundred times that is negligible. Unless you're going strictly for historical accuracy, you'll probably want to add more RAM to your replica design. Figure 7.15 shows the memory map for Briel Computers' Replica I.

Figure 7.15 Replica I Memory Map

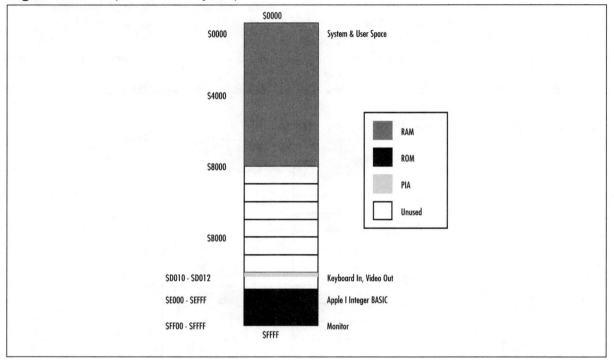

The first thing you'll notice about Briel's design is all the extra RAM. The first 32KB (*$0000–$8000*) are all dedicated to system and user space. This is memory you're free to play around with. This is eight times the amount of system and user space in the original design, and that kind of expansion can make a big difference. Next, look at locations *$E000* to *$EFFF*. Instead of being in RAM, Integer BASIC is now in ROM. This means BASIC is permanently stored on the Apple I and is immediately available when the system is turned on. If you're a hardy assembly language programmer who scorns BASIC, this might be superfluous, but for everybody else, it saves a tremendous amount of time and frustration. Finally, note that addresses *$F000* to *$FE99* are mapped to ROM but aren't labeled. If there's some program you use very frequently, you could potentially put it in ROM here, but right now, the space is wasted. Dedicating the entire 4KB block, *$F000–$FFFF,* to ROM makes addressing easier and decreases the number of chips we need to place on the circuit board.

Implementing 8KB RAM

The original Apple I used 16 MK4096 ICs to get 8KB RAM. You can do the same with a single Cypress CY6264 (see Figure 7.16). Let's now briefly take a look at the function of the more interesting pins.

Figure 7.16 A CY6264 Pinout

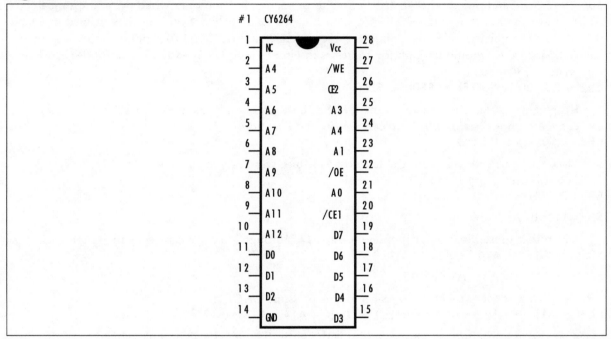

Address Lines (*A0–A12*)

You'll see that there are 13 address lines, which is enough to address 2^{13}, or 8,192, locations. It's no coincidence that works out to 8KB. For the most part, these pins will be connected directly to the address bus, but there are some tricks we can play to divide the RAM into two separate blocks.

Data Lines (*D0–D7*)

All eight data lines are connected directly to the data bus.

Chip Enable (*/CE1, CE2*)

When Chip Enable 1 is low and Chip Enable 2 is high, the chip is "turned on" and will attempt either to read data from the bus or write data to it.

Write Enable (/*WE*)

When the chip is enabled and Write Enable is low, the data on the data bus is written to memory.

Output Enable (/*OE*)

When the chip is enabled and Output Enable is low, data from memory is output onto the data bus.

The difficulty in wiring up the RAM comes from having to divide it into two blocks, one at *$0000—$0FFF* and one at *$E000–$EFFF*. We must enable the chip only when the address on the address bus is within those ranges. The CY6264 has two chip enables. Both must be enabled to enable the chip. For simplicity, we're just going to use one (*CE2*) and tie /*CE1* to ground so that it is always enabled. Since *CE2* should be high for addresses in either range *$0000–$0FFF* or *$E000–$EFFF*, we can write the statement:

CE2 = ($0000 to $0FFF) + ($E00 to $EFFF)

Keep in mind that the + here means *OR*. Since the lowest 12 bits in each part of the statement can change without having *CE2*, we can rewrite the equation:

CE2 = ($0xxx) + ($Exxx)

Now we just need to look at the leftmost four bits, which represent pins *A15, A14, A13*, and *A12*. Converting *0* and *E* to binary, we get:

$0 = 0000b

$E = 1110b

Given that those binary digits represent pins *A15* through *A12*, we can write the statements:

$0xxx = A15 ′ • A14 ′ • A13 ′ • A12 ′

$Exxx = A15 • A14 • A13 • A12 ′

Then we put them together to realize our expression for *CE2*:

CE2 = (A15 ′ • A14 ′ • A13 ′ • A12 ′) + (A15 • A14 • A13 • A12 ′)

The circuit created from this expression is shown in Figure 7.17. The implementation of the latter half is straightforward (four signals, one inverted, going into a quad-*AND* gate). To implement the former half, we could have used four inverters going into a quad-*AND* gate, but instead we took advantage of DeMorgan's Law to create an equivalent circuit using *OR* gates. Since four *OR* gates come to a chip, this approach lent itself to a more efficient design.

Our RAM chip will be enabled whenever an address on the address bus is within its range. We need to add some circuitry to the chip's address lines to make it map to two separate blocks. Since we have 8KB and we want two blocks of 4KB, we can use one of the address lines as a switch. *A12* can be that address line. Let's make *A12* high when the address is in the *$Exxx* region. *A12* is low for every other region, but because our chip is only enabled for *$Exxx* and *$0xxx,* that effectively means *A12* is only low for *$0xxx.*

When enabled, our memory chip is always either reading or writing data, as dictated by the processor's Read/Write line. The Read/Write line is high when the processor is reading and low when the processor is writing. We need to connect this Read/Write line directly to the Output Enable (/*OE*) line of memory. We also connect the inverted Read/Write line to the chip's Write Enable

(/*WE*), but since we don't want to write until the data is available, we *AND* the inverted R/W with the Phi 2 clock, which is used for timing memory writes. Both lines are active–low (are activated by a low signal, as opposed to a high). "Output Enable" corresponds to "Read." Because Read/Write is low when the processor wants to write and Write Enable is active–low, we can hook the Read/Write line directly to the Write Enable pin. Whenever we're not writing, we're reading; consequently, Output Enable should be high whenever Write Enable is low, and vice versa. This means Output Enable should be hooked up to the inverted Read/Write signal. See the complete schematic in Figure 7.17.

Figure 7.17 An 8KB RAM Schematic

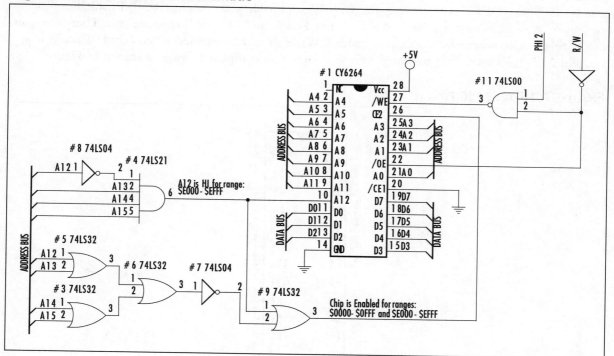

NEED TO KNOW...

The original Apple I was built using dynamic RAM, which is still prevalent in computers today. In dynamic RAM, each memory cell (1 bit) is made up of a transistor and a capacitor. If the capacitor loses its charge, the content of memory is forgotten. A capacitor will discharge after just a couple milliseconds; therefore, dynamic memory relies on external refresh circuitry to keep the capacitor charged. Static memory, by contrast, uses a flip-flop (see section XX) for each bit. A flip-flop, of course, requires no refreshing, so static memory is much easier to work with. It's also faster. Unfortunately, a flip-flop is much more complex than a mere transistor and capacitor; therefore, static memory is a lot more expensive, which is why dynamic memory remains so common today. A static RAM chip of mere kilobytes costs only a couple dollars, so for our project it's perfectly economical.

Implementing 32KB RAM

The 32KB RAM design used in the Replica I is far more simple than the 8KB example we just examined. The chip used is a 62256 static RAM IC (see Figure 7.18). The design for the 62256 mirrors our earlier example. The chip should be enabled whenever the lower half of memory is addressed. This occurs whenever $A15$ is low, yielding the result of $CE = A15$. Your only chip enable line is $/CE1$, so $/CE1 = A15$, leaving you with Write Enable and Output (Read) Enable lines to configure. Writing takes precedence if both Write Enable and Output Enable are true. Therefore, you can enable output whenever the chip is enabled. Write should be enabled when Read/Write is low and Phi 2 (the clock used for memory writes) is high. The completed design is shown in Figure 7.19.

Figure 7.18 A 62256 Pinout

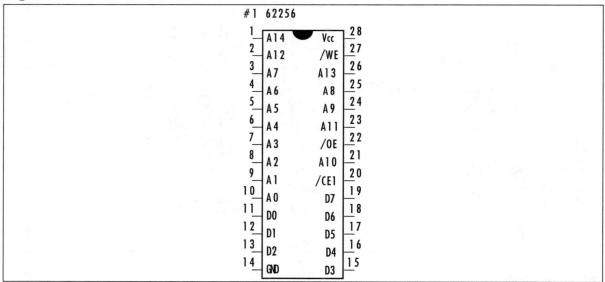

Figure 7.19 A 32KB RAM Schematic

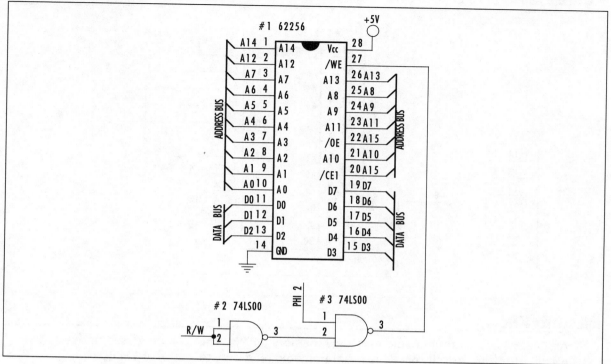

Implementing the EPROM

If you want to use an erasable programmable read-only memory (EPROM) solely for the Monitor program, as the Apple I does, the circuit is straightforward. This design uses a 2716 EPROM, which is much bigger than we need; so, address lines *A8* through *A10* are permanently tied low. This leaves us with 2^8, or 256, bytes of addressable space—exactly the amount we need for the monitor ROM range of *$FF00* to *$FFFF*. Address lines *A0* through *A7* can be connected to the address bus, and the data lines can be connected to the data bus.

Output Enable, which is active-low, should be low whenever read is high; subsequently, */OE* is connected to the R/W line through an inverter. Lastly, the chip should be enabled whenever the address is in the *$FFxx* range. Refer to the schematic in Figure 7.20.

Figure 7.20 A 2716 EPROM Schematic

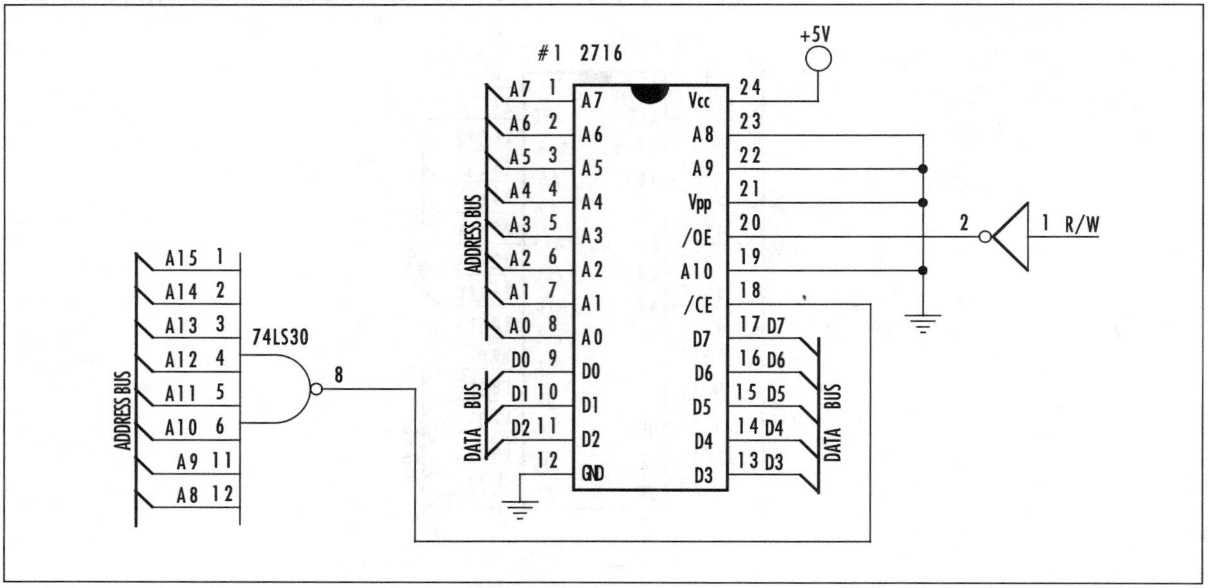

NEED TO KNOW...

An EPROM is a programmable read-only memory (PROM) that can be erased under ultraviolet light. An electrically erasable programmable read-only memory, or EEPROM, is an EPROM that can be erased with an electrical charge. Both EPROMs and EEPROMs can be read an unlimited number of times, but erasing or writing is typically limited to a few hundred thousand times. EPROM is pronounced "ee-prom." EEPROM is pronounced "ee-ee-prom."

Implementing the Expanded ROM

The Replica I uses an alternative chip for the ROM, a 28c64. It also uses a more complex method for chip enable. The EEPROM can be enabled for the entire range from *$E000* to *$FFFF.* This can be conveniently done with a 74LS138 decoder. This same decoder can also be used to decode the addresses for our 6821 PIA, discussed in the next section; therefore, it is advantageous to become familiar with its use at this point.

Wiring the 74LS138

The 74LS138 is a one-of-eight decoder, yielding eight possible outputs. The EEPROM requires addresses *$E000* through *$FFFF.* The 6821 PIA discussed later uses the *$Dxxx* range. Ranges *$Axxx,* *$Bxxx,* and *$Cxxx,* aren't used, but since you have extra outputs, you can make them available for future projects. Table 7.3 shows the ranges expressed as hexadecimal and binary values.

Table 7.3 Addresses for the 74LS138 Decoder

Hexadecimal	Binary
$Axxx	1010 xxxx xxxx xxxxb
$Bxxx	1011 xxxx xxxx xxxxb
$Cxxx	1100 xxxx xxxx xxxxb
$Dxxx	1101 xxxx xxxx xxxxb
$Exxx	1110 xxxx xxxx xxxxb
$Fxxx	1111 xxxx xxxx xxxxb

The highest bit ($A15$) is 1 for all the ranges we're working with, so $A15$ can simply be used as an enable line ($G1$). Bits $A12, A13$, and $A14$ all vary, so they will be the input lines, A, B, C. For the range $Fxxx, ABC = 111b. 111b$ equals 7, making the output $Y7$ true. For $Exxx, ABC = 110b$, which is 6 in binary, making $Y6$ true. The EEPROM should be enabled whenever $Y6$ or $Y7$ is true. Since $/CE, Y6,$ and $Y7$ are all active low, we should have an *OR* gate with an inverter at each input and output. Using DeMorgan's law, this is equivalent to an *AND* gate. Since this design already has a 7400 IC on board, a *NAND* followed by another *NAND* (to invert) is equivalent.

Wiring the 28c64

Since you're using this EEPROM as a simple ROM, write Enable (*/WE*) is permanently tied to High. The chip is only enabled when data is to be read from it, so it follows that */OE = /CE*. The address lines go directly to the address bus, and the data lines go directly to the data bus. See Figure 7.21.

Figure 7.21 A 28c64 EEPROM Schematic

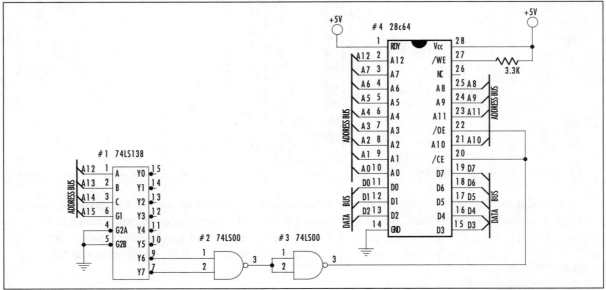

I/O with the 6821

The Motorola 6821 (see Figure 7.22) is a peripheral interface adapter (PIA), which means that it is used for interfacing peripherals, such as keyboard and video, to the computer. The 6821 has two configurable 8-bit ports, PA and PB (for "port A" and "port B"), which can be used either for output or input. The Apple I uses PA for input from the keyboard and PB for output to the video circuit. The data is transferred to and from the computer via the data bus.

This section provides a rather in-depth look at the operation of the 6821. If you plan to use the Apple I's standard interfaces for keyboard in and video out, this information might not interest you. If, on the other hand, you intend to substantially modify the Apple I circuit for some special purpose or if you are interested in building your own microcomputer using the 6821, this information will be very helpful.

Figure 7.22 A PIA 6821 Pinout

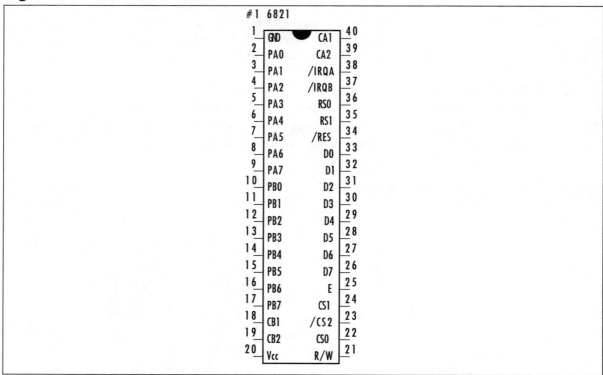

Each 8-bit port can be configured for either input or output. In fact, each bit direction in each port can be individually specified. When the Apple I is reset, the monitor configures the 6821 to work with our circuit. On reset, both ports default to being inputs and the keyboard port is left untouched. The video port is set to outputs except for the highest bit, which is used as the "Data Available" line.

The monitor uses the information in Table 7.4 for setting up the address lines. Changing the value of the bits *CRA 2* and *CRB 2* can alter which register lines *RS1* and *RS0* address. The bits in the Control Register A (*CRA*), including bit 2 (*CRA 2*), can be set when *RS1* = 1 and *RS2* = 0. First, set *CRA 2* to 0. Next, make *RS1* = 0 and *RS0* = 0. This allows you to pass 8 bits to the 6821 that will set the data direction for Register A. Then set *RS1* high and *RS0* low to access *CRA,* and set *CRA 2* to 0. Now when *RS1* = 0 and *RS0* = 0, Peripheral Register A will be accessed, whether for reading or writing, depending on which data direction bits were set. The same technique applies to Peripheral Register B.

Table 7.4 Internal Addressing

| RS1 | RS0 | Control Register Bit | | Location Selection |
		CRA 2	CRB 2	
0	0	1	X	Peripheral Register A
0	0	0	X	Data Direction Register A
0	1	X	X	Control Register A
1	0	X	1	Peripheral Register B
1	0	X	0	Data Direction Register B
1	1	X	X	Control Register B

Take a look at Figure 7.23. The Register Select lines *RS0* and *RS1* are connected to the Address lines *A0* and *A1*, respectively. The chip select line *CS0* goes to *A4*. For the other chip select, *CS2,* you use the same 74LS138 as in the memory section to decode the high bits in the address, giving us everything in the *$Dxxx* range. This combination of decoding enables you to use the addresses shown in Table 7.5.

Figure 7.23 A 6821 Schematic

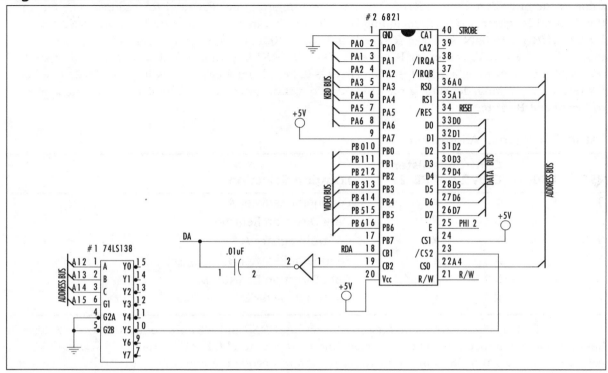

Table 7.5 External Addressing

Mnemonic	Apple I Name	6821 Name	Address	Description
DSP	Display Register	Peripheral Register B	$D012	A character being sent to the display is held in this register until the video section is ready to take it
DSPCR	Display Control Register	Control Register B	$D013	Defines the behavior of the display register
KBD	Keyboard Register	Peripheral Register A	$D010	A character from the keyboard is held in this register until it is requested by the processor
KBDCR	Keyboard Controller Register	Control Register A	$D011	Defines the behavior of the keyboard register

When the circuit is reset, the DSP and KBD ports are in configuration mode (i.e., bits *CRA 2* and *CRB 2* are low). This means that when we send data to DSP or KBD, it will go to the data direction register instead of the peripheral register. By sending *$7F* (that's *0111 1111b*) to DSP, the lower 7 bits are set to outputs and the highest bit is set to an input.

Next, the control registers (Figures 7.24 and 7.25) need to be configured. They are set to the same configuration (see Figure 7.26).

Figure 7.24 Keyboard Control Register

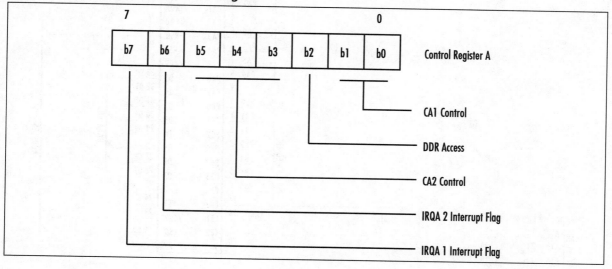

Figure 7.25 Display Control Register

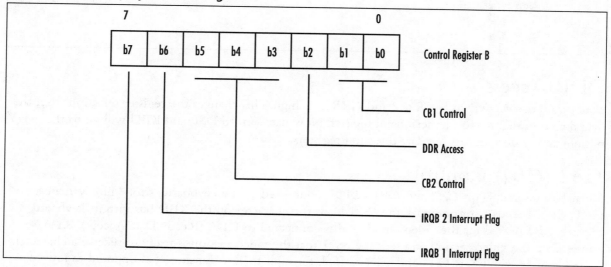

Figure 7.26 Control Registers A and B

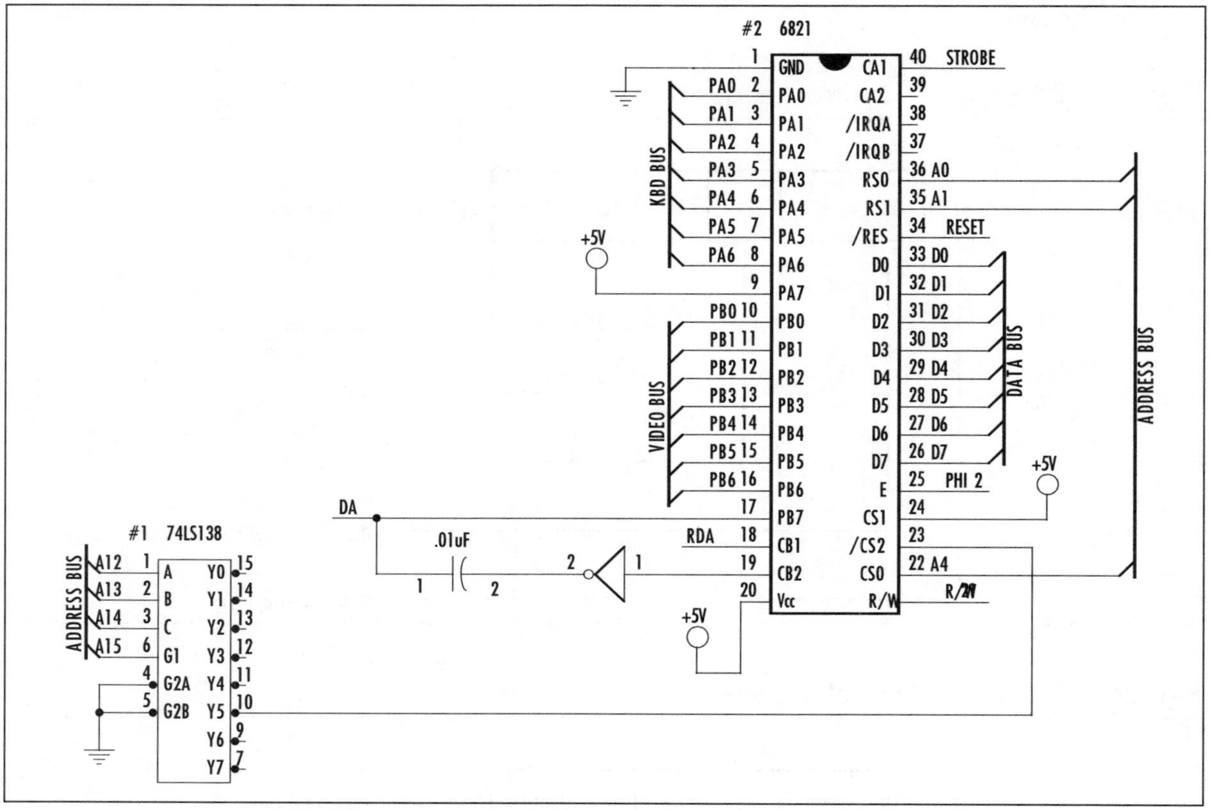

DDR Access

You'll note that *b2*, which is *CRA 2* and *CRB 2,* is high. This changes the register selection from the data direction register to the peripheral register. Now data sent to DSP and KBD will go to the peripheral registers, not to the data direction registers.

CA1 (CB1) Control

b0 enables interrupts on *CA1* and *CB1. CA1* is connected to the keyboard's strobe line. Whenever the keyboard sends a strobe signal, the 6821 loads the character on the KBD bus into its keyboard register. *CB1* is used for the video circuit and is connected to RDA (Ready Data Accept). RDA comes from the video section and tells the 6821 that the video section is ready to receive a character.

b1 is high, which sets *CA1* and *CB1* to look for high-to-low transitions, as opposed to low-to-high transitions. This means that a change from 0 to 1 will cause an interrupt, whereas a change from 1 to 0 will not.

CA2 (CB2) Control

The keyboard's *CA2* has no connection; consequently, these settings are only important for the video's *CB2*. *b5* is high, which means *CB2* is an output. *b4* does nothing in this configuration. *b3* is a flag that goes high when *CB1*, which is connected to the RDA line, goes high. The flag is cleared on the clock pulse (Phi 2 on pin E) after data is loaded into the display register.

IRA Interrupt Flags

IRQA and *IRQB* are not used.

Behavior of Apple 1 Components

Let's now take a brief look at the performance of various Apple 1 components.

The Keyboard

When a pulse arrives on the STROBE line, the character from the keyboard is loaded into the keyboard register and a flag is set in the keyboard control register. In the Apple I's memory map, the keyboard register is at *$D010*, and the keyboard control register is at *$D011*. The processor checks for the flag at *$D011*. When it sees it, the processor goes to *$D010* and loads the character.

Video

The processor sends a character to the 6821, which sends it out to the video section. The display register is at *$D012*. Before sending data, the processor checks bit 7 at memory location *$D012*. If this bit is high, it means the "Data Available" line is high, and the 6821 currently has data it is waiting to send to the video section. The processor waits until the bit goes low, indicating that the 6821 has sent its data and is now ready to talk to the processor. The processor then sends its character to the display register, which is located at *$D012* in the memory map. The 6821 loads this character into the display register and tells the video section that it has data available by setting DA (Data Available) high. When the video section is ready, it responds by setting RDA (Ready Data Accept) high. The 6821 sends the character to the video section and sets DA to low.

The completed 6821 circuit is shown in Figure 7.23. See Chapter 6 for a simple program that reads a character from the keyboard and then outputs it to the display.

Keyboard In

The Apple I uses a very simple ASCII keyboard (see Figure 7.27). When a key is pressed, that character's 7-bit ASCII value is placed on the keyboard's data lines. A pulse on the strobe line indicates the data is ready. Many ASCII keyboards will also have a Reset button. This button is connected to the processor's reset line. The rest of the signals, including data lines and strobe, go to the 6821. See Figure 7.28.

An ASCII keyboard is the simplest way to get data into your Apple I replica. Unfortunately, these keyboards are becoming very hard to find. The most reliable source is an Apple II+, but that computer is becoming a rarity in its own right. If you do borrow a II+ keyboard, treat the computer gently. The Apple II+ is a fun computer you'll want to keep around.

Figure 7.27 An ASCII Keyboard

Figure 7.28 An ASCII Keyboard Schematic

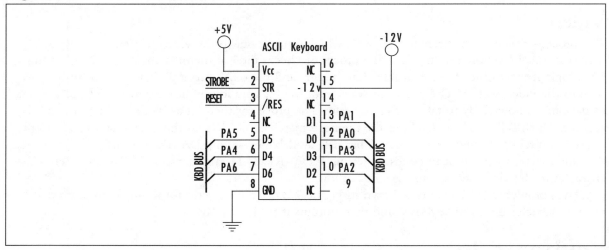

For those who can't find or don't want an ASCII keyboard, there is an alternative. Briel Computers has designed a PS/2 interface around an ATMEGA microcontroller (see Figure7.29). The PS/2 keyboard sends its scancodes to the microcontroller. The microcontroller converts them to ASCII and sends them to the 6821, using the STROBE line to indicate when data is available.

You'll need an 8MHz crystal and two 18pF capacitors to provide a clock for the microcontroller and a PS/2 connector to plug your keyboard into. If you want the option of switching between a PS/2 keyboard and an ASCII keyboard, provide a jumper between the ATMega's reset pin and ground (as shown in Figure 7.29). Since Reset is active-low, jumpering it to ground will disable the ATMEGA by placing it permanently into reset mode, letting you use your ASCII keyboard without conflict.

NEED TO KNOW...

A *microcontroller* is a specialized microcomputer contained on a single chip. Microcontrollers are often used to control intelligent peripherals such as hard drives and are now common even in simple devices such as keyboards and mice. You'll find many Web sites and books devoted to the microcontroller hobby.

Figure 7.29 A PS/2 Keyboard Schematic

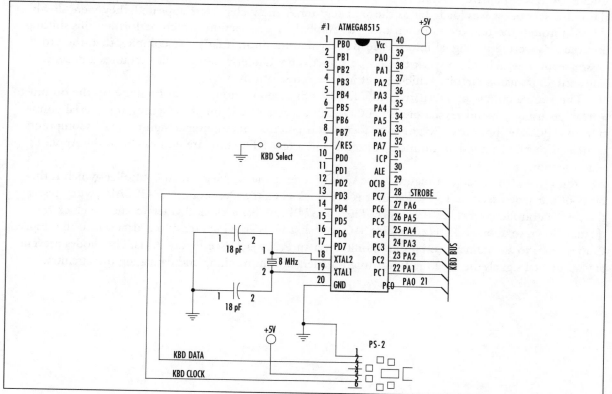

Video Out

The Apple I has very limited video capabilities. Most computers have video mapped to memory. On a black-and-white display, each pixel is represented in memory by a single bit—1 for black and 0 for white. The Apple I's video section is text only. Instead of storing each individual pixel for a character, it stores the character's ASCII code. The video section has a ROM containing the pixel layouts for every character it supports. The layout table is referenced for each pixel of each character that is being displayed. This process saves a tremendous amount of space, but at significant expense in versatility. Only the characters stored in that ROM can be displayed on screen. Thus, no graphics can be displayed.

Even more limiting is the fact that once a character is sent to the display, it cannot be modified. It's there until you enter enough lines that it scrolls off the top of the screen or until you manually clear the entire display. In this way, the function of the video is very similar to a typewriter or a teletype.

Why did Apple make these choices? At that time, memory—which would have allowed full graphics—was expensive. Instead, to save money, shift registers were used. When a character is sent to the video section, it was loaded into the shift register. As new characters appeared, they were slowly shifted through the register and then out. The Apple I's video section, which performed this shifting and then converted the signal into one readable video monitor, is far more complex than the processor section, which we've spent this chapter discussing. Understanding it also requires a decent knowledge of analog circuits, which is outside the scope of this book.

There are a couple of alternatives to a full-blown video section, such as hooking up the output to a teletype, using a liquid crystal display (LCD) that accepts ASCII input, or setting up a serial connection to a PC. The option we're going to focus on uses a microcomputer design by Briel Computers to deliver output to a video monitor. This chip and a few TTL chips are equivalent to the Apple I's video section.

You can see the circuit in Figure 7.30. At the center is the ATMega microcontroller, which is the heart of our video section. To the left of it is the clock circuitry. Depressing the CLEAR switch resets the microcontroller and clears the display. The 74LS74 is used as a clock divider, to cut the clock frequency down to about 7.1MHz. The 74LS166 is a shift register, which sends our data out to the display. Output goes to an ordinary composite monitor via an RCA jack (see Figure 7.31). The diodes prevent any accidental signals the video monitor might generate from reaching and damaging the circuitry.

Figure 7.30 A Video Section Schematic

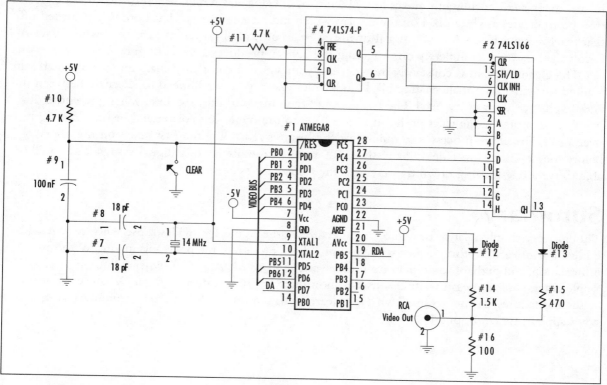

Figure 7.31 An RCA Phono Jack

The electron beam in the video monitor's cathode ray tube scans the display line by line. It starts in the upper-right corner and moves left. The display is black and white. When turned on, the electron beam creates a white pixel on the display, which indicates its current location. When turned off, that pixel remains black. A 0-volt signal turns the beam on to full power and creates a white pixel. A 3-volt signal turns it completely off. Anything in between produces a shade of gray.

The electron beam is constantly moving, and your signal is constantly changing its voltage. If you wanted to send a line of alternating black-and-white pixels, you would need to alternate between 0 and 3 volts every for every pixel. The beam would then move to the next line. When the entire display has been drawn, the electron beam moves back to the upper-left corner and begins drawing it over again. The entire process is so quick that the beam is redrawing the first pixels on the display before they even start to fade. Look at the CRT through the display of a digital camera and you'll be able to see a line moving down the screen as the display refreshes.

Summary

Though very simple relative to microcomputers today, the Apple 1 provides those who study it with quite a bit to learn. In this chapter we've examined the processor, memory, and in/out. With this information, and perhaps some help from other members of the Apple I Owners Club on Applefritter, you can begin writing software and modifying the hardware design. Whatever your successes and failures, be sure to share what you learn with the rest of the Apple I community at www.applefritter.com/apple1.

ASCII Codes

Dec	Hex	Char	Dec	Hex	Char	Dec	Hex	Char	Dec	Hex	Char
0	0	NUL (null)	32	20	Space	64	40	@	96	60	`
1	1	SOH (start of heading)	33	21	!	65	41	A	97	61	a
2	2	STX (start of text)	34	22	"	66	42	B	98	62	b
3	3	ETX (end of text)	35	23	#	67	43	C	99	63	c
4	4	EOT (end of trans.)	36	24	$	68	44	D	100	64	d
5	5	ENQ (enquiry)	37	25	%	69	45	E	101	65	e
6	6	ACK (acknowledge)	38	26	&	70	46	F	102	66	f
7	7	BEL (bell)	39	27	'	71	47	G	103	67	g
8	8	BS (backspace)	40	28	(	72	48	H	104	68	h
9	9	TAB (horizontal tab)	41	29	)	73	49	I	105	69	i
10	A	LF (line feed)	42	2A	*	74	4A	J	106	6A	j
11	B	VT (vertical tab)	43	2B	+	75	4B	K	107	6B	k
12	C	FF (form feed)	44	2C	,	76	4C	L	108	6C	l
13	D	CR (carriage return)	45	2D	-	77	4D	M	109	6D	m
14	E	SO (shift out)	46	2E	.	78	4E	N	110	6E	n
15	F	SI (shift in)	47	2F	/	79	4F	O	111	6F	o
16	10	DLE (data link escape)	48	30	0	80	50	P	112	70	p
17	11	DC1 (device control 1)	49	31	1	81	51	Q	113	71	q
18	12	DC2 (device control 2)	50	32	2	82	52	R	114	72	r
19	13	DC3 (device control 3)	51	33	3	83	53	S	115	73	s
20	14	DC4 (device control 4)	52	34	4	84	54	T	116	74	t
21	15	NAK (neg. acknowledge)	53	35	5	85	55	U	117	75	u
22	16	SYN (synchronous idle)	54	36	6	86	56	V	118	76	v
23	17	ETB (end of trans.)	55	37	7	87	57	W	119	77	w
24	18	CAN (cancel)	56	38	8	88	58	X	120	78	x
25	19	EM (end of medium)	57	39	9	89	59	Y	121	79	y
26	1A	SUB (substitute)	58	3A	:	90	5A	Z	122	7A	z

Dec	Hex	Char	Dec	Hex	Char	Dec	Hex	Char	Dec	Hex	Char
27	1B	ESC (escape)	59	3B	;	91	5B	[	123	7B	{
28	1C	FS (file separator)	60	3C	<	92	5C	\	124	7C		
29	1D	GS (group separator)	61	3D	=	92	5D	]	125	7D	}
30	1E	RS (record separator)	62	3E	>	94	5E	^	126	7E	~
31	1F	US (unit separator)	63	3F	?	95	5F	_	127	7F	DEL

Operation Codes and Status Register

Mnemonic	a	(a,x)	a,x	a,y	(a)	A	#	i	r	zp	(zp,x)	zp,x	zp,y	(zp),y	Processor Status Register							
															7 N	6 V	5 1	4 1	3 D	2 I	1 Z	0 C
ADC	6D		7D	79			69			65	61	75		71	N	V					Z	C
AND	2D		3D	39			29			25	21	35		31	N						Z	
ASL	0E		1E			0A				06		16			N						Z	C
BCC									90													
BCS									B0													
BEQ									F0													
BIT	2C						89			24					M7	M6					Z	
BMI									30													
BNE									D0													
BPL									10													
BRA									80													
BRK								00										1		1		
BVC									50													
BVS									70													
CLC								18														0
CLD								D8											0			
CLI								58												0		
CLV								B8								0						
CMP	CD		DD	D9			C9			C5	C1	D5		D1	N						Z	C
CPX	EC						E0			E4					N						Z	C
CPY	CC						C0			C4					N						Z	C
DEC	CE		DE							C6		D6			N						Z	
DEX								CA							N						Z	
DEY								88							N						Z	
EOR	4D		5D	59			49			45	41	55		51	N						Z	
INC	EE		FE							E6		F6			N						Z	
INX								E8							N						Z	
INY								C8							N						Z	

Continued

Processor Status Register instruction / addressing-mode table (6502)

Mnemonic	a	(a,x)	a,x	a,y	(a)	A	#	i	r	zp	(zp,x)	zp,x	zp,y	(zp),y	N 7	V 6	1 5	1 4	D 3	I 2	Z 1	C 0
JMP	4C	7C			6C																	
JSR	20																					
LDA	AD		BD	B9			A9			A5	A1	B5		B1	N						N	
LDX	AE			BE			A2			A6			B6		N						N	
LDY	AC		BC				A0			A4		B4			N						N	
LSR	4E		5E			4A				46		56			0						N	C
NOP								EA														
ORA	0D		1D	19			09			05	01	15		11	N						N	
PHA								48														
PHP								08														
PLA								68							N						N	
PLP								28							N	V		–	D	–	N	C
ROL	2E		3E			2A				26		36			N						N	C
ROR	6E		7E			6A				66		76			N						N	C
RTI								40							N	V		1	F	–	N	C
RTS								60														
SBC	ED		FD	F9			E9			E5	E1	F5		F1	N	V					N	C
SEC								38														1
SED								F8											1			
SEI								78												1		
STA	8D		9D	99						85	81	95		91								
STX	8E									86			96									
STY	8C									84		94										
TAX								AA							N						N	
TAY								AB							N						N	
TSX								BA							N						N	
TXA								8A							N						N	
TXS								9A														
TYA								98							N						N	

OpCode Matrix

	0	1	2	3	4	5	6	7	8	9	A	B	C	D	E	F
0	BRK i	ORA (zp,x)				ORA zp	ASL zp		PHP i	ORA #	ASL A			ORA a	ASL a	0
1	BPL r	ORA (zp),y				ORA zp,x	ASL zp,x		CLC i	ORA a,y				ORA a,x	ASL a,x	1
2	JSR a	AND (zp,x)			BIT zp	AND zp	ROL zp		PLP i	AND #	ROL A		BIT a	AND a	ROL a	2
3	BMI r	AND (zp),y				AND zp,x	ROL zp,x		SEC i	AND a,y				AND a,x	ROL a,x	3
4	RTI i	EOR (zp,x)				EOR zp	LSR zp		PHA i	EOR #	LSR A		JMP a	EOR a	LSR a	4
5	BVC r	EOR (zp),y				EOR zp,x	LSR zp,x		CLI i	EOR a,y				EOR a,x	LSR a,x	5
6	RTS s	ADC (zp,x)				ADC zp	ROR zp		PLA i	ADC #	ROR A		JMP (a)	ADC a	ROR a	6
7	BVS r	ADC (zp),y				ADC zp,x	ROR zp,x		SEI i	ADC a,y				ADC a,x	ROR a,x	7
8		STA (zp,x)			STY zp	STA zp	STX zp		DEY i		TXA i		STY a	STA a	STX a	8
9	BCC r	STA (zp),y			STY zp,x	STA zp,x	STX zp,y		TYA i	STA a,y	TXS i			STA a,x		9
A	LDY #	LDA (zp,x)	LDX #		LDY zp	LDA zp	LDX zp		TAY i	LDA #	TAX i		LDY a	LDA a	LDX a	A
B	BCS r	LDA (zp),y			LDY zp,x	LDA zp,x	LDX zp,x		CLV i	LDA a,y	TSX i		LDY a,x	LDA a,x	LDX a,y	B
C	CPY #	CMP (zp,x)			CPY zp	CMP zp	DEC zp		INY i	CMP #	DEX i		CPY a	CMP a	DEC a	C
D	BNE r	CMP (zp),y				CMP zp,x	DEC zp,x		CLD i	CMP a,y				CMP a,x	DEC a,x	D
E	CPX #	SBC (zp,x)			CPX zp	SBC zp	INC zp		INX i	SBC #	NOP i		CPX a	SBC a	INC a	E
F	BEQ R	SBC (zp),y				SBC zp,x	INC zp,x		SED i	SBC a,y				SBC a,x	INC a,x	F
	0	1	2	3	4	5	6	7	8	9	A	B	C	D	E	F

Instructions by Category

Load and Store

LDA – Load Accumulator with Memory

M → A

Flags: N, Z

Addressing Mode	Opcode
a	AD
a,x	BD
a,y	B9
#	A9
zp	A5
(zp,x)	A1
zp,x	B5
(zp),y	B1

LDX – Load Index X with Memory

M → X

Flags: N, Z

Addressing Mode	Opcode
a	AE
a,y	BE
#	A2
zp	A6
zp,y	B6

LDY – Load Index Y with Memory

M → Y

Flags: N, Z

Addressing Mode	Opcode
a	AC
a,x	BC
#	A0
zp	A4
zp,x	B4

STA – Store Accumulator in Memory

A → M

Flags: *none*

Addressing Mode	Opcode
a	8D
a,x	9D
a,y	99
zp	85
(zp,x)	81
zp,x	95
(zp),y	91

STX – Store Index X in Memory

X → M

Flags: *none*

Addressing Mode	Opcode
a	8E
zp	86
zp,y	96

STY – Store Index Y in Memory

Y → M

Flags: *none*

Addressing Mode	Opcode
a	8C
zp	84
zp,x	94

Arithmetic

ADC – Add Memory to Accumulator with Carry

$A + M + C \rightarrow A$

Flags: N, V, Z, C,

Addressing Mode	Opcode
a	6D
a,x	7D
a,y	79
#	69
zp	65
(zp,x)	61
zp,x	75
(zp),y	71

SBC – Subtract Memory from Accumulator with Borrow

$A - M - \sim C \rightarrow A$

Difference between C and ~C is...?

Flags: N, V, Z, C

Addressing Mode	Opcode
a	ED
a,x	FD
a,y	F9
#	E9
zp	E5
(zp,x)	E1
zp,x	F5
(zp),y	F1

Increment and Decrement

INC – Increment Memory by One

M + 1 $\rightarrow$ M

Flags: N, Z

Addressing Mode	Opcode
a	EE
a,x	FE
zp	E6
zp,x	F6

INX – Increment Index X by One

X + 1 $\rightarrow$ X

Flags: N, Z

Addressing Mode	Opcode
i	E8

INY – Increment Index Y by One

Y + 1 $\rightarrow$ Y

Flags: N, Z

Addressing Mode	Opcode
i	C8

DEC – Decrement Memory by One

$M - 1 \rightarrow M$

Flags: N, Z

Addressing Mode	Opcode
a	CE
a,x	DE
zp	C6
zp,x	D6

DEX – Decrement Index X by One

$X - 1 \rightarrow X$

Flags: N, Z

Addressing Mode	Opcode
i	CA

DEY – Decrement Index Y by One

$Y - 1 \rightarrow Y$

Flags: N, Z

Addressing Mode	Opcode
i	88

Shift and Rotate

ASL – Accumulator Shift Left One Bit

C ▪ 7 6 5 4 3 2 1 0 ▪ 0

Flags: N, Z, C

Addressing Mode	Opcode
a	0E
a,x	1E
A	0A
zp	06
zp,x	16

LSR – Logical Shift Right One Bit

0 → 7 6 5 4 3 2 1 0 → C

Flags: N, Z, C

Addressing Mode	Opcode
a	4E
a,x	5E
A	4A
zp	46
zp,x	56

ROL – Rotate Left One Bit

C ▪ 7 6 5 4 3 2 1 0 ▪ C

Flags: N, Z, C

Addressing Mode	Opcode
a	2E
a,x	3E
A	2A
zp	26
zp,x	36

ROR – Rotate Right One Bit

C → 7 6 5 4 3 2 1 0 → C

Flags: N, Z, C

Addressing Mode	Opcode
a	6E
a,x	7E
A	6A
zp	66
zp,x	76

Logic

AND – AND Memory with Accumulator

$A \wedge M \rightarrow A$

Flags: N, Z

Addressing Mode	Opcode
a	2D
a,x	3D
a,y	39
#	29
zp	25
(zp,x)	21
zp,x	35
(zp),y	31

ORA – OR Memory with Accumulator

$A \vee M \rightarrow A$

Flags: N, Z

Addressing Mode	Opcode
a	0D
a,x	1D
a,y	19
#	09
zp	05
(zp,x)	01
zp,x	15
(zp),y	11

EOR – Exclusive-OR Memory with Accumulator

A v M → A

Flags: N, Z

Addressing Mode	Opcode
a	4D
a,x	5D
a,y	59
#	49
zp	45
(zp,x)	41
zp,x	55
(zp),y	51

Compare and Test Bit

For all Compare instructions:

Condition	N	Z	C
Register < Memory	1	0	0
Register = Memory	0	1	1
Register > Memory	0	0	1

CMP – Compare Memory and Accumulator

A – M

Flags: N, Z, C

Addressing Mode	Opcode
a	CD
a,x	DD
a,y	D9
#	C9
zp	C5
(zp,x)	C1
zp,x	D5
(zp),y	D1

CPX – Compare Memory and Index X

X – M

Flags: N, Z, C

Addressing Mode	Opcode
a	EC
#	E0
zp	E4

CPY – Compare Memory and Index Y

Y - M

Flags: N, Z, C

Addressing Mode	Opcode
a	CC
#	C0
zp	C4

BIT – Test Bits in Memory with Accumulator

A ^ M

Flags: N = M7, V = M6, Z

Addressing Mode	Opcode
a	2C
#	89
zp	24

Branch

BCC – Branch on Carry Clear

Branch if C = 0

Flags: *none*

Addressing Mode	Opcode
r	90

BCS – Branch on Carry Set

Branch if C = 1

Flags: *none*

Addressing Mode	Opcode
r	B0

BEQ – Branch on Result Zero

Branch if Z = 1

Flags: *none*

Addressing Mode	Opcode
r	F0

BMI – Branch on Result Minus

Branch if N = 1

Flags: *none*

Addressing Mode	Opcode
r	30

BNE – Branch on Result not Zero

Branch if Z = 0

Flags: *none*

Addressing Mode	Opcode
r	D0

BPL – Branch on Result Plus

Branch if N = 0

Flags: *none*

Addressing Mode	Opcode
r	10

BVC – Branch on Overflow Clear

Branch if V = 0

Flags: *none*

Addressing Mode	Opcode
r	50

BVS – Branch on Overflow Set

Branch if V = 1

Flags: *none*

Addressing Mode	Opcode
r	70

Transfer

TAX – Transfer Accumulator to Index X

A → X

Flags: N, Z

Addressing Mode	Opcode
i	AA

TXA – Transfer Index X to Accumulator

X → A

Flags: N, Z

Addressing Mode	Opcode
i	8A

TAY – Transfer Accumulator to Index Y

A → Y

Flags: N, Z

Addressing Mode	Opcode
i	AB

TYA – Transfer Index Y to Accumulator

Y → A

Flags: N, Z

Addressing Mode	Opcode
i	98

TSX – Transfer Stack Pointer to Index X

S → X

Flags: N, Z

Addressing Mode	Opcode
i	BA

TXS – Transfer Index X to Stack Register

X → S

Flags: N, Z

Addressing Mode	Opcode
i	9A

Stack

PHA – Push Accumulator on Stack

A → S

Flags: *none*

Addressing Mode	Opcode
i	48

PLA – Pull Accumulator from Stack

S → A

Flags: N, Z

Addressing Mode	Opcode
i	68

PHP – Push Processor Status on Stack

P → S

Flags: *none*

Addressing Mode	Opcode
i	08

PLP – Pull Processor Status from Stack

S → P

Flags: *all*

Addressing Mode	Opcode
i	28

Subroutines and Jump

JMP – Jump to New Location

Jump to new location

Flags: *none*

Addressing Mode	Opcode
a	4C
(a,x)	7C
(a)	6C

JSR – Jump to New Location Saving Return Address

Jump to Subroutine

Flags: *none*

Addressing Mode	Opcode
a	20

RTS – Return from Subroutine

Return from Subroutine

Flags: *none*

Addressing Mode	Opcode
i	60

RTI – Return from Interrupt

Return from Interrupt

Flags: *none*

Addressing Mode	Opcode
i	40

Set and Clear

SEC – Set Carry Flag

1 → C

Flags: *none*

Addressing Mode	Opcode
i	38

SED – Set Decimal Mode

1 → D

Flags: *none*

Addressing Mode	Opcode
i	F8

SEI – Set Interrupt Disable Status

1 → I

Flags: *none*

Addressing Mode	Opcode
i	78

CLC – Clear Carry Flag

$0 \rightarrow C$

Flags: $C = 0$

Addressing Mode	Opcode
i	18

CLD – Clear Decimal Mode

$0 \rightarrow D$

Flags: $D = 0$

Addressing Mode	Opcode
i	D8

CLI – Clear Interrupt Disable Bit

$0 \rightarrow I$

Flags: $I = 0$

Addressing Mode	Opcode
i	58

CLV – Clear Overflow Flag

$0 \rightarrow V$

Flags: V = 0

Addressing Mode	Opcode
i	B8

Miscellaneous

NOP – No Operation

No Operation

Flags: *none*

Addressing Mode	Opcode
i	EA

BRK – Break

Force an interrupt

Flags: B = 1, I = 1

Addressing Mode	Opcode
i	00

Hacking Macintosh

Compubrick SE

As computer hardware became a commodity in the mid-1980s, the importance of focusing on software became increasingly apparent to many at Apple, as did the need for an open platform. Apple's John Fitch devised the Jonathan architecture, consisting of a simple backplane that would accept book-like modules. Using this design, modules for running a variety of operating systems could be developed and placed on the same backplane. This would allow users to easily experiment with new operating systems—a feature Fitch believed would work very much to Apple's advantage. However, John Sculley, CEO of Apple, feared just the opposite would occur, and the project was canceled.

Jonathan could have changed the way we think about computers, each user starting out with a bare-bones system and then adding and upgrading individual components as needed. Jonathan's modular design lends itself very well to building blocks. Need a new hard drive? Snap off the old one and snap a new one into place. Each computer component is a giant building block, allowing the user to mix and match any combination of components and snap them together in whatever form factor is most convenient. The Compubrick SE is a proof-of-concept artist's rendering of this methodology.

Fanaticism meets fanaticism with the Compubrick SE, combining the thrill of hardware hacking with the joy of building. We start with a Macintosh SE, strip it down to its individual parts, then build it back up again in cases of multicolored plastic Mega Bloks. Each component becomes its own block, attached to the system however the builder chooses.

NOTE

More information on the Jonathan concept is available in *AppleDesign* by Paul Kunkel, published by Graphics Inc., 1997.

Preparing for the Hack

Before we begin the Compubrick SE hack, you will need to gather all required materials and tools. Figure E.1 shows most of the items.

Figure E.1 Getting Ready for the Compubrick SE Hack

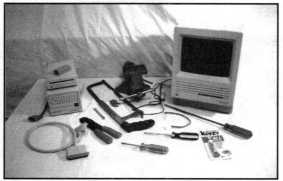

Table E.1 is a list of components that you will need to build a Compubrick SE.

Table E.1 Required Components for the Compubrick SE

Component	Notes
Macintosh SE	
800K external drive	Model number M0131
Mega Bloks, about 2,500	A few of Mega Bloks' 600-piece bins will work. Be careful when estimating the number you'll need; many of the smaller pieces won't be usable in this project.
Erector set	
Internal-to-external SCSI cable	Found in external hard drives
SCSI terminator	
18-22AWG wire, 26 feet	

Table E.2 presents a list of tools that you will also need to build a Compubrick SE.

Table E.2 Required Tools for the Compubrick SE

Tool	Notes
Super Glue	
T15 x 6 in. screwdriver	Sears Craftsman part #47431
Straight screwdriver	
Philips screwdriver	
Wire stripper/crimper	Found in external hard drives
Wire snips or hobby knife	
Vise	
Hacksaw	

A Craftsman T15 x 6 in. screwdriver is available at Sears for under $5. A longer shaft is convenient but not necessary. Mega Bloks and Erector sets can be found at any toy store. Try salvaging an internal-to-external SCSI cable from an old external hard drive. Computer swap meets will often have used hard drives, disk drives, and the Mac SE for pennies on the dollar. If you're not inclined to go searching, you can easily purchase all these components online for a few dollars plus the cost of shipping. Here are a few sources to consider:

- eBay: www.ebay.com
- USENET Groups: groups.google.com
- Applefritter Forums: www.applefritter.com

Performing the Hack

The disassembly and reassembly of the Compubrick is a multistep process. To make this process easier to understand, we have broken the hack into different modules, as follows:

- Taking Apart the Mac
- Speaker
- Keyboard and Mouse
- Disk Drive
- Hard Drive
- Motherboard
- Cathode Ray Tube (CRT)

Taking Apart the Mac

Steve Jobs saw the Macintosh as an appliance not meant to be taken apart. As such, the compact Macs are very difficult to open. In order to disassemble the Mac, complete the following steps:

1. Locate the four T15 Torx screws that need to be removed. Two are on the back, just above the line of ports. The other two are inside the handle, for which the long screwdriver shaft is necessary. You can see the removal process for the screws inside the handle in Figures E.2 and E.3.

Figure E.2 Locations of Screws

Figure E.3 Unscrewing the Screws

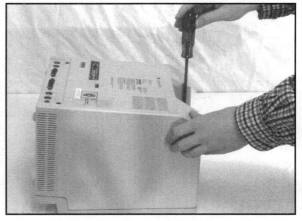

2. Once you have removed the screws, pry open the case by gently tugging at each corner of the case until the two pieces separate (see Figure E.4).

Figure E.4 Prying the Case Apart

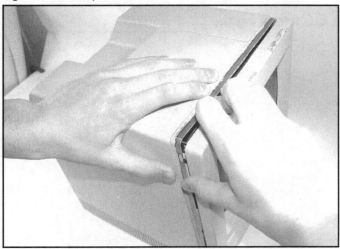

3.   Once the case is open, discharge the CRT. This is a dangerous and critical step.

WARNING: PERSONAL INJURY

The CRT inside a compact Macintosh can potentially hold a charge of up to 13,000 volts, which can give you quite a shock. Take extreme caution to discharge the CRT properly. An example of discharge procedure can be found at www.jagshouse.com/CRT.html. Never perform a CRT discharge alone—always have a friend present in case of emergency.

4.   Next, remove the analog cable from the motherboard. Figure E.5 shows a photo of the inside of the Mac with the analog cable in place. The cable is a snug fit; be careful not to bump the CRT's neck when the cable gives way, because it could easily snap off and destroy the monitor!

Figure E.5 Inside the Mac SE with the Analog Cable in Place

5. Now slide the motherboard upward about an inch and pop it out (see Figure E.6).

Figure E.6 Removing the Motherboard

With the case opened, we can now begin to dismantle the chassis:

1. Remove the two screws (shown in Figure E.7) that hold the hard drive and floppy enclosure in place. The drive unit will now easily lift out of the case and can be set aside.

Figure E.7 Hard Drive Screws

2. Next, detach the frame from the front cover. The frame has five screws holding it in place; four of these screws are pictured in Figure E.8.

Figure E.8 Frame Screws: Four of the Five

3. To be able to remove the fifth screw that attaches the front cover, we have to first detach the power supply, which is mounted to the analog board with six screws on its right side.

NEED TO KNOW...

The analog board is the circuit board mounted vertically beside the power supply. It provides power to the CRT and motherboard.

4. Push the power supply out of the way, as shown in Figure E.9, to reach the last screw.

Figure E.9 Removing the Fifth Frame Screw

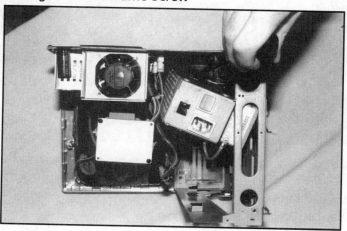

5. With the frame now disconnected, lift it out of the case and set it aside (see Figure E.10).

Figure E.10 Frame Removed from the Case

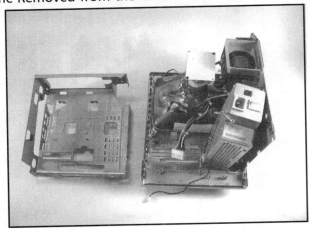

6. Next, remove the power supply after disconnecting it from the analog board. Disconnect the short cable that connects the CRT to the analog board (see Figure E.11). This allows you to spread out the remaining parts as shown in Figure E.12.

Figure E.11 Disconnect the Power Supply

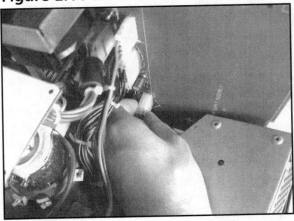

Figure E.12 The Analog Board

7. Finally, disconnect the CRT from the front plate by removing the four screws, one in each corner of the CRT. This is done so that you can remove the speaker from the front case. The speaker is held in place by two flimsy plastic tabs, as shown in Figure E.13. Just break these off using the wire snips or a hobby knife.

Figure E.13 Moving the Speaker

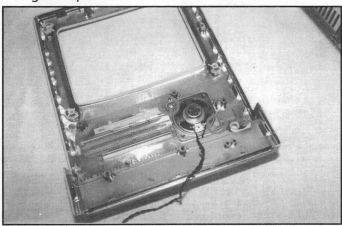

Need to Know... Building Techniques

The Compubrick design is based primarily upon the use of 2x4 bricks, making flat regions a bit tricky because the block segments are so short. These regions are built using two layers of bricks, with the second layer offset from the first, as shown in Figures E.14 and E.15. This technique is known as *layering*.

Figure E.14 Mega Blok Layering Example, Underside

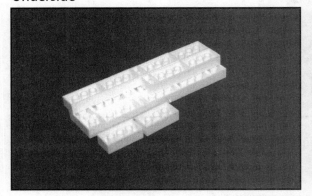

Figure E.15 Mega Blok Layering Example, Top

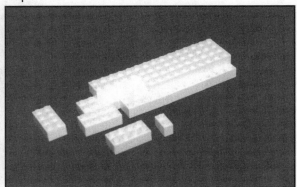

Assembling the bricks in this manner is adequate for use on small surfaces such as the top or bottom of the hard drive or disk drive. For the larger areas, however, this technique results in a connection that is too flimsy. In this case, it is necessary to reinforce the assembly with Super Glue. Figure E.16, the top of the CRT case, is an example of an area so large that it requires gluing for strength. Place a dab of glue on the edges of a few studs on the brick, then quickly snap the piece above it into place. Avoid placing glue on the sides of the bricks. It will seep out when you press them together.

Figure E.16 Mega Blok Layering Example, Top of the CRT Case

Encasing the Speaker

The first task of assembling the Compubrick is constructing the speaker encasement. This is a relatively simple step. You need to encase the speaker with blocks, using cylindrical 1x1s for the speaker grill. Any color or size brick that you prefer to use is acceptable; however, the case should be relatively the same size as the example shown in Figure E.17.

Figure E.17 Partially Assembled Speaker

A completed version of the speaker encased in blocks is shown in Figure E.18.

Figure E.18 Completed Speaker

Covering the Mouse and the Keyboard

The blocks on the keyboard and mouse serve only aesthetic purposes, in keeping with the theme of covering a Macintosh SE with Mega Bloks. The Compubrick mouse is completed by gluing blocks to the surface and has no function other than a visual one. The ADB Mouse I that shipped with the Mac SE has a flat surface, making the gluing fairly simple. The Mega Blok-covered ADB Mouse I is shown in Figure E.19.

Figure E.19 Completed ADB Mouse I

Figure E.20 ADB Mouse II

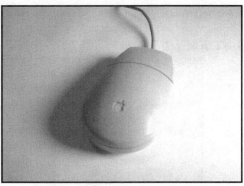

The choice of keyboards is unimportant; any keyboard will do. For this example, an Apple Extended Keyboard II was used.

1. Dismantle the keyboard by removing both the top and bottom pieces of the case. The top and bottom of the keyboard case is usually connected by a variety of simple screws that can be accessed from the bottom of the keyboard. In the case of the Extended Keyboard II, there is only one screw (see Figure E.21). Remove it, then pry the keyboard apart.

2. Now remove the keyboard mechanism from the case (see Figure E.22). To do this, first release the keyboard from underneath the snaps, then pop out the ADB connectors. Finally, slide the keyboard upward out of the tabs. Once you have separated the top and bottom portions of the keyboard case, discard the top piece.

Figure E.21 Bottom of Keyboard

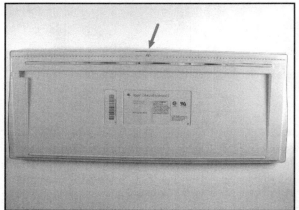

Figure E.22 Removing the Keyboard Mechanism

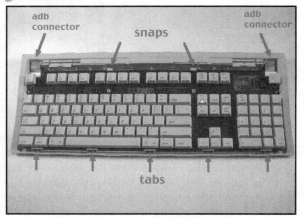

3. Next, take the bottom half of the keyboard and, using the hacksaw, saw off any tabs that protrude from the case (Figure E.23). This is done so you have as smooth a surface as possible on which to place the bricks.

Figure E.23 Sawing Off the Tabs

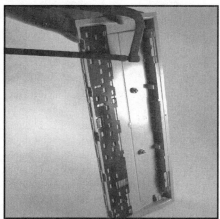

4. Now place the keyboard back into the lower case and build your frame around it, filling in the spaces between rows of keys with blocks (see Figure E.24). When you have a frame that you're happy with, remove it, apply glue to the keyboard, and press the frame into place. The finished keyboard will resemble Figure E.25.

Figure E.24 Partially Assembled Keyboard

Figure E.25 Completed Keyboard

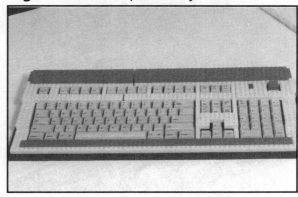

Encasing the Disk Drive

To encase the disk drive with the Mega Bloks, you will first have to remove the disk drive from its plastic case, but keep the metal chassis and cable intact.

1. There are four screws on the bottom of the case (see Figure E.26). Remove these, and remove the bottom piece of plastic.

Figure E.26 Bottom of the Floppy Drive

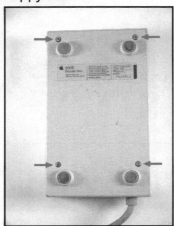

2. To remove the drive's chassis from the remaining plastic, remove the two screws shown in Figure E.27 and lift out the metal enclosure. These uncased elements are shown in Figure E.28.

Figure E.27 Inside the Floppy Drive

Figure E.28 Disk Drive Mechanism

3. Now that the disk drive is uncovered, you can begin by building the base using the previously described layering technique. Then add two rows of blocks for the sides, leaving a hole for the cable. The assembled base is shown in Figure E.29.

Figure E.29 Partially Assembled Disk Drive

4. The third row should have a slot in the front to allow a disk to be inserted (see Figure E.30). On the right-hand side, we used an angular block so that the eject mechanism could still be reached (but only with a paperclip—this being a Macintosh, after all!). A fourth row finishes the sides, and the top is built using the layering technique, for a more aesthetically pleasing crown (see Figure E.31).

Figure E.30 Eject Mechanism

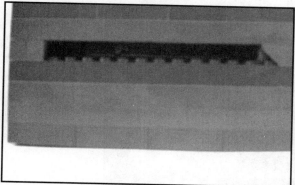

Figure E.31 Completed Disk Drive

Encasing the Hard Drive

The goal of this step is to remove the SCSI internal hard drive from your Mac SE and create an external, modular SCSI drive. To do this:

1. Take the hard drive out of your Mac SE (or use any other SCSI hard drive) and the internal-to-external SCSI cable you salvaged from the external hard drive.

2. Connect them together, and then connect the SCSI cable and terminator. Now build the base and the top using layering, and build up the sides around the drive and cables, as shown in Figure E.32.

Figure E.32 Partially Assembled Hard Drive

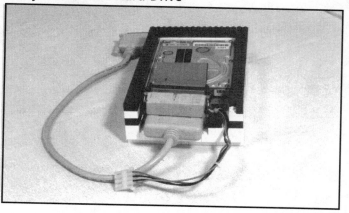

3. If you used a cable and terminator as shown in Figure E.32, you'll find that the two stacked components are just barely too high to allow the top to fit on. The difference is slight enough that shaving a layer of plastic off the SCSI terminator will allow everything to fit properly, so stick the terminator in a vice and grab a hacksaw (see Figure E.33).

Figure E.33 Hacksawing the SCSI Terminator

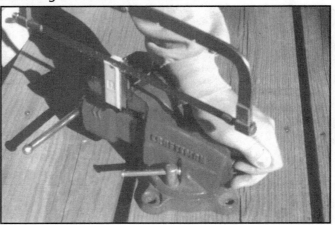

Figures 5.34 and 5.35 show the finished product: a nice square unit with the cables neatly protruding from the back.

Figure E.34 Completed Hard Drive, Front

Figure E.35 Completed Hard Drive, Back

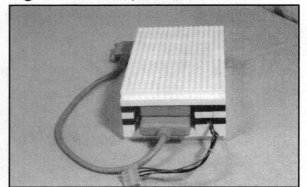

Encasing the Motherboard

The Mac SE motherboard is exactly 28 2x4 bricks wide, which will sit perfectly upon a baseplate (see Figure E.36). However, doing so makes it nearly impossible to securely snap the motherboard on top of another component, but it gives us a lower-profile motherboard.

Figure E.36 Baseplate

If you lack a baseplate or want the ability to snap the motherboard on top of another component, layering and gluing 2x4 bricks will also work well here. For this example, we used a baseplate for the bottom. The layering scheme, with gluing, is used for the top (see Figure E.38). The back is left open, but cutting the shielding down to the right height (see Figure E.37) will give it a nice, finished look, as shown in Figure E.38. Figure E.40 shows the top, with the hole left for the analog cable. I used black bricks for part of the underside because I was short on green.

Figure E.37 Cutting the Shielding

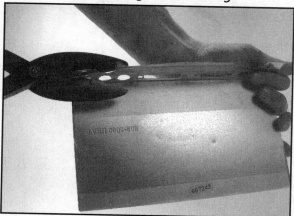

Figure E.38 Underside of the Motherboard's Cover

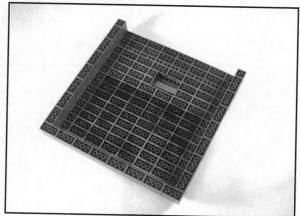

Figure E.39 Partially Assembled Motherboard

Figure E.40 shows us the completed motherboard case. Note the hole left for the analog cable, denoted by the arrow.

Figure E.40 The Finished Motherboard Enclosure

Encasing the CRT

Mounting the CRT to the analog board is tricky because we're no longer using the original plastic encasements. We will first use Erector set beams to build a frame across the top and bottom and down the side of the CRT, then connect it to the analog board using the holes already available (see Figure E.41). Use whatever Erector set pieces you have available to build a frame that extends from the back, affixing to the analog board using the holes already present. Then extend beams from the CRT to the brackets in the back (see Figure E.42) Connect the grounding wires (circled in Figure E.43) anywhere on the frame. Figures 5.43 and 5.44 show the back of the completed CRT and analog board structure.

Figure E.41 CRT and Analog Board Structure, Front View

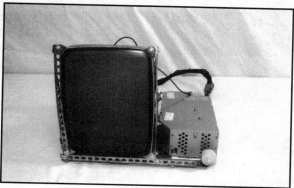

Figure E.42 Affixing Erector Set Pieces

Figure E.43 Completed CRT Structure, Top View

Figure E.44 Completed CRT Structure, Bottom View

Since the cable that runs from the analog board to the motherboard must reach outside of your CRT case, it must be extended. To do this:

1. Cut the cable in half (see Figure E.45) and use your stripper to bare the edges (see Figure E.46).

2. Then crimp both ends to a new series of wires (see Figure E.47), each about two feet long.

Figure E.45 Cutting the Wire

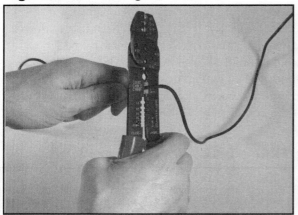

Figure E.46 Stripping the Wire

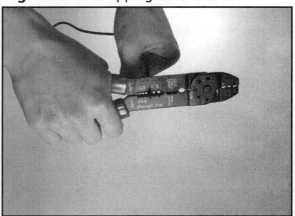

Figure E.47 Crimping the Wire

3. Begin the Mega Bloks construction by building a base large enough for the CRT, analog board, and power supply (Figure E.48). Build support beams for the CRT and glue them into place. You can see these black beams in Figure E.48, holding up the CRT. The beams are then built up the sides.

Figure E.48 CRT on a Mega Bloks Base

4. As you build, leave a hole in the front around the contrast knob. You'll also need to leave a hole in the back for the cable. The cable is already wired into place, so when you reach the height at which you want it, just build around it. Likewise, build around the power supply and the fan, so they are even with the back.

5. Build the top using the layering technique (Figure E.49) and gently snap it into place. Figure E.50 shows an almost complete CRT encasement.

Figure E.49 Top of the CRT, Built with Layering

Figure E.50 CRT Nearing Completion

How the Hack Works

Now that we're finished preparing the individual components, we can snap them together and arrange them in whatever manner you desire. Using a few extra blocks to widen the top of the

Compubrick, we can place the floppy drive and hard drive side by side, as shown in Figure E.51, or we can spread everything out, like Figure E.52.

Figure E.51 Compubrick SE, Partially Stacked Setup

Figure E.52 Compubrick SE, Wide Setup

If we want a compact, minimalist system, the hard drive and speaker can be removed and the motherboard stacked on top of the CRT. The analog cable that comes out of the top of the motherboard prevents us from putting the disk drive directly on top, but a set of legs (in white) for the floppy drive quickly fixes that problem (see Figure E.53).

Figure E.53 Compubrick SE, Minimal Setup

Building a UFO Mouse

"Today we brought romance and innovation back into the industry," Steve Jobs proclaimed as he introduced the iMac on May 6, 1998. It was the dawn of a new era for Apple. Gone was SCSI, gone was ADB, and *gone was beige*. Heralded as the most innovative computer since the original Macintosh, the iMac was as revolutionary in its industrial design as it was in its architecture. Curved sheets of translucent

"Bondi Blue" plastics replaced the old beige metal cases with rigid corners. Apple's new design was an instant hit, and soon the entire industry was following suit, rounding their corners and making their plastics translucent. Few matched the elegance of the iMac, with its close attention to detail.

Even the iMac's mouse sported a unique new design (see Figure E.54). Perfectly round, the iMac mouse was denounced for its ergonomics but lauded for its style. At the iMac's introduction, the translucent mouse was set upon a lighted pedestal, causing it to glow and leading to rumors the mouse itself was lit. The rumors were false but, for the aspiring hacker, inspirational.

The goal of this hack is to modify a standard Apple USB Mouse to add an LED, giving the mouse a glowing appearance.

Figure E.54 Apple USB Mouse

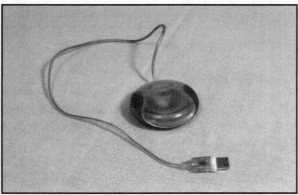

 # Preparing for the Hack

The UFO mouse is a simple hack to perform and requires relatively few parts or tools. A picture of the materials is shown in Figure E.55. The components that you will need outlined in Table E.3.

Figure E.55 Getting Ready for the UFO Mouse Hack

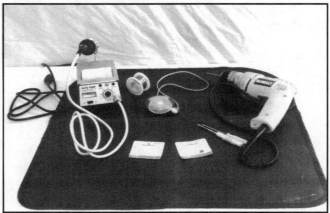

Table E.3 Required Components for the UFO Mouse Hack

Component	Notes
Apple USB mouse	Also known as the "puck mouse"
Blue LED	Radio Shack Part #276-311, 5V, T1 3/4 size

The tools that are required for this hack are described in Table E.4.

Table E.4 Required Tools for the UFO Mouse Hack

Tool	Notes
Soldering iron and solder	
Drill and 7/32-inch drill bit	
Small flat-head screwdriver	
Small Philips screwdriver	
Small jeweler's screwdriver	

As an alternative to the blue LED, Radio Shack also sells a blinking red LED, part #276–036, that runs off 5V and will work in the mouse. If you want something a bit wilder (and potentially headache inducing), consider this LED in lieu of the blue one.

Performing the Hack

Building an illuminated puck mouse consists of four steps:

1. Opening the mouse
2. Drilling the hole
3. Soldering the LED
4. Reassembling the mouse

Opening the Mouse

1. You'll see a translucent blue plastic covering on both the right and left sides of the mouse. To open the mouse, you'll have to remove this covering. The plastic coverings are each attached to the body of the mouse with three tabs. The locations of the tabs are shown in Figure E.56.

Figure E.56 Tab Locations on the Plastic Covering

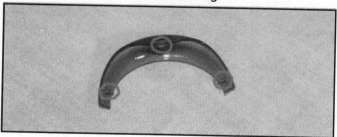

2. With a small flat screwdriver, gently pry the two tabs on the mouse's underside loose and then wiggle the third one free (see Figure E.57).

Figure E.57 Removing the Plastic Coverings

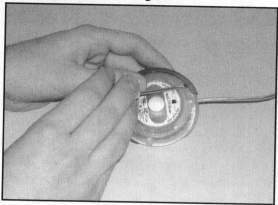

3. With the plastic coverings removed, locate the two screws on the bottom of the mouse that were previously hidden (Figure E.58). Using a small jeweler's screwdriver, remove these two screws and then pry upward on the back end of the plastic casing to remove the top cover.

Figure E.58 Unscrewing the Mouse

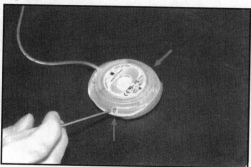

Drilling the Hole

To achieve a more diffused glow that really illuminates your puck mouse, you need to drill a hole into the ball chamber and point the LED into it.

1. Remove the circuit board from the mouse and place it as far away as the cable will allow (see Figure E.59).

Figure E.59 The Circuit Board Removed from the Case

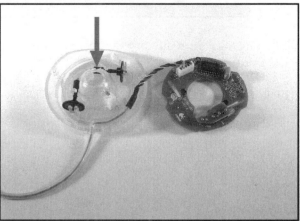

2. Using the 7/32-inch drill bit, drill a hole into the backside of the mouse housing (the side opposite the button), as indicated by the arrow in Figure E.59. The hole should be just low enough so that the rim around the top of the chamber will not be broken. The proper positioning of the drill is shown in Figure E.60.

Figure E.60 Drilling the Hole

Soldering the LED

Now that the hole is prepared in the plastic mouse housing, it's time to attach the LED to the mouse.

NEED TO KNOW... LED POLARITY

An LED typically has two leads projecting from its base (see Figure E.61). The longer lead is the positive lead (also known as the *anode*). The shorter lead is the negative lead (also known as the *cathode*). The cathode is also denoted by a flat edge on the plastic LED housing. The anode will connect to a positive voltage (5V in this case) and the cathode will connect to ground.

Figure E.61 LED Diagram

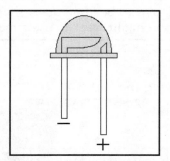

1. Turn the mouse so that the cable is facing away from you (Figure E.62). Opposite the cable, you should notice that there are five pins outlined in white.

Figure E.62 Close-Up of the Pins

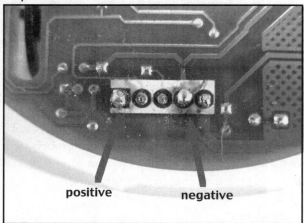

2. Snip the leads on the LED so that they are the appropriate length to reach from these pins into the hole that you drilled.

3. Now solder the positive lead of the LED to the leftmost pin (Figure E.63). If you turn the circuit board over, you'll see that the wire going into this pin is red.

4. Next, solder the negative lead (the flat side of the LED) to the second pin from the right. If you turn the circuit board over, you'll see that the wire going into this pin is black.

WARNING: HARDWARE HARM

When soldering the LED to the circuit board, be careful not to heat up the device too much or cause any surrounding pins to be lifted up or shorted together with solder. The pins are very close together, and you might want to use a magnifying glass to inspect your work.

Figure E.63 Soldering the LED

Reassembling the Mouse

Now put your mouse back together:

1. Carefully adjust the head of the LED to stick into the hole you drilled in the plastic housing. Be careful not to snap the LED off the circuit board. Make sure the circuit board is firmly connected to the base. Two spokes stick up from the base, one in the upper right and one in the lower left. Make sure these spokes go through the appropriate holes in the circuit board, rather than allowing the board to rest on top of them. When properly aligned, the board will fit snugly on the posts (see Figure E.64).

Figure E.64 Properly Aligned Mouse

2. Finally, take the plastic cover and place the tabs on its front into the corresponding slots on the base. Then snap the backside of the two pieces together (see Figure E.65).

Figure E.65 Closing the Mouse

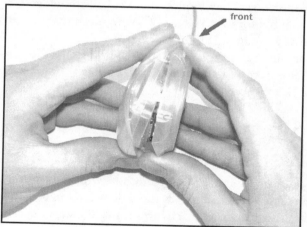

3. Return the two screws and snap the plastic sides into place. The hack is now complete!

Figure E.66 shows a picture of the completed UFO mouse in all its glowing glory.

Figure E.66 Completed UFO Mouse

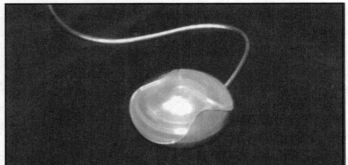

How the Hack Works

This hack is extremely simple—all we need to do is add an LED onto the circuit board of the USB mouse. The LED receives its power directly from the USB port, which provides a 5VDC supply. The LED is connected to the power supply using the two pads provided for us on the circuit board. Since we are using an LED with a forward voltage of 5V, we do not see a need to include a current-limiting resistor. Note that if any other LED is used, you may have to add a current-limiting resistor between the 5V supply line from the mouse and the positive lead of the LED—otherwise, you could damage the LED when it received power. See the "Electrical Engineering Basics" chapter and other LED hacks in this book for more details.

Adding Colored Skins to the Power Macintosh G4 Cube

One of the most popular consumer-based Macintosh systems from Apple Computer Inc. was the Power Mac G4 Cube (also known simply as the Cube), announced at MacWorld New York 2001. This machine's compact size and high CPU power made it an instant hit with users in every market who wanted a full-powered desktop in a tastefully artistic and compact enclosure. The G4 Cube was built to accept many of the same components as a full-size desktop computer, such as 3.5-inch hard disks, standard PC100 memory, and processor expansion cards.

Of course, the big downfall to all modern computer designs is the rapidly changing pace of technology. Eventually a machine, no matter how cool and sexy it is, is overtaken by the next new interesting design. Although the G4 Cube's lifespan far exceeds that of most personal computers, it is true that this wonderful machine is leaning toward obsolescence. However, a growing community of die-hard Cube fans, including myself, will go to great lengths to keep their machines useful.

This hack allows you to change the external appearance of your G4 Cube from the original, boring gray to any design you choose. You can make your Cube any color you want. Since the Cube comes in a gray metal box suspended inside a clear plastic box, any design that can be put to paper can be inlaid inside the cube.

This construction also has the advantage of protecting your artwork from external abrasions due to handling. However, the clear plastic case is far from scratch proof, so handle with care.

 # Preparing for the Hack

To prepare for this hack, you need to choose the artwork for your case design. Literally thousands of public domain textures are available online for free download, or you could create your own custom design in any number of art programs, such as Adobe Illustrator. A "wrappable" texture design flows from the edge of one sheet of paper perfectly to the second sheet, creating an appearance of the design being on one single, long sheet of paper. Instructions on how to create your own wrappable artwork for your cube are available at www.resexcellence.com/hack_html_00/12-15-00.shtml.

WARNING: HARDWARE HARM

 If you decide to print out your own texture, be aware that the pigments printed by thermal printers (e.g., laser or dye sublimation) can adhere to the plastic shell of the Cube when the machine heats up. This will cause inconsistencies in the appearance of the texture, and if the shell is removed later, the texture will be destroyed. Excess pigment left inside the clear shell can be removed with rubbing alcohol and a soft cotton cloth.

The parts required for this hack are shown in Table E.5.

Table E.5 Required Components for the Colored Skins Hack

Component	Notes
Custom texture design	Paper design 7.25 inches square, 5 sheets of 8.5 x 11-inch paper
Glossy clear tape	Scotch Transparent Tape 600, 1/2-inch width
Felt-tip marker	As close to texture color as possible

The tools required for this hack are listed in Table E.6.

Table E.6 Required Tools for the Colored Skins Hack

Tool	Notes
Small Phillips screwdriver	
Scissors	
Torx screwdriver, size T-10	Available at most hardware stores
X-ACTO knife	
Cloth gloves	Optional—to prevent leaving fingerprints on the plastic casing

Performing the Hack

1. The first step in the hack is to open your G4 Cube by removing the screws that hold the acrylic cube in place. Remove the Cube core (the actual CPU that sits inside the clear case) and set it aside someplace safe.

2. Inside the shell you will find two Phillips head screws and four T-10 Torx screws (see Figure E.67). Remove all six screws.

Figure E.67 Screw Locations Inside the G4 Cube

3. Next, you must remove the black screen grate that covers the vent slots on top, also shown in Figure E.67. The easiest way to do this is to unhook the screen and then lift up the shell. The grill should drop away. Once the grill is gone, you can remove the metal shell from inside the plastic shell. Be careful not to touch the inside of the plastic shell unless you're wearing cloth gloves or you'll leave fingerprints in it.

WARNING: PERSONAL INJURY

The hobby knife used for preparing your custom skin is extremely sharp. Extra care should be taken to always cut in a direction away from your body.

4. The next step in the hack is to prepare the texture sheets to be inserted into the Cube case. The hardest part of this exercise is the top sheet. Fortunately, Apple was kind enough to provide a "template." For our purposes, the template is a plastic sheet with all the slots and holes traced in it. This sheet lies between the metal shell and the acrylic case. Simply lay the Apple template on top of your printed texture and use it as a guide to carefully cut out the openings with an X-ACTO knife (see Figure E.68). The smaller holes should be traced with a pencil or fine-point marker before cutting.

Figure E.68 Using the Included Template

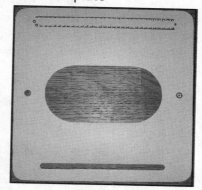

5. Run a felt marker that matches the color scheme of your wrappable skin all around the top and bottom edges of the metal box. This will help conceal your seams once you apply your texture sheets to the Cube core.

6. Tape two pages of the artwork to the Cube core, as shown in Figure E.69. You will have to pull these sheets rather tightly to avoid any wrinkling of the paper when you slide the clear case back over the core.

Figure E.69 Applying the Texture Sheets

7. Apply the two remaining panels for the top and the rear of the Cube core, lining up the edges with the front of the Cube. Secure these sheets using a piece of clear tape at least 8 inches long. Make sure that the ends of the tape are cut with scissors, rather than torn with your fingers, to ensure a smooth edge. Make sure to trim any excess tape once you have tightly wrapped the Cube design. Using this method, your seams will be placed on the corners and thus make the seams much less visible. Figure E.70 shows a close-up of the finished seam.

Figure E.70 Taping the Seams

8. After every sheet is secure, carefully return the wrapped core Cube back into the acrylic shell. You might want to run a clean cloth around the inside of the shell to remove any fingerprints or debris.

Once the Cube is fully assembled, your hack is complete! Figure E.70 shows my personal G4 Cube with a custom skin.

Figure E.71 G4 Cube with a Custom Skin

Under the Hood: How the Hack Works

All we are doing for this hack is slipping colored paper between the clear plastic outer shell and the gray metal box of the G4 Cube. The thick plastic causes some interesting visual effects with certain abstract designs, so experiment with various colors and shapes. The protection of the clear shell will keep your art looking great for years to come. Just be sure to keep your custom Cube away from direct sunlight.

Other Hacks and Resources

This chapter includes only the beginning of the things that you can do to your Mac. The following are lists of some of our favorites!

Desktop Hacks

- **Compubrick 160: www.applefritter.com/compubrick/compubrick160** The original Mega Blocks Macintosh.

- **DLZ-3: www.applefritter.com/hacks/dlz3** Devin Durham's Mac in a 1940's Zenith Radio case. Note the beautiful CD-ROM drive.

- **030 MacAquarium: www.applefritter.com/hacks/68Kfish** Jeff Knox turned his SE/30 into an aquarium—and it still runs!

- **Duo Digital Frame: www.applefritter.com/hacks/duodigitalframe** This elegant hack by James Roos places a Powerbook screen inside a picture frame.

- **Ze PowerSuitcase: www.applefritter.com/hacks/zepowersuitcase** Bernard Bélanger built his Macintosh into a suitcase.

- **Red Rocket: www.applefritter.com/hacks/redrocket** This rugged case was built from scratch by Mark Fisher to house his Power Mac 7300.

- **21" iMac: www.applefritter.com/hacks/21imac** Don Hardy rebuilt the original iMac, with its 15-inch display, into a 21-inch Nokia monitor.

Laptop Hacks

- **Tron Book: www.applefritter.com/hacks/tronbook** icruise stripped the paint off his iBook with alcohol, then painted the case a translucent blue.

- **ZebraBook: www.applefritter.com/hacks/zebrabook** In this simple hack, Mark Herbert replaced half of his Powerbook's black keys with white keys from an iBook, creating an elegant "zebra" effect.

- **Monster Ti: www.applefritter.com/hacks/monster_ti** Ted Warren painted his Powerbook G4 black, then added flames.

- **TiDrag: www.applefritter.com/hacks/tidrag** Artist Marek Jusiega used aerograph painting techniques to create this masterpiece on the back of a Powerbook G4.

Electrical and Optical Hacks

- **IlluminatedMac: www.applefritter.com/hacks/illuminatedmac** Matt Riley used electro-luminescent string to make this iMac glow.

- **Metamorphosis: www.applefritter.com/hacks/metamorphosis** Mad Dog soldered two additional PCI slots into his Umax J700 Macintosh clone.

- **Blue Ice G4: www.applefritter.com/hacks/blueiceg4** Kent Salas used neon and cold cathode tubes to make this G4 glow an icy blue.

- **BlueCube: www.applefritter.com/hacks/bluecube** Richard Chang added cold cathode tubes to his Power Mac Cube.

Case Mods

- **Mercury: www.applefritter.com/hacks/mercury** Myles Robinson used automotive paint to make this Mac Classic look stunning. Wax regularly.

- **Hal: www.applefritter.com/hacks/hal** This Mac Classic by Shane Hale features a case window and an eerie paint job.
- **MacRock: www.applefritter.com/hacks/macrock** Mike @ pigpen digital used "Stone Creation" paint to give his Mac a rugged look.
- **Candy Apple: www.applefritter.com/hacks/candy_apple** Alison Friedman used Clear Candy Apple Red Spray to paint this stunning Power Mac 7300.

Software

- **ResExcellence: www.resexcellence.com** Mac OS customizations.
- **The Iconfactory: www.iconfactory.com** A collection of beautifully rendered icons.
- **Kaleidoscope: www.kaleidoscope.net** This software allows complete customization of the Macintosh interface.

Discussion

- **Applefritter Forums:** www.applefritter.com
- **MacAddict Forums:** www.macaddict.com/phpBB2

Electrical Engineering Basics

Topics in this Appendix:

- Introduction
- Fundamentals
- Basic Device Theory
- Soldering Techniques
- Common Engineering Mistakes
- Web Links and Other Resources

Note: Not all hacks in this book require electrical engineering.

Introduction

Understanding how hardware hacks work usually requires an introductory-level understanding of electronics. This appendix describes electronics fundamentals and the basic theory of the most common electronic components. We also look at how to read schematic diagrams, how to identify components, proper soldering techniques, and other engineering topics.

NEED TO KNOW...LIMITATIONS OF THIS APPENDIX

Engineering, like hardware hacking, is a skill that requires time and determination if you want to be proficient in the field. There is a lot to discuss, but we have a limited amount of space. This appendix is not going to turn you into an electronics guru, but it will teach you enough about the basics so that you can start to find your way around. For more detail on the subject, see the suggested reading list at the end of this appendix.

Fundamentals

It is important to understand the core fundamentals of electronics before you venture into the details of specific components. This section provides a background on numbering systems, notation, and basic theory used in all facets of engineering.

Bits, Bytes, and Nibbles

At the lowest level, electronic circuits and computers store information in binary format, which is a base-2 numbering system containing only 0 and 1, each known as a *bit* (derived from a combination of the words *binary*, which is defined as something having two parts or components, and *digit*). The common decimal numbering system that we use in everyday life is a base-10 system, which consists of the digits 0 through 9.

Electrically, a 1 bit is generally represented by a positive voltage (5V, for example), and a 0 bit is generally represented by a zero voltage (or ground potential). However, many protocols and definitions map the binary values in different ways.

A group of 4 bits is a *nibble* (also known as a *nybble*), a group of 8 bits is a *byte*, and a group of 16 bits is typically defined as a *word* (though a *word* is sometimes defined differently, depending on the system architecture you are referring to). Figure F.1 shows the interaction of bits, nibbles, bytes, and words. This visual diagram makes it easy to grasp the concept of how they all fit together.

Figure F.1 Breakdown of a 16-Bit Word into Bytes, Nibbles, and Bits

Word															
Byte 1 (High)								Byte 0 (Low)							
Nibble 3				Nibble 2				Nibble 1				Nibble 0			
Bit 15	Bit 14	Bit 13	Bit 12	Bit 11	Bit 10	Bit 9	Bit 8	Bit 7	Bit 6	Bit 5	Bit 4	Bit 3	Bit 2	Bit 1	Bit 0

The larger the group of bits, the more information that can be represented. A single bit can represent only two combinations (0 or 1). A nibble can represent 2^4 (or 16) possible combinations (0 to 15 in decimal), a byte can represent 2^8 (or 256) possible combinations (0 to 255 in decimal), and a word can represent 2^{16} (or 65,536) possible combinations (0 to 65,535 in decimal).

Hexadecimal format, also called *hex*, is commonly used in the digital computing world to represent groups of binary digits. It is a base-16 system in which 16 sequential numbers are used as base units before adding a new position for the next number (digits 0 through 9 and letters A through F). One hex digit can represent the arrangement of 4 bits (a nibble). Two hex digits can represent 8 bits (a byte). Table F.1 shows equivalent number values in the decimal, hexadecimal, and binary number systems. Hex digits are sometimes prefixed with 0x or $ to avoid confusion with other numbering systems.

Table F.1 Number System Equivalents: Decimal, Binary, and Hexadecimal

Decimal	Binary	Hex	
0	0	0	
1	1	1	
2	10	2	
3	11	3	
4	100	4	
5	101	5	
6	110	6	
7	111	7	
8	1000	8	
9	1001	9	

Continued

Table F.1 Number System Equivalents: Decimal, Binary, and Hexadecimal

Decimal	Binary	Hex
10	1010	A
11	1011	B
12	1100	C
13	1101	D
14	1110	E
15	1111	F
16	10000	10
17	10001	11
18	10010	12
19	10011	13
20	10100	14
21	10101	15
22	10110	16
23	10111	17
24	11000	18
25	11001	19
26	11010	1A
27	11011	1B
28	11100	1C
29	11101	1D
30	11110	1E
31	11111	1F
32	100000	20
...	...	...
63	111111	3F
...	...	...
127	1111111	7F
...	...	...
255	11111111	FF

The American Standard Code for Information Interchange, or ASCII (pronounced *ask-key*), is the common code for storing characters in a computer system. The standard ASCII character set (see Table F.2) uses 1 byte to correspond to each of 128 different letters, numbers, punctuation marks, and special characters. Many of the special characters are holdovers from the original specification created in 1968 and are no longer commonly used for their originally intended purpose. Only the decimal values 0 through 127 are assigned, which is half of the space available in a byte. An extended ASCII character set uses the full range of 256 characters available in a byte. The decimal values of 128 through 255 are assigned to represent other special characters that are used in foreign languages, graphics, and mathematics.

Table F.2 The Standard ASCII Character Set

Hex	Symbol	Hex	Symbol	Hex	Symbol	Hex	Symbol
0x00	NUL (null)	0x20	SP (space)	0x40	@	0x60	' (Single quote)
0x01	SOH (start of heading)	0x21	!	0x41	A	0x61	a
0x02	STX (start of text)	0x22	"	0x42	B	0x62	b
0x03	ETX (end of text)	0x23	#	0x43	C	0x63	c
0x04	EOT (end of transmission)	0x24	$	0x44	D	0x64	d
0x05	ENQ (enquiry)	0x25	%	0x45	E	0x65	e
0x06	ACK (acknowledge)	0x26	&	0x46	F	0x66	f
0x07	BEL (bell)	0x27	' (apostrophe)	0x47	G	0x67	g
0x08	BS (backspace)	0x28	(	0x48	H	0x68	h
0x09	HT (horizontal tab)	0x29	)	0x49	I	0x69	i
0x0A	LF (line feed/new line)	0x2A	*	0x4A	J	0x6A	j
0x0B	VT (vertical tab)	0x2B	+	0x4B	K	0x6B	k
0x0C	FF (form feed)	0x2C	, (comma)	0x4C	L	0x6C	l
0x0D	CR (carriage return)	0x2D	-	0x4D	M	0x6D	m
0x0E	SO (shift out)	0x2E	. (period)	0x4E	N	0x6E	n
0x0F	SI (shift in)	0x2F	/	0x4F	O	0x6F	o
0x10	DLE (data link escape)	0x30	0	0x50	P	0x70	p
0x11	DC1 (device control 1)	0x31	1	0x51	Q	0x71	q
0x12	DC2 (device control 2)	0x32	2	0x52	R	0x72	r
0x13	DC3 (device control 3)	0x33	3	0x53	S	0x73	s
0x14	DC4 (device control 4)	0x34	4	0x54	T	0x74	t
0x15	NAK (negative acknowledge)	0x35	5	0x55	U	0x75	u
0x16	SYN (synchronous idle)	0x36	6	0x56	V	0x76	v
0x17	ETB (end of transmission block)	0x37	7	0x57	W	0x77	w
0x18	CAN (cancel)	0x38	8	0x58	X	0x78	x
0x19	EM (end of medium)	0x39	9	0x59	Y	0x79	y
0x1A	SUB (substitute)	0x3A	: (colon)	0x5A	Z	0x7A	z

Continued

Table F.2 The Standard ASCII Character Set

Hex	Symbol	Hex	Symbol	Hex	Symbol	Hex	Symbol
0x1B	ESC (escape)	0x3B	;	0x5B	[	0x7B	{
0x1C	FS (file separator)	0x3C	<	0x5C	\	0x7C	|
0x1D	GS (group separator)	0x3D	=	0x5D	]	0x7D	}
0x1E	RS (record separator)	0x3E	>	0x5E	^	0x7E	~
0x1F	US (unit separator)	0x3F	?	0x5F	_ (underscore)	0x7F	Del (delete)

Reading Schematics

Before we get into the theory of individual electronic components, it is important to learn how circuit designs are drawn and described. A *schematic* is essentially an electrical road map of a circuit. Reading basic schematics is a good skill to have, even if it is just to identify a particular component that needs to be removed during a hack. Reading schematics is much easier than it may appear, and with practice it will become second nature.

On a schematic, each component of the circuit is assigned its own symbol, unique to the type of device that it is. The United States and Europe sometimes use different symbols, and there are even multiple symbols to represent one type of part. A resistor has its own special symbol, as does a capacitor, a diode, or an integrated circuit. Think of schematic symbols as an alphabet for electronics. Table F.3 shows a selection of basic components and their corresponding designators and schematic symbols. This is by no means a complete list, and, as mentioned, a particular component type may have additional symbols that aren't shown here.

A *part designator* is also assigned to each component and is used to distinguish between two parts of the same type and value. The designator is usually an alphanumeric character followed by a unique numerical value (R1, C4, or SW2, for example). The part designator and schematic symbol are used as a pair to define each discrete component of the circuit design.

Table F.3 Designator and Schematic Symbols for Basic Electronic Components

Component	Designator	Symbol
Resistor	R	
Potentiometer (variable resistor)	R	
Capacitor (nonpolarized)	C	

Continued

Table F.3 Designator and Schematic Symbols for Basic Electronic Components

Component	Designator	Symbol
Capacitor (polarized)	C	
Diode	D	
LED	D	
Photodiode	D	
Transistor (NPN)	Q	
Transistor (PNP)	Q	
Crystal	Y	
Switch	SW	
Pushbutton switch	SW	
Speaker	LS	
Fuse	F	
Battery	BT	

Continued

Table F.3 Designator and Schematic Symbols for Basic Electronic Components

Component	Designator	Symbol
	None	
Ground	None	
	None	

Figure F.2 An Example Circuit: A Basic LED with a Current-Limiting Resistor and Switch

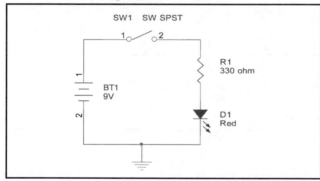

Voltage, Current, and Resistance

Voltage and current are the two staple quantities of electronics. *Voltage*, also known as a *potential difference*, is the amount of work (energy) required to move a positive charge from a lower potential (a more negative point in a circuit) to higher potential (a more positive point in a circuit). Voltage can be thought of as an electrical pressure or force and has a unit of volts (*V*). It is denoted with a symbol *V*, or sometimes *E* or *U*.

Figure F.2 shows an example circuit using some of the basic schematic symbols. It describes a light–emitting diode (LED) powered by a battery and controlled by a switch. When the switch is off, no current is able to flow from the battery through the rest of the circuit, so the LED will not illuminate. When the switch is enabled, current will flow and the LED will illuminate.

Current is the rate of flow (the quantity of electrons) passing through a given point. Current has a unit of amperes, or *amps* (*A*), and is denoted with a symbol of *I*. Kirchhoff's Current Law states that the sum of currents into a point equals the sum of the currents out of a point (corresponding to a conservation of charge).

Power is a "snapshot" of the amount of work being done at that particular point in time and has a unit of watts (W). One watt of power is equal to the work done in 1 second by 1 volt moving 1 coulomb of charge. Furthermore, 1 coulomb per second is equal to 1 ampere. A coulomb is equal to

6.25×10^{18} electrons (a very, very large amount). Basically, the power consumed by a circuit can be calculated with the following simple formula:

$P = V \times I$

where

- P = Power (W)
- V = Voltage (V)
- I = Current (A)

NEED TO KNOW... DIFFERENTIATING BETWEEN VOLTAGE AND CURRENT

We use special terminology to describe voltage and current. You should refer to voltage as going *between* or *across* two points in a circuit—for example, "The voltage across the resistor is 1.7V." You should refer to current going *through* a device or connection in a circuit—for example, "The current through the diode is 800mA." When we're measuring or referring to a voltage at a single given point in a circuit, it is defined with respect to ground (typically 0V).

Direct Current and Alternating Current

Direct current (DC) is simple to describe because it flows in one direction through a conductor and is either a steady signal or pulses. The most familiar form of a DC supply is a battery. Generally, aside from power supply or motor circuitry, DC voltages are more commonly used in electronic circuits.

Alternating current (AC) flows in both directions through a conductor (see Figure F.3) and is arguably more difficult to analyze and work with than DC. The most familiar form of an AC supply is an electrical outlet in your home. In the United States and Canada, these outlets provide 120V AC at 60Hz (cycles per second). In other parts of the world, varying AC voltages and line frequencies are used.

Several terms are used to describe the AC signal:

- **Peak voltage (V$_{\text{PEAK}}$)** The maximum positive and negative points of the AC signal from a center point of reference.

Figure F.3 An Example of an Alternating Current Waveform

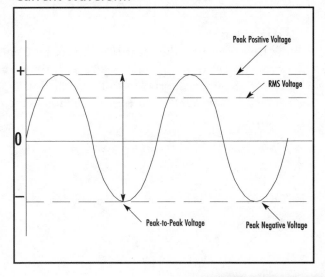

- **Peak-to-peak voltage (V_{PP})** The total voltage swing from the most positive to the most negative point of the AC signal.

- **Root-mean-square (RMS) voltage (V_{RMS})** The most common term used to describe an AC voltage. Since an AC signal is constantly changing (as opposed to DC, in which the signal is constant), the RMS measurement is the most accurate way to determine how much work will be done by an AC voltage.

For a typical sinusoidal AC signal (like the one shown in Figure F.3), the following four formulas can be used:

Average AC Voltage (V_{AVG}) = 0.637 x V_{PEAK} = 0.9 x V_{RMS}

V_{PEAK} = 1.414 x V_{RMS} = 1.57 x V_{AVG}

V_{RMS} = 0.707 x V_{PEAK} = 1.11 x V_{AVG}

V_{PP} = 2 x V_{PEAK}

Resistance

Resistance can be described with a simple analogy of water flowing through a pipe: If the pipe is narrow (high resistance), the flow of water (current) will be restricted. If the pipe is large (low resistance), water (current) can flow through it more easily. If the pressure (voltage) is increased, more current will be forced through the conductor. Any current prevented from flowing (if the resistance is high, for example) will be dissipated as heat (based on the first law of thermodynamics, which states that energy cannot be created or destroyed, simply changed in form). Additionally, there will be a difference in voltage on either side of the conductor.

Resistance is an important electrical property and exists in any electrical device. *Resistors* are devices used to create a fixed value of resistance. (For more information on resistors, see the "Basic Device Theory" section in this appendix.)

Ohm's Law

Ohm's Law, proven in the early 19th century by George Simon Ohm, is a basic formula of electronics that states the relationship among voltage, current, and resistance in an ideal conductor. The current in a circuit is directly proportional to the applied voltage and inversely proportional to the circuit resistance. Ohm's Law can be expressed as the following equations:

V = I x R

Or...

I = V / R

Or...

R = V / I

Where...

- V = Voltage (V)
- I = Current (A)
- R = Resistance (in ohms, designated with the omega symbol, Ω)

Basic Device Theory

This section explores the basic device theory of the five most common electronic components: resistors, capacitors, diodes, transistors, and integrated circuits. Understanding the functionality of these parts is essential to any core electronics knowledge and will prove useful in designing or reverse-engineering products.

Resistors

Resistors are used to reduce the amount of current flowing through a point in a system. Resistors are defined by three values:

- Resistance (Ω)
- Heat dissipation (in watts, W)
- Manufacturing tolerance (%)

Figure F.4 Various Resistor Types

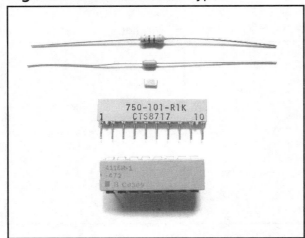

A sampling of various resistor types is shown in Figure F.4. Resistors are not polarized, meaning that they can be inserted in either orientation with no change in electrical function.

The value of a resistor is indicated by an industry-standard code of four or five colored bands printed directly onto the resistor (see Figure F.5). The bands define the resistance, multiplier, and manufacturing tolerance of the resistor. The manufacturing tolerance is the allowable skew of a resistor value from its ideal rated value.

A resistor's internal composition can consist of many different materials, but typically one of three are used: carbon, metal film, or wire-wound. The material is usually wrapped around a core, with the wrapping type and length corresponding to the resistor value. The carbon-filled resistor, used in most general-purpose applications such as current limiting and nonprecise circuits, allows a +/-5 % tolerance on the resistor value. Metal film resistors are for more precise applications such as amplifiers, power supplies, and sensitive analog circuitry; they usually allow a +/-1 or 2 % tolerance. Wire-wound resistors can also be very accurate.

When resistors are used in series in a circuit (see Figure F.6), their resistance values are *additive*, meaning that you simply add the values of the resistors in series to obtain the total resistance. For example, if *R1* is 220 ohm and *R2* is 470 ohm, the overall resistance will be 690 ohm.

Parallel circuits provide alternative pathways for current flow, although the voltage across the components in parallel is the same. When resistors are used in parallel (see Figure F.7), a simple equation is used to calculate the overall resistance:

$$1 / R_{TOTAL} = (1 / R1) + (1 / R2) + ...$$

This same formula can be extended for any number of resistors used in parallel. For example, if *R1* is 220 ohm and *R2* is 470 ohm, the overall resistance will be 149.8 ohm.

For only two resistors in parallel, an alternate formula can be used:

$$R_{TOTAL} = (R1 \times R2) / (R1 + R2)$$

Figure F.5 Resistor Color Code Chart

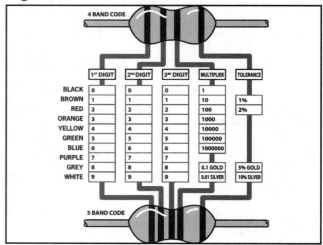

Figure F.6 Resistors in Series

Figure F.7 Resistors in Parallel

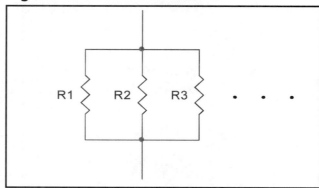

Carbon and metal film resistors typically come in wattage values of 1/16W, 1/8W, 1/4W, 1/2W and 1W. This corresponds to how much power they can safely dissipate. The most commonly used resistors are 1/4W and 1/2W. For large current applications, wire-wound resistors are typically used because they can support wattages greater than 1W. The wattage of the resistor usually corresponds to its physical size and surface area. For most consumer electronics, resistors greater than 1W are typically not used. To calculate the required wattage value for your application, use the following equation:

$$P = V \times I$$

Or...

$$P = I^2 \times R$$

Where...

- P = Power (W)
- V = Voltage across the resistor (V)
- I = Current flowing through the resistor (A)
- R = Resistance value (Ω)

Capacitors

A *capacitor's* primary function is to store electrical energy in the form of electrostatic charge. Consider a simple example of a water tower, which stores water (charge): When the water system (circuit) produces more water than a town or building needs, the excess is stored in the water tower (capacitor). At times of high demand, when additional water is needed, the excess water (charge) flows out of the water tower to keep the pressure up.

A capacitor is usually implemented for one of three uses:

- **To store a charge** Typically used for high-speed or high-power applications, such as a laser or a camera flash. The capacitor will be fully charged by the circuit in a fixed length of time, and then all of its stored energy will be released and used almost instantaneously, just like the water tower example previously described.

- **To block DC voltage** If a DC voltage source is connected in series to a capacitor, the capacitor will instantaneously charge and no DC voltage will pass into the rest of the circuit. However, an AC signal flows through a capacitor unimpeded because the capacitor will charge and discharge as the AC fluctuates, making it appear that the alternating current is flowing.

- **To eliminate ripples** Useful for filtering, signal processing, and other analog designs. If a line carrying DC voltage has ripples or spikes in it, also known as "noise," a capacitor can smooth or "clean" the voltage to a more steady value by absorbing the peaks and filling in the valleys of the noisy DC signal.

Capacitors are constructed of two metal plates separated by a *dielectric*. The dielectric is any material that does not conduct electricity, and varies for different types of capacitors. It prevents the plates from touching each other. Electrons are stored on one plate of the capacitor and they discharge through the other. Consider lightning in the sky as a real-world example of a capacitor: One plate is formed by the clouds, the other plate is formed by the earth's ground, and the dielectric is the air in between. The lightning is the charge releasing between the two plates.

Depending on their construction, capacitors are either *polarized*, meaning that they exhibit varying characteristics based on the direction they are used in a circuit, or *nonpolarized*, meaning that they can be inserted in either orientation with no change in electrical function. A sampling of various capacitor types is shown in Figures F.8 and A.9.

Figure F.8 Various Nonpolarized Capacitor Types (Ceramic Disc and Multilayer)

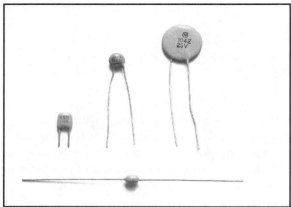

Figure F.9 Various Polarized Capacitor Types (Electrolytic and Tantalum)

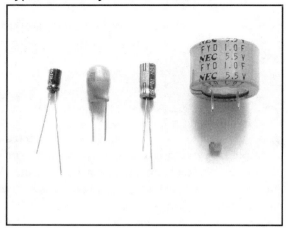

Capacitors have a unit of farad (F). A 1 farad capacitor can store 1 coulomb of charge at 1 volt (equal to 1 amp-second of electrons at 1 volt). A single farad is a very large amount. Most capacitors store a miniscule amount of charge and are usually denoted in uF (microfarads, $10^{-6} \times F$) or pF (pico-farads, $10^{-12} \times F$). The physical size of the capacitor is usually related to the dielectric material and the amount of charge that the capacitor can hold.

Unlike resistors, capacitors do not use a color code for value identification. Today, most mono-lithic and ceramic capacitors are marked with a three-number code called an *IEC marking* (see Figure F.10). The first two digits of the code indicate a numerical value; the last digit indicates a multiplier. Electrolytic capacitors are always marked in uF. These devices are polarized and must be oriented cor-rectly during installation. Polarized devices have a visible marking denoting the negative side of the device (in the case of surface-mount capacitors, the marking is on the positive side). There may be additional markings on the capacitor (sometimes just a single character); these usually denote the capacitor's voltage rating or manufacturer.

Figure F.10 Examples of Some Capacitor IEC Markings

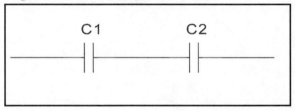

The calculations to determine effective capacitance of capacitors in series and parallel are essentially the reverse of those used for resistors. When capacitors are used in series (see Figure F.11), a simple equation is used to calculate the effective capacitance:

$$1 / C_{TOTAL} = (1 / C1) + (1 / C2) + ...$$

This same formula can be extended for any number of capacitors used in series. For example, if *C1* is 100uF and *C2* is 47uF, the overall capacitance will be 31.9uF.

For only two capacitors in series, an alternate formula can be used:

$$C_{TOTAL} = (C1 \times C2) / (C1 + C2)$$

When using capacitors in series, you store effectively less charge than you would by using either one alone in the circuit. The advantage to capacitors in series is that it increases the maximum working voltage of the devices.

When capacitors are used in parallel in a circuit (see Figure F.12), their effective capacitance is additive, meaning that you simply add the values of the capacitors in parallel to obtain the total capacitance. For example, if *C1* is 100uF and *C2* is 47uF, the overall capacitance will be 147uF.

Capacitors are often used in combination with resistors in order to control their charge and discharge time. Resistance directly affects the time required to charge or discharge a capacitor (the larger the resistance, the longer the time).

Figure F.13 shows a simple RC circuit. The capacitor will charge as shown by the curve in Figure F.14. The amount of time for the capacitor to become fully charged in an RC circuit depends on the values of the capacitor and resistor in the circuit.

Figure F.11 Capacitors in Series

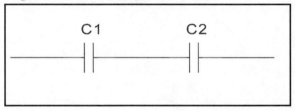

Figure F.12 Capacitors in Parallel

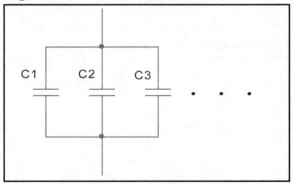

Figure F.13 A Simple RC Circuit to Charge a Capacitor

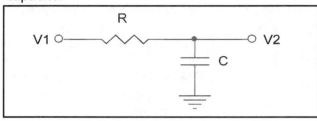

The variable τ (called the *time constant*) is used to define the time it takes for the capacitor to charge to 63.2 % of its maximum capacity. The time constant can be calculated by the following formula:

$$\tau = R \times C$$

Where…

- τ = Time constant (seconds)
- C = Capacitance (F)
- R = Resistance (Ω)

A capacitor reaches 63.2 % of its charge in one-fifth of the time it takes to become fully charged. Capacitors in actual applications are usually not charged to their full capacity because it takes too long.

Figure F.14 Capacitor-Charging Curve

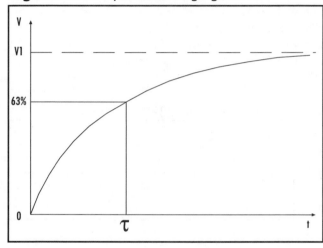

Diodes

In the most basic sense, *diodes* pass current in one direction while blocking it from the other. This allows for their use in rectifying AC into DC, filtering, limiting the range of a signal (known as a *diode clamp*), and as "steering diodes," in which diodes are used to allow voltage to be applied to only one part of the circuit.

Most diodes are made with semiconductor materials such as silicon, germanium, or selenium. Diodes are polarized, meaning that they exhibit varying characteristics depending on the direction they are used in a circuit. When current is flowing through the diode in the direction shown in Figure F.15 (from anode, left, to cathode, right), the diode appears as a short circuit. When current tries to pass in the opposite direction, the diode exhibits a high resistance, preventing the current from flowing.

Figure F.15 Various Diode Types Showing Direction of Current Flow

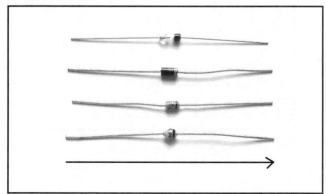

Diodes come in many types and sizes, each with varying electrical properties. You need to consider characteristics such as breakdown voltage, forward voltage, forward current, and reverse recovery time when designing with diodes or replacing one in a circuit:

- **Breakdown/reverse voltage (V_R)**, also known as the *peak inverse voltage* (P_{IV}), is the maximum voltage you can apply across a diode in the reverse direction and still have it block conduction. If this voltage is exceeded, the diode goes into "avalanche breakdown" and conducts current, essentially rendering the diode useless (unless it's a Zener diode, which is designed to operate in this breakdown region).

- **Forward voltage (V_F)** is the voltage drop across the diode. This usually corresponds to the forward current (the greater the current flowing through the diode, the larger the voltage drop). Typical forward voltage of a general-purpose diode is between 0.5V and 0.8V at 10mA.

- **Forward current (I_F)** is the maximum current that can flow through the diode. If current flowing through the diode is more than it can handle, the diode will overheat and can melt down and cause a short circuit.

- **Reverse recovery time (T_{RR})** is the time it takes a diode to go from forward conduction to reverse blocking (think of a revolving door that goes in both directions and the people coming in and going out acting as the current). If the turnaround time is too slow, current will flow in the reverse direction when the polarity changes and cause the diode junction to heat up and possibly fail. This is primarily of concern for AC-rectifying circuits commonly used in power supplies.

Figure F.16 The Diode V-I Curve

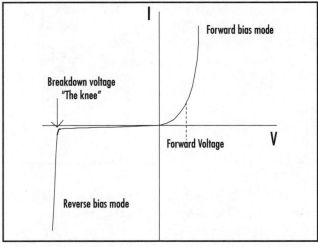

Figure F.16 shows the diode V-I curve, a standard curve that describes the relationship between voltage and current with respect to a diode.

In normal forward bias operation (shown on the right side of the graph), the diode begins to conduct and act as a short circuit after the forward voltage drop is met (usually between 0.5V and 0.8V). In reverse bias operation (shown on the left side of the graph), reverse current is generally measured in the nA range (an extremely small measure of current). When the diode is reverse biased, current is essentially prevented from flowing in that direction, with the exception of a very small leakage current. The point at which the diode begins its avalanche breakdown is called "the knee," as shown by the visible increase in reverse current on the curve, looking somewhat similar to a profile of a knee. Breakdown is not a desirable mode to which to subject the diode, unless the diode is of a Zener type (in which case proper current limiting should be employed).

Transistors

The *transistor* is arguably the greatest invention of the 20th century and the most important of electronic components. It is a three-terminal device that essentially serves as an amplifier or switch to control electronic current. When a small current is applied to its base, a much larger current is allowed to flow from its collector. This gives a transistor its switching behavior, since a small current can turn a larger current on and off.

The first transistor was demonstrated on December 23, 1947, by William Shockley, John Bardeen, and Walter Brattain, all scientists at the Bell Telephone Laboratories in New Jersey. The transistor was the first device designed to act as both a transmitter, converting sound waves into electronic waves, and a resistor, controlling electronic current. The name *transistor* comes from the *trans* of *transmitter* and the *sistor* of *resistor*. Although its use has gone far beyond the function that combination implies, the name remains.

Figure F.17 Various Discrete Transistor Types

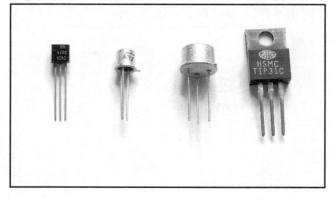

The transistor became commercially available on May 10, 1954 from Texas Instruments, and quickly replaced the bulky and unreliable vacuum tubes, which were much larger and required more power to operate. Jumping ahead 50 years, to 2004, transistors are now an essential part of engineering, used in practically every circuit and by the millions in single integrated circuits taking up an area smaller than a fingernail. Companies such as AMD, NEC, Samsung, and Intel are pushing the envelope of transistor technology, continuing to discover new ways to develop smaller, faster, and cheaper transistors.

This appendix only scratches the surface of transistor theory and focuses only on the most general terms. A sampling of various discrete transistors is shown in Figure F.17.

The transistor is composed of a three-layer "sandwich" of semiconductor material. Depending on how the material's crystal structure is treated during its creation (in a process known as *doping*), it becomes more positively charged (P-type) or negatively charged (N-type). The transistor's three-layer structure contains a P-type layer between N-type layers (known as an NPN configuration) or an N-type layer sandwiched between P-type layers (known as a PNP configuration).

The voltages at a transistor terminal (*C* for the collector, *E* for the emitter, and *B* for the base) are measured with respect to ground and are identified by their pin names, V_C, V_E, and V_B, respectively. The voltage drop measured between two terminals on the transistor is indicated by a double-subscript (for example, V_{BE} corresponds to the voltage drop from the base to the emitter). Figure F.18 shows the typical single NPN and PNP schematic symbols and notations.

A trick to help you remember which diagram corresponds to which transistor type is to think of NPN as meaning "not pointing in" (in reference to the base-emitter diode). With that said, the other transistor is obviously the PNP type.

An NPN transistor has four properties that must be met (the properties for the PNP type are the same, except the polarities are reversed):

1. The collector must be more positive than the emitter.

2. The base-emitter and base-collector circuits look like two diodes back to back (see Figure F.19). Normally the base-emitter diode is conducting (with a forward voltage drop, V_{BE}, of approximately 0.7V) and the base-collector diode is reverse-biased.

3. Each transistor has maximum values of I_C, I_B, and V_{CE} that cannot be exceeded without risk of damaging the device. Power dissipation and other limits specified in the manufacturer's data sheet should also be obeyed.

4. The current flowing from collector to emitter (I_C) is roughly proportional to the current input to the base (I_B), shown in Figure F.20, and can be calculated with the following formula:

$$I_C = h_{FE} \times I_B$$

or

$$I_C = \beta \times I_B$$

Figure F.18 NPN (Left) and PNP (Right) Transistor Diagrams

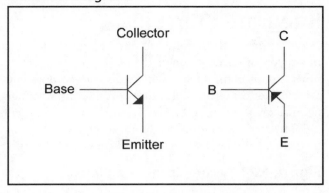

Figure F.19 Diode Representation of a Transistor, NPN (Left) and PNP (Right)

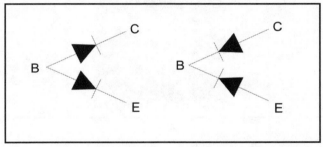

Figure F.20 NPN Transistor Characteristic Curve

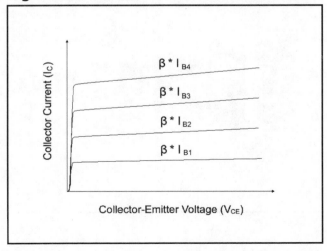

Where h_{FE} (also known as beta, β) is the current gain of the transistor. Typically, β is around 100, though it is not necessarily constant.

Integrated Circuits

Integrated circuits (ICs) combine discrete semiconductor and passive components onto a single microchip of semiconductor material. These may include transistors, diodes, resistors, capacitors, and other circuit components. Unlike discrete components, which usually perform a single function, ICs are capable of performing multiple functions. There are thousands of IC manufacturers, but some familiar ones are Intel, Motorola, and Texas Instruments.

The first generation of commercially available ICs were released by Fairchild and Texas Instruments in 1961 and contained only a few transistors. In comparison, the latest Pentium 4 processor by Intel contains over 175 million transistors in a die area of only 237mm² (approximately the size of your thumbnail).

ICs are easy to identify in a circuit by their unique packaging. Typically, the silicon die (containing the microscopic circuitry) is mounted in a plastic or ceramic housing with tiny wires connected to it (see Figure F.21). The external housing (called a *package*) comes in many mechanical outlines and various pin configurations and spacings.

With the constant advances in technology, ICs are shrinking to inconceivable sizes. Figure F.22 shows a variety of IC packages, including, from left to right, Dual Inline Package (DIP), Narrow DIP, Plastic Leadless Chip Carrier (PLCC), Thin Small Outline Package (TSOP) Type II, TSOP Type I, Small Outline Integrated Circuit (SOIC), Shrink Small Outline Package (SSOP), and Small Outline Transistor (SOT-23).

Ball Grid Array (BGA) is a relatively new package type that locates all the device leads underneath the chip, which reduces the area necessary for the device (see Figure F.23). However, it is extremely difficult to access the balls of the BGA without completely removing the device, which could be a problem for hardware hacking. BGA devices are becoming more popular due to their

Figure F.21 Silicon Die Inside an Integrated Circuit

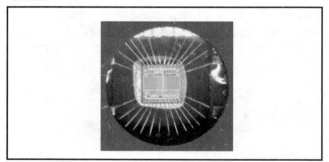

Figure F.22 Various IC Package Types

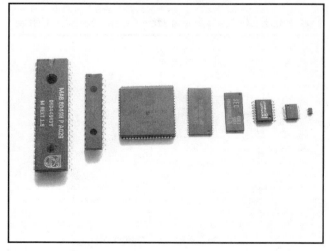

small footprint and low failure rates. The testing process (done during product manufacturing) is more expensive than other package types due to the fact that X-rays need to be used to verify that the solder has properly bonded to each of the ball leads.

With Chip-on–Board (COB) packaging, the silicon die of the IC is mounted directly to the PCB and protected by epoxy encapsulation (see Figure F.24).

Figure F.23 BGA Packaging

Figure F.24 COB Packaging

Proper IC positioning is indicated by a dot or square marking (known as a *key*) located on one end of the device (see Figure F.25). Some devices mark pin 1 with an angled corner (for square package types such as PLCC). On the circuit board, pin 1 is typically denoted by a square pad, whereas the rest of the IC's pads will be circular. Sometimes, a corresponding mark will be silkscreened or otherwise noted on the circuit board. Pin numbers start at the keyed end of the case and progress counter-clockwise around the device, unless noted differently in the specific product data sheet.

Figure F.25 IC Package Showing Pin Numbers and Key Marking

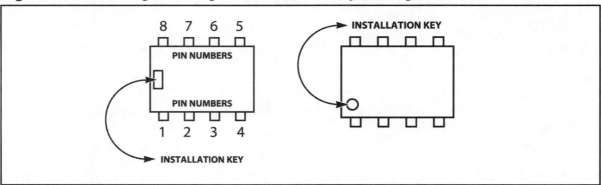

Microprocessors and Embedded Systems

A microprocessor – also known as a microcontroller or CPU (central processing unit), though there are slight technical differences – is essentially a general-purpose computer and is the heart of any embedded system. It is a complete computational engine fabricated on a single integrated circuit. In embedded systems, there is a union of hardware (the underlying circuitry) and software/firmware (code that is executed on the processor). You cannot have one without the other. Just about every electronic device you own can be considered an embedded system.

In November 1971, Intel released the first microprocessor, the Intel 4004. There are now thousands of microprocessors available each with their own benefits and features, including:

- Cost

- Size

- Clock speed

- Data width (for example, 8-, 16-, or 32-bit)

- On-chip peripherals (such as on-chip memory, I/O pins, LCD control, RS232/serial port, USB support, wireless support, analog-to-digital converters, or voltage references)

Common microprocessors include the Intel x86/Pentium-family (used on most personal computers), Motorola 6800- and 68000-families (such as the 68020 or 68030 used in some Macintosh computers or the DragonBall MC68328 used in some Palm PDA devices), ZiLOG Z8, Texas Instruments OMAP, and Microchip PIC.

While we don't cover the specifics of various microprocessors here, we wanted to mention their ubiquity inside hardware products. When you're hardware hacking or reverse engineering a product, chances are that you will encounter a microprocessor of some type. But fear not: Microprocessor data sheets, usually available from the manufacturer, contain instruction sets, register maps, and device-specific details that will give you the inside scoop on how to operate the device. And, once you understand the basic theory of how microprocessors work and the low-level assembly language that they execute, it is fairly trivial to apply that knowledge to a new device or processor family.

Soldering Techniques

Soldering is an art form that requires proper technique in order to be done right. With practice, you will become comfortable And experienced with it. The two key parts of soldering are good heat distribution and cleanliness of the soldering surface and component. In the most basic sense, soldering requires a soldering iron and solder. There are many shapes and sizes of tools to choose from (you can find more details in Chapter 1 "Tools of the Warranty Voiding Trade"). This section uses hands-on examples to demonstrate proper soldering and desoldering techniques.

WARNING: PERSONAL INJURY

Improper handling of the soldering iron can lead to burns or other physical injuries. Wear safety goggles and other protective clothing when working with solder tools. With temperatures hovering around 700 degrees F, the tip of the soldering iron, molten solder, and flux can quickly sear through clothing and skin. Keep all soldering equipment away from flammable materials and objects. Be sure to turn off the iron when it is not in use and store it properly in its stand.

Hands-On Example:
Soldering a Resistor to a Circuit Board

This simple example shows the step-by-step process to solder a through-hole component to a printed circuit board (PCB). We use a piece of prototype PCB and a single resistor (see Figure F.26). Before you install and solder a part, inspect the leads or pins for oxidation. If the metal surface is dull, sand with fine sandpaper until shiny. In addition, clean the oxidation and excess solder from the soldering iron tip to ensure maximum heat transfer.

Figure F.26 Prototype PCB and Resistor Used in the Example

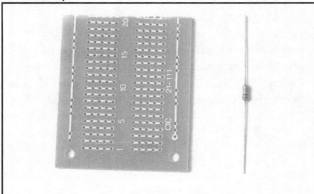

Bend and insert the component leads into the desired holes on the PCB. Flip the board to the other side. Slightly bend the lead you will be soldering to prevent the component from falling out when the board is turned upside down (see Figure F.27).

Figure F.27 Resistor Inserted into PCB

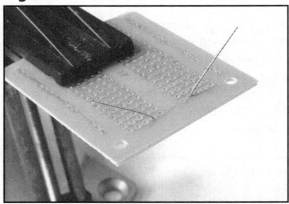

Figure F.28 Heating the Desired Solder Connection

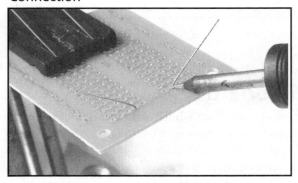

Figure F.29 Applying Heat and Solder to the Connection

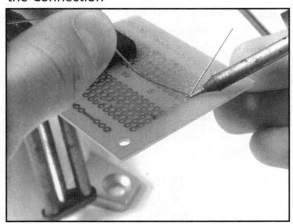

To begin the actual soldering process, allow the tip of your iron to contact both the component lead and the pad on the circuit board for about 1 second before feeding solder to the connection. This will allow the surface to become hot enough for solder to flow smoothly (see Figure F.28).

Next, apply solder sparingly and hold the iron in place until solder has evenly coated the surface (see Figure F.29). Ensure that the solder flows all around the two pieces (component lead and PCB pad) that you are fastening together. Do not put solder directly onto the hot iron tip before it has made contact with the lead or pad; doing so can cause a cold solder joint (a common mistake that can prevent your hack from working properly). Soldering is a function of heat, and if the pieces are not heated uniformly, solder may not spread as desired. A cold solder joint will loosen over time and can build up corrosion.

When it appears that the solder has flowed properly, remove the iron from the area and wait a few seconds for the solder to cool and harden. Do not attempt to move the component during this time. The solder joint should appear smooth and shiny, resembling the image in Figure F.30. If your solder joint has a dull finish, reheat the connection and add more solder if necessary.

Once the solder joint is in place, snip the lead to your desired length (see Figure F.31). Usually, you will simply cut the remaining portion of the lead that is not part of the actual solder joint (see Figure F.32). This prevents any risk of short circuits between leftover component leads on the board.

Figure F.30 Successful Solder Joint

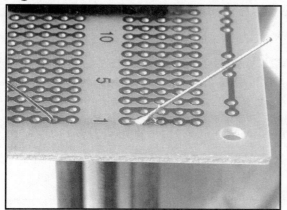

Figure F.31 Snipping Off the Remaining Component Lead

Every so often during any soldering process, use a wet sponge to lightly wipe the excess solder and burned flux from the tip of your soldering iron. This allows the tip to stay clean and heat properly. Proper maintenance of your soldering equipment will also increase its life span.

Figure F.32 Completed Soldering Example

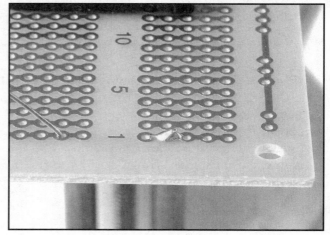

Desoldering Tips

Desoldering, or removing a soldered component from a circuit board, is typically more tricky than soldering, because you can easily damage the device, the circuit board, or surrounding components.

For standard through-hole components, first grasp the component with a pair of needle-nose pliers. Heat the pad beneath the lead you intend to extract and pull gently. The lead should come out. Repeat for the other lead. If solder fills in behind the lead as you extract it, use a spring-loaded solder sucker to remove the excess solder.

For through-hole ICs or multipin parts, use a solder sucker or desoldering braid to remove excess from the hole before attempting to extract the part. You can use a small flat-tip screwdriver or IC extraction tool to help loosen the device from the holes. Be careful to not overheat components, since they can become damaged and may fail during operation. If a component is damaged during extraction, simply replace it with a new part. For surface mount devices (SMDs) with more than a few pins, the easiest method to remove the part is by using the ChipQuik SMD Removal Kit, as shown in the following step-by-step example. Removal of SMD and BGA devices is normally accomplished with special hot-air rework stations. These stations provide a directed hot-air stream used with specific nozzles, depending on the type of device to be removed. The hot air can flow freely around and under the device, allowing the device to be removed with minimal risk of overheating. Rework stations are typically priced beyond the reach of hobbyist hardware hackers, and the ChipQuik kit works quite well as a low-cost alternative.

Hands-On Example: SMD Removal Using ChipQuik

The ChipQuik SMD Removal Kit (www.chipquik.com) allows you to quickly and easily remove surface mount components such as PLCC, SOIC, TSOP, QFP, and discrete packages. The primary component of the kit is a low-melting temperature solder (requiring less than 300 degrees F) that reduces the overall melting temperature of the solder on the SMD pads. Essentially, this enables you to just lift the part right off the PCB.

WARNING: HARDWARE HARM

Please read through this example completely before attempting SMD removal on an actual device. When removing the device, be careful to not scratch or damage any of the surrounding components or pull up any PCB traces. After following the instructions on the package (which consists of simply applying a standard no-clean flux to the SMD pins and then applying a low-melting-point solder), you can easily remove the surface mount part from the board.

Figure F.33 shows the contents of the basic ChipQuik SMD Removal Kit, from top to bottom: alcohol pads for cleaning the circuit board after device removal, the special low-melting temperature alloy, standard no-clean flux, and application syringe.

Figure F.33 ChipQuik SMD Removal Kit Contents

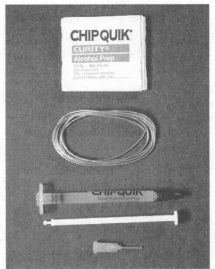

Figure F.34 Circuit Board Before Part Removal

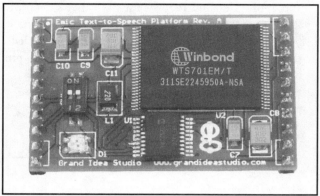

Figure F.35 Applying Flux to the Leads

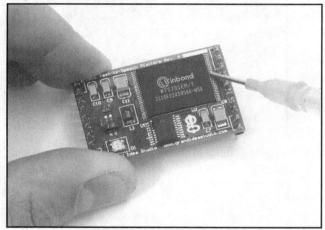

Figure F.36 Chip with Flux Applied

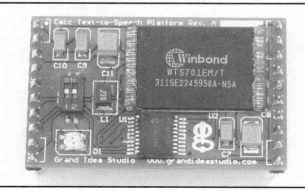

Figure F.34 shows the circuit board before the SMD part removal. Our target device to remove is the largest device on the board, the Winbond WTS701EM/T 56-pin TSOP IC.

The first step is to assemble the syringe, which contains the no-clean flux. Simply insert the plunger into the syringe and push down to dispense the compound (see Figure F.35). The flux should be applied evenly across all the pins on the package you will be removing (see Figure F.36). Flux is a chemical compound used to assist in the soldering or removal of electronic components or other metals. It has three primary functions:

1. Cleans metals surfaces to assist the flow of filler metals (solder) over base metals (device pins)

2. Assists with heat transfer from heat source (soldering iron) to metal surface (device pins)

3. Helps in the removal of surface metal oxides (created by oxygen in the air when the metal reaches high temperatures)

Once the flux is evenly spread over the pins of the target device, the next step is to apply the special ChipQuik alloy to the device (see Figure F.37). This step is just like soldering: Apply heat to the pins of the device and the alloy at the same time. The alloy has a melting point of approximately 300 degrees F, which is quite low. You should not have to heat the alloy with the soldering iron for very long before it begins to melt. The molten alloy should flow around and under the device pins (see Figure F.38).

Figure F.37 Applying Heat and Alloy to the Leads

Now that the alloy has been properly applied to all pins of the device, it is time to remove the device from the board. After making sure that the alloy is still molten by reheating all of it with the soldering iron, gently slide the component off the board (see Figure F.39). You can use a small jeweler's flathead screwdriver to help with the task. If the device is stuck, reheat the alloy and wiggle the part back and forth to help the alloy flow underneath the pads of the device and loosen the connections.

The final step in the desoldering process is to clean the circuit board. This step is important because it will remove any impurities left behind from the ChipQuik process and leave you ready for the next step in your hardware hack.

First, use the soldering iron to remove any stray alloy left on the device pads or anywhere else on the circuit board. Next, apply a thin, even layer of flux to all of the pads that the device was just soldered to. Use the included alcohol swab or a flux remover spray to remove the flux and clean the area (see Figure F.40).

Starting at one end of the device, simply heat and apply the alloy. Repeat for the other side(s) of the device. The flux will help with ensuring a nice flow of the alloy onto the device pins. Ensure that the alloy has come in contact with every single pin by gently moving the soldering iron around the edges of the device. Avoid touching nearby components on the PCB with the soldering iron.

Figure F.38 Chip with Alloy Applied

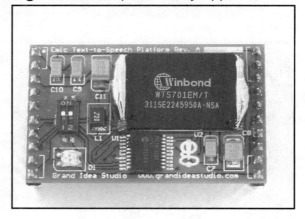

Figure F.39 Removing the Device from the Board

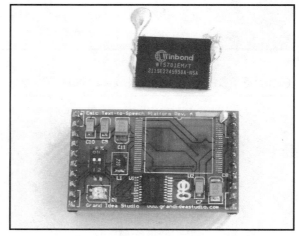

Figure F.40 Using Flux and Alcohol Swab to Clean Area

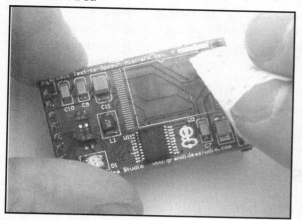

Figure F.41 Circuit Board with Part Successfully Removed

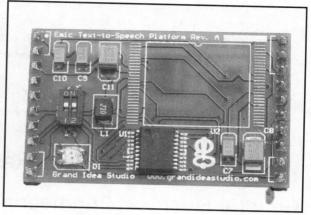

The desoldering process is now complete. The surface mount device has been removed and the circuit board cleaned (see Figure F.41). If you intend to reuse the device you just removed, use the soldering iron to remove any stray alloy or solder left over on and in between the pins and ensure there are no solder bridges between pins. If you do not want to reuse the device, simply throw it away.

Common Engineering Mistakes

During engineering design and debugging, you should remember the important maxim K.I.S.S.—or Keep It Simple, Stupid—at all times. It can be frustrating to troubleshoot a problem for hours or days on end and then discover the cause was a simple oversight. The most common engineering mistakes for hardware hacking are listed here. Although there are hundreds of other simple mistakes that can cause an engineer to quickly lose his or her hair, this list should get you started:

- **Faulty solder connections** After soldering, inspect the connections for cold solder joints and solder bridges. Cold solder joints happen when you don't fully heat the connection or when metallic corrosion and oxide contaminate a component lead or pad. Cold solder joints are the most common mistake for amateur and hobbyist electronics builders. Solder bridges form when a trail of excess solder shorts pads or tracks together (see the "Soldering Techniques" section in this appendix).

- **Installing the wrong part** Verify the part type and value before you insert and solder the component to the circuit board. Although many devices appear to look similar (e.g., a 1K and a 10K resistor look almost the same except for the color of one band), they have different operating characteristics and may act very differently in an electronic circuit. Surface mount components are typically harder to distinguish from one another. Double check to ensure that each part is installed properly. Keep in mind that the only way to properly test a component's value is to remove it from the board and then test it.

- **Installing parts backward** ICs have a notch or dot at one end indicating the correct direction of insertion. Electrolytic capacitors have a marking to denote the negative lead (on polarized surface mount capacitors, the positive lead has the marking). Through-hole capacitors also have a shorter-length negative lead than the positive lead. Transistors have a flat side or emitter tab to help you identify the correct mounting position and are often marked to identify each pin. Diodes have a banded end indicating the cathode side of the device.

- **Verify power** Ensure that the system is properly receiving the desired voltages from the power supply. If the device uses batteries, check to make sure that they have a full charge and are installed properly. If your device isn't receiving power, chances are it won't work.

Web Links and Other Resources

General Electrical Engineering Books

- Radio Shack offers a wide variety of electronic hobby and "how to" books, including an Engineer's Notebook series of books that provide an introduction to formulas, tables, basic circuits, schematic symbols, integrated circuits, and optoelectronics (light-emitting diodes and light sensors). Other books cover topics on measurement tools, amateur radio, and computer projects.

- *Nuts & Volts* (www.nutsvolts.com) and *Circuit Cellar* (www.circuitcellar.com) magazines are geared toward both electronics hobbyists and professionals. Both are produced monthly and contain articles, tutorials, and advertisements for all facets of electronics and engineering.

- Horowitz and Hill, *The Art of Electronics*, Cambridge University Press, 1989, ISBN 0-52-137095-7. Essential reading for basic electronics theory. It is often used as a course textbook in university programs.

- C. R. Robertson, *Fundamental Electrical & Electronic Principles*, Newnes, 2001, ISBN 0-75-065145-8. Covers the essential principles that form the foundations for electrical and electronic engineering courses.

- M. M. Mano, *Digital Logic and Computer Design,* Prentice-Hall, 1979, ISBN 0-13-214510-3. Digital logic design techniques, binary systems, Boolean algebra and logic gates, simplification of Boolean functions, and digital computer system design methods.

- K. R. Fowler, *Electronic Instrument Design*, Oxford University Press, 1996, ISBN 0-19-508371-7. Provides a complete view of the product development life cycle. Offers practical design solutions, engineering trade-offs, and numerous case studies.

Electrical Engineering Web Sites

- **ePanorama.net: www.epanorama.net** A clearing house of electronics information found on the Web. The content and links are frequently updated. Copious amounts of information for electronics professionals, students, and hobbyists.

- **The EE Compendium, The Home of Electronic Engineering and Embedded Systems Programming: http://ee.cleversoul.com** Contains useful information for professional electronics engineers, students, and hobbyists. Features many papers, tutorials, projects, book recommendations, and more.

- **Discover Circuits: www.discovercircuits.com** A resource for engineers, hobbyists, inventors, and consultants, Discover Circuits is a collection of over 7,000 electronic circuits and schematics cross-references into more than 500 categories for finding quick solutions to electronic design problems.

- **WebEE, The Electrical Engineering Homepage: www.web-ee.com** Large reference site of schematics, tutorials, component information, forums, and links.

- **Electro Tech Online: www.electro-tech-online.com** A community of free electronic forums. Topics include general electronics, project design, microprocessors, robotics, and theory.

- **University of Washington EE Circuits Archive: www.ee.washington.edu/circuit_archive** A large of collection of circuits, data sheets, and electronic-related software.

Data Sheets and Component Information

When reverse engineering a product for hardware hacking purposes, identifying components and device functionality is typically an important step. Understanding what the components do may provide detail of a particular area that could be hacked. Nearly all vendors post their component data sheets on the Web for public access, so simple searches will yield a decent amount of information. The following resources will also help you if the vendors don't:

- **Data Sheet Locator: www.datasheetlocator.com** A free electronic engineering tool that enables you to locate product data sheets from hundreds of electronic component manufacturers worldwide.

- **IC Master: www.icmaster.com** The industry's leading source of integrated circuit information, offering product specifications, complete contact information, and Web site links.

- **Integrated Circuit Identification (IC-ID): www.elektronikforum.de/ic-id** Lists of manufacturer logos, names, and datecode information to help identifying unknown integrated circuits.

- **PartMiner: www.freetradezone.com** Excellent resource for finding technical information and product availability and for purchasing electronic components.

Major Electronic Component and Parts Distributors

- Digi-Key, 1–800–344–4539, www.digikey.com
- Mouser Electronics, 1–800–346–6873, www.mouser.com
- Newark Electronics, 1–800–263–9275, www.newark.com
- Jameco, 1–800–831–4242, www.jameco.com

Obsolete and Hard-to-Find Component Distributors

When trying to locate obscure, hard-to-find materials and components, don't give up easily. Sometimes it will take hours of phone calls and Web searching to find exactly what you need. Many companies that offer component location services have a minimum order (upward of $100 or $250), which can easily turn a hobbyist project into one collecting dust on a shelf. Some parts-hunting tips:

- Go to the manufacturer Web site and look for any distributors or sales representatives. For larger organizations, you probably won't be able to buy directly from the manufacturer. Call your local distributor or representative to see if they have access to stock. They will often sample at small quantities or have a few-piece minimum order.

- Be creative with Google searches. Try the base part name, manufacturer, and combinations thereof.

- Look for cross-reference databases or second-source manufacturers. Many chips have compatible parts that can be used directly in place.

The following companies specialize in locating obsolete and hard-to-find components. Their service is typically not inexpensive, but as a last resort to find the exact device you need, these folks will most likely find one for you somewhere in the world:

- USBid, www.usbid.com
- Graveyard Electronics, 1–800–833–6276, www.graveyardelectronics.com
- Impact Components, 1–800–424–6854, www.impactcomponents.com
- Online Technology Exchange, 1–800–606–8459, www.onlinetechx.com

Index

Numerics

A

WE GIVE YOU PCB DESIGN IN SPADES

♠ SCHEMATICS
♠ SIMULATION
♠ PCB LAYOUT
♠ SMT LAYOUT
♠ AUTO ROUTING
♠ GERBER PHOTOPLOT

McCAD™

Deal Yourself a Winning Hand
With the Most
Complete...Powerful...
Flexible...Simple...Affordable
CAE/CAD System

Syngress: *The Definition of a Serious Security Library*

Syn·gress (sin–gres): *noun, sing.* Freedom from risk or danger; safety. See *security*.

Game Console Hacking

Joe Grand and Albert Yarusso

In November of 1977, Atari shipped its first 400,000 Video Computer Systems. Since that time, over 1.2 billion consoles have been sold worldwide, and a large percentage of those are still hanging around as "classic systems". An avid community of video game hackers and hard-core gamers has developed around a common passion to push their consoles, and the games themselves, beyond the functionality originally intended by the manufacturers. This book provides detailed instructions on how to customize and reconfigure consoles to a wide variety of ends---from the cosmetic case modifications to the ambitious porting of Linux to the Nintendo GameCube..

ISBN: 1-931836-31-0

Price: $39.95 US $57.95 CA

Hardware Hacking

Joe Grand, Ryan Russell, Kevin D. Mitnick (Editor)

"If I had this book 10 years ago, the FBI would never have found me!"— Kevin Mitnick

This book has something for everyone---from the beginner hobbyist with no electronics or coding experience to the self-proclaimed "gadget geek." Take an ordinary piece of equipment and turn it into a personal work of art. Build upon an existing idea to create something better. Have fun while voiding your warranty!

ISBN: 1-932266-83-6

Price: $39.95 US $59.95 CA

SYNGRESS®

Syngress: *The Definition of a Serious Security Library*

Syn·gress (sin–gres): *noun, sing.* Freedom from risk or danger; safety. See *security*.

Wireless Hacking: Projects for Wi-Fi Enthusiasts

Lee Barken, with Matt Fanady, Debi Jones, Alan Koebrick, and Michael Mee
As the cost of wireless technology drops, the number of Wi-Fi users continues to grow. Millions of people have discovered the joy and delight of "cutting the cord." Many of those people are looking for ways to take the next step and try out some of the cutting edge techniques for building and deploying "homebrew" Wi-Fi networks, both large and small. This book shows Wi-Fi enthusiasts and consumers of Wi-Fi LANs who want to modify their Wi-Fi hardware how to build and deploy "homebrew" Wi-Fi networks, both large and small.

ISBN: 1-931836-37-X
Price: $39.95 US $57.95 CAN

Google Hacking for Penetration Testers

Johnny Long, Foreword by Ed Skoudis
What many users don't realize is that the deceptively simple components that make Google so easy to use are the same features that generously unlock security flaws for the malicious hacker. Vulnerabilities in website security can be discovered through Google hacking, techniques applied to the search engine by computer criminals, identity thieves, and even terrorists to uncover secure information. This book beats Google hackers to the punch, equipping web administrators with penetration testing applications to ensure their site is invulnerable to a hacker's search.

ISBN: 1-931836-36-1
Price: $44.95 US $65.95 CA

SYNGRESS®

Syngress: *The Definition of a Serious Security Library*

Syn·gress (sin–gres): *noun, sing.* Freedom from risk or danger; safety. See *security.*

Inside the SPAM Cartel
Spammer X

Authored by a former spammer, this is a methodical, technically explicit expose of the inner workings of the SPAM economy. Readers will be shocked by the sophistication and sheer size of this underworld. "Inside the Spam Cartel" is a great read for people with even a casual interest in cyber-crime. In addition, it includes a level of technical detail that will clearly attract its core audience of technology junkies and security professionals.

ISBN: 1932266-86-0

Price: $49.95 US   72.95 CAN

Stealing the Network: How to Own a Continent
Ryan Russell, FX, Joe Grand, Tim Mullen, Jay Beale, Russ Rogers, Ken Pfeil, Paul Craig, Tom Parker, Fyodor
The first book in the "Stealing the Network" series was called a "blockbuster" by Wired magazine, a "refreshing change from more traditional computer books" by Slashdot.org, and "an entertaining and informative look at the weapons and tactics employed by those who attack and defend digital systems" by Amazon.com. This follow-on book once again combines a set of fictional stories with real technology to show readers the danger that lurks in the shadows of the information security industry... Could hackers take over a continent?

ISBN: 1-931836-05-1

Price: $49.95 US $69.95 CAN

SYNGRESS®

Syngress: *The Definition of a Serious Security Library*

Syn·gress (sin-gres): *noun, sing.* Freedom from risk or danger; safety. See *security*.

The Mezonic Agenda: Hacking the Presidency

Dr. Herbert H. Thompson and Spyros Nomikos

The Mezonic Agenda: Hacking the Presidency is the first Cyber-Thriller that allows the reader to "hack along" with both the heroes and villains of this fictional narrative using the accompanying CD containing real, working versions of all the applications described and exploited in the fictional narrative of the book. The Mezonic Agenda deals with some of the most pressing topics in technology and computer security today including: reverse engineering, cryptography, buffer overflows, and steganography. The book tells the tale of criminal hackers attempting to compromise the results of a presidential election for their own gain.

ISBN: 1-931836-83-3

Price: $34.95 U.S. $50.95 CAN

"This novel is scarily realistic."
—James A. Whittaker, Ph.D., Chief Scientist and Founder of Security Innovation

THE **Mezonic**
HACKING THE PRESIDENCY
Agenda

A Novel by
Dr. Herbert H. Thompson
Spyros Nomikos

Hacking a Terror Network: The Silent Threat of Covert Channels
Russ Rogers

Written by a certified Arabic linguist from the Defense Language Institute with extensive background in decoding encrypted communications, this cyber-thriller uses a fictional narrative to provide a fascinating and realistic "insider's look" into technically sophisticated covert terrorist communications over the Internet. The accompanying CD-ROM allows readers to "hack along" with the story line, by viewing the same Web sites described in the book containing encrypted, covert communications.

ISBN: 1-928994-98-9

Price: $39.95 US $57.95 CAN

4 FREE BOOKLETS
YOUR SOLUTIONS MEMBERSHIP

Hacking a Terror Network
THE SILENT THREAT OF COVERT CHANNELS

A terrorist plot against the United States is planned where the terrorists use the Internet's covert channels to communicate and hide their trails. Loyal U.S. agents must locate and decode this plot before innocent American citizens are harmed. Hack along with them... Can you decode the Internet's covert terrorists communications?

Russ Rogers
Matthew G. Devost Technical Editor

SYNGRESS®
HACK ALONG!
DO YOU HAVE WHAT IT TAKES?

SYNGRESS®

Syngress: *The Definition of a Serious Security Library*

Syn·gress (sin‑gres): *noun, sing.* Freedom from risk or danger; safety. See *security*.

WarDriving: Drive, Detect, Defend
A Guide to Wireless Security

Chris Hurley, Frank Thornton, Michael Puchol, Russ Rogers
The act of driving or walking through urban areas with a wireless-equipped laptop to map protected and un-protected wireless networks has sparked intense debate amongst law-makers, security professionals, and the telecommunications industry. This first ever book on WarDriving is written from the inside perspective of those who have created the tools that make WarDriving possible.

ISBN: 1-931836-03-5

Price: $49.95 US $69.95 CAN

Cyber Adversary Characterization:
Auditing the Hacker Mind

Tom Parker, Marcus Sachs, Eric Shaw, Ed Stroz, Matt Devost

The ever-increasing emphasis and reliance on the use of computers and the Internet, has come in hand with the increased threat of cyber-crime. Many systems and infrastructures are exceedingly vulnerable to attacks, as the complexity of computer networks is growing faster than the ability to understand and protect them. Heightened vigilance is not enough, but needs to be coupled with active defensive measures to guarantee the best protection. This book provides the reader with understanding of and an ability to anticipate that "cyber adversary" silently waiting in the wings to attack.

ISBN: 1-931836-11-6

Price: $49.95 US $69.95 CAN